STUDY GUIDE FOR USE WITH

PSYCHOLOGY

FRONTIERS AND APPLICATIONS

SECOND CANADIAN EDITION

Michael W. Passer
University of Washington

Ronald E. Smith
University of Washington

Michael L. Atkinson
University of Western Ontario

John B. Mitchell
Brescia University College, University of Western Ontario

Darwin W. Muir
Queen's University

Prepared by
David K. Jones
Westminster College

Steve Charlton
Kwantlen University College

Rhonda Snow
University College of the Fraser Valley

 **McGraw-Hill**
Ryerson

Toronto Montréal Boston Burr Ridge, IL Dubuque, IA Madison, WI New York San Francisco
St. Louis Bangkok Bogotá Caracas Kuala Lumpur Lisbon London Madrid
Mexico City Milan New Delhi Santiago Seoul Singapore Sydney Taipei

The McGraw-Hill Companies

Study Guide
for use with
Psychology: Frontiers and Applications
Second Canadian Edition

ISBN: 0-07-0939926

1 2 3 4 5 6 7 8 9 10 TRI 0 9 8 7 6 5

Printed and bound in Canada

Executive Sponsoring Editor: James Buchanan
Developmental Editor: Suzanne Simpson Millar
Senior Production Coordinator: Jennifer Wilkie
Printer: Tri-Graphic Printing Limited

CONTENTS

Chapter 3 - Biological Foundations of Behaviour

Chapter 4 - Genes, Evolution, and Behaviour

Chapter 5 - Sensation and Perception

Chapter 6 - States of Consciousness

Chapter 7 - Learning and Adaptation: The Role of Experience

Chapter 8 – Memory

Chapter 9 – Thought, Language, and Intelligence

Chapter 10 – Motivation and Emotion

Chapter 11 - Development Over the Lifespan

Chapter 15. Stress, Coping, and Health

Chapter 16. Behaviour in a Social Context

Introduction

Welcome to the world of psychology! During this course you will study many aspects of the science of psychology as psychologists try to provide answers to some of the classic questions about human nature and behaviour. Questions such as:

Do humans behave the way they do because it is our basic nature or because of the experiences we've had?
Can people really change, especially if their genes influence their behaviour?
Can you teach an old dog new tricks, and if so, how?
Is it really possible to develop an exceptional memory?
Does hypnosis work?
Can the way we think and live affect our health and well-being?
How can we know which human behaviours are abnormal when people around the world believe such different things, hold such different values, and behave so differently?
Why is there so much human conflict in the world? Are prejudice and racism part of human nature?

Psychology: Frontiers and Applications (2nd Canadian Edition) is designed to help you understand how psychologists investigate important issues. It focuses on three major approaches to explaining human behaviour and thought: biological, psychological, and environmental causes. As you read through the book, focus on how each of the three causes helps you to understand behaviour. Also, keep in mind that the explanations are not mutually exclusive; that is, all three may be needed to fully explain the complex behaviour of humans.

This study guide is designed to help you get the most out of this course, and to work well with your textbook. In your text, chapter 8 on Memory is filled with information on how to improve your memory and academic learning (see page 313 for example). In addition, the authors discuss time management, study skills, test-preparation strategies, and test-taking skills (see textbook chapter 1). Let's consider each of those in turn.

Time Management Skills

It is extremely important when you arrive at university to develop solid time management skills. If you are new to university, you will soon find this out. If you are already a seasoned student, you know what I'm talking about. Students find themselves with many obligations in addition to their classes. Many have jobs, raise children, and most would like to maintain some kind of social life. In order to do the things you have to do and the things you want to do, you need to figure out how to utilize your available time well. Form an attachment to your day planner, and consult it often. You have 168 hours in a week. Sit down with your planner, and determine how to distribute your time. When planning for studying, try to distribute it across each day and week. Leaving it until it becomes a necessary and urgent task, makes it much more difficult. The difference between successful and unsuccessful students is often the effectiveness of the skills they employ, rather than differences in their ability. Monitor your progress. If the schedule you planned for yourself isn't working, examine your priorities.

To study more effectively, there are a number of things that psychologists recommend. First, find a quiet place to study, preferably somewhere similar to the environment in which you will take the exam. Do not study while lying on your bed. Your body has learned that lying down is conducive to sleep. When you do find a good place for study, study <u>actively</u>. To study actively, you can use the SQ3R or PQ4R methods. First, preview the chapter to see what major topics it will explore. Then, read the chapter and take notes on it. Highlighting sections of the chapter with a marker is not as effective as taking notes and <u>rewriting</u> sections of the chapter in your own words. Finally, review the chapter to make sure that you understand the main points covered. . It is also helpful to think of the lecture time as 'study time'. Read the chapter in advance, ask questions, take notes, and review your notes after class. Keep your text with you to consult during and after the lecture. Do not be afraid to ask questions in class. If students do not ask questions, it is difficult for an instructor to know whether this is due to the material being easily understood or very difficult to understand. Keep in mind that if it seems difficult to you, it's likely difficult for many of your classmates, who will be relieved when someone asks a question.

To prepare for tests, it is again good to distribute your studying. If you have kept up with the material as it was being presented, you won't need to learn everything from scratch at exam time. The study guide contains some useful exercises to help you prepare for an exam. For example, the directed questions cover the key points of each chapter, the matching questions permit you to check your understanding of the concepts by identifying their definition, the fill in the blanks review tests your ability to 'recall' important information, and the multiple-choice, true/false, short-answer, and essay questions for each chapter provide good coverage of the main topics in each chapter

Although, some multiple-choice questions may focus on your understanding of terms, many require you to apply the knowledge you've learned. If you find you do very well on the study guide multiple-choice questions, but poorly on the actual exam, the following may help. Compile into one exam the multiple-choice questions for the chapters to be covered on the exam. Then, after you've finished studying, sit down and write the exam you've compiled. Limit the time you give yourself to write it, in order to simulate an actual exam (no looking at the answers until you've completed it). You'll find you will have a more accurate assessment of how you will do on that component of the actual exam. Further, you should be able to tell in which topic areas/chapters you need to expend more effort. If you need help, visit the professor or teaching assistant 'before' the exam.

While actually taking the test, you can apply a few strategies as well. On multiple-choice items, try to anticipate the answer by reading the question carefully before looking at the answer alternatives. You can also try to eliminate as many items as you possibly can. Sometimes students think the questions are more vague than they really are. If you don't know an item, don't waste time while fretting over it. Go on and come back to it later. If you have time, go back over each question to ensure you haven't misread the question. If you do change an answer, do it because you believe it is the best answer. You may have heard that 'c' is the most likely option, or that there cannot be a whole series of answers that have the same letter as the correct answer (e.g., 5 or 6 'b's in a row) – in fact, odd sequences are possible when items are selected from large test banks, rather than created by the instructor.

If you think you are better at short answer questions, treat the multiple choice question as a short answer and jot your answer down on the exam booklet – then, see if your answer is there in the options provided.

On short-answer or essay questions, organize your thoughts in advance before you start writing. Begin with a quick outline that organizes the material systematically, and includes all the points you want to make. Make sure that you organize your time wisely on exams.

After taking the exam, you miss an important opportunity if you do not ask to review the exam you've taken. By looking at the multiple choice questions you answered incorrectly, you may be able to determine if you have a problem with a particular type of question (e.g., a double negative), a particular topic within a chapter, or a particular chapter. If your mistakes are equally distributed across topics, chapters, and question types, you simply may not have dedicated enough time to studying for the exam, or you may need to adjust your strategy for handling the material. With the short answers, explain to your instructor that you are trying to improve your performance on future exams; the instructor may be able to show you how another student approached the same question and performed well. Remember to keep an open mind, and try to learn from the experience your instructor has in working with students.

We know that this sounds like an awful lot of work, and it is. You will likely find, though, that success in university doesn't come without blood, sweat, and sometimes tears.

Steve Charlton
Kwantlen University College

David K. Jones
Westminster College

Rhonda Snow
University College of the Fraser Valley

Chapter 1. Psychology: The Science of Behaviour

Learning Objectives

The importance of defining learning objectives for students cannot be overstated. Learning objectives orient students to the most important topics in each chapter, enable them to be better prepared for class, and facilitate studying for quizzes and exams. The following list of learning objectives is related to material presented in Chapter 1 of the Passer, Smith, Atkinson, Mitchell, Muir Psychology: Frontiers and Applications textbook.

1.1 Define psychology and indicate what kind of behaviours it incorporates.

1.2 Define critical thinking and describe types of questions involved in critical thinking.

1.3 Differentiate basic and applied research, and describe studies illustrating the relation between them.

1.4 List and describe the five goals of scientific research in psychology.

1.5 Describe how mind-body interactions help explain behavioural phenomena like voodoo death.

1.6 Contrast the positions of dualism and monism as they apply to the mind-body problem.

1.7 Describe how British empiricism, early work in physiology and psychophysics, and Darwin's theory of evolution paved the way for the field of psychology.

1.8 Describe the goals of structuralism and functionalism and identify researchers from each school.

1.9 Describe the method of introspection.

1.10 Describe the psychodynamic perspective, highlighting Freud's psychoanalytic theory.

1.11 Contrast Freud's psychoanalytic theory with modern psychodynamic theories.

1.12 Describe the behavioural perspective, highlighting the work of Pavlov, Thorndike, Watson, and Skinner.

1.13 Describe the humanistic perspective, highlighting the work of Maslow and Rogers.

1.14 Describe the cognitive perspective, including Gestalt psychology, cognitive neuroscience, artificial intelligence, and social constructivism.

1.15 Describe the sociocultural perspective and define culture, norms, and socialization.

1.16 Differentiate individualist and collectivist societies.

1.17   Describe the purpose, methods, and results of research on love and marriage across cultures by Levene et al.

1.18   Describe the biological perspective, highlighting research in behavioural neurosciences, behavioural genetics, and evolutionary psychology.

1.19   Contrast evolutionary and sociocultural perspectives in explaining behavioural phenomena.

1.20   Differentiate the six psychological perspectives in explaining behaviour: behavioural, biological, cognitive, humanistic, psychodynamic, and sociocultural.

1.21   Describe the Three Levels of Analysis and explain how it integrates the perspectives of psychology.

1.22   Using the Three Levels of Analysis, outline possible causal factors in depression.

1.23   Describe how the Three Levels of Analysis addresses the nature-nurture controversy.

1.24   List and describe the activities associated with various specialty areas within psychology.

1.25   List and describe the major professional associations of psychologists.

1.26   Describe the training needed for the various types of psychologists or psychiatrists.

1.27   Describe research-based strategies to improve academic performance, including effective time management, improving study habits, and preparing for and taking tests.

Chapter Overview

This chapter gives an introduction to some of the basic aspects of psychology. One of the most important things to understand is that psychology is both a basic and applied science, meaning that psychologists both search for knowledge about human behaviour for its own sake and also use that knowledge to solve practical problems in personal lives, education, business, law, health and medicine, and other areas. As psychology is a science, psychologists use the scientific method to help satisfy their four basic goals: describing, understanding, predicting, and controlling behaviour. Psychology is an empirical science, which means that it favours direct observations of behaviour.

Psychologists use several different perspectives to understand behaviour, including the biological, cognitive, psychodynamic, behavioural, humanistic, and sociocultural perspectives.

The biological perspective suggests that behaviour is best explained by studying how the brain, biochemical processes, and genetic factors influence actions. A modern-day movement in psychology has pointed to evidence that evolutionary factors may influence current behaviours. The cognitive perspective grew out of the early distinction between adherents of the structuralist approach, which contrasted with the functionalist approach. The cognitive perspective views humans as information processors and problem solvers. Social constructivists believe that each person creates his or her own "reality" from his or her cognitive perceptions. Adherents of the psychodynamic perspective believe that unconscious conflicts and unresolved conflicts from the past influence our personalities and behaviour. The behavioural perspective suggests that the environment, rather than individual characteristics such as cognitions or personality, is the primary determinant of our behaviour. On the other hand, humanists stress the importance of motives, freedom, and choice as we move toward our full potential, or self-actualization. The sociocultural perspective suggests that cultural norms, or rules for behaviour, shape our actions. Because it is likely that none of the perspectives provides a complete explanation for behaviour, many psychologists stress the need to integrate the perspectives to provide a more complete explanation of human behaviour.

There are a number of different specialty areas within psychology as a whole. These specialties include clinical, counselling, educational, experimental, industrial, developmental, social, personality, physiological, and quantitative psychologies.

Chapter Outline

The Nature of Psychology
  Psychology as a Basic and Applied Science
    From Robber's Cave to the Jigsaw Classroom Goals of Psychology

Perspectives on Behaviour: Guides to Understanding and Discovery
  The Importance of Perspectives
  The Biological Perspective: Brain, Genes, and Behaviour
    Discovery of Brain-Behaviour Relations
    Evolution and Behaviour: From Darwin to Evolutionary Psychology
    Behaviour Genetics
  The Cognitive Perspective: The Thinking Human
    Origins of the Cognitive Perspective
    Modern Cognitive Science
    Social Constructivism

Research Foundations: The Social Construction of Reality: They Saw A Game

  The Psychodynamic Perspective: The Forces Within
    Psychoanalysis: Freud's Great Challenge
    Current Developments
  The Behavioural Perspective
    Origins of the Behavioural Perspective
    Behaviourism
    Cognitive Behaviourism
  The Humanistic Perspective: Freedom and Self-Actualization
  The Sociocultural Perspective: The Embedded Human
    Cultural Learning and Diversity

Research Frontiers: Nature and *Nurture: Biology, Culture and Behaviour*

  The Perspectives In Historical Context

Integrating the Perspectives: Three Levels of Analysis
  An Example: Understanding Depression

Fields Within Psychology

Psychological Applications: Academic Performance Enhancement Strategies

Problem-Based Learning

History

http://www.cwu.edu/~warren/today.html
Today in the History of Psychology-This site based on Warren Street's book is the APA's history of psychology database with short descriptions of over 3100 events.

http://psychclassics.yorku.ca
Classics in the History of Psychology-This is Chris Green's website at York University in Toronto. It contains a large collection of original historical material.

Terrorism

http://www.cpa.ca/contents.html
Canadian Psychological Association-This is the CPA's website and it contains information about careers, regulatory bodies, professional associations, clinical disorders, and issues that concern psychology in Canada. This site contains a Canadian report on the terrorist attacks in the United States.

General

www.psychologicalscience.org
American Psychological Society-This site is the home page for the American Psychological Society and it contains a wealth of information including student tips, teaching resources, journal articles, news and events and links to many areas of psychology.

http://www.psy.pdx.edu/PsiCafe
The PSI CAFÉ-This is a comprehensive and well organized gateway to psychology links in all areas of psychology.

http://Kenstange.com/psycsite
Psyc Site-This very extensive site, designed by Ken Stange from the department of psychology at Nipissing University, contains information about employment and professional associations, general information for students, links to other psychology sites, chat rooms, etc..

http://www.rider.edu/users/suler/gradschl.html
This site contains information about graduate schools and careers in psychology.

http://www.psychref.com
This is a large website that contains information on all areas of psychology.

http://www.psychwww.com
PsychWeb-This is a comprehensive website that contains links to all areas of psychology, information about careers, student tips, psychology departments and other resources.

Key Terms: *Write the letter of the definition next to the term in the space provided.*

The Nature of Psychology / Perspectives on Behaviour / The Biological Perspective

1. ___ applied research
    a. research involving the application of scientific knowledge to solve practical problems

2. ___ basic research
    b. research designed to obtain knowledge for its own sake

3. ___ behaviour genetics
    c. the scientific study of the role of genetic inheritance in behaviour

4. ___ biological perspective
    d. a perspective that focuses on the role of biological factors in behaviour, including biochemical and brain processes as well as genetic and evolutionary factors

5. ___ evolutionary psychology
    e. a field of study that focuses on the role of evolutionary processes (especially natural selection) in the development of adaptive psychological mechanisms and social behaviour in humans

6. ___ jigsaw program
    f. an applied research program in which knowledge gained from basic research on factors that increase and decrease intergroup hostility was translated into a cooperative learning program designed to reduce interracial hostility in racially integrated schools

7. ___ mind-body dualism
    g. the philosophical position that the mind is a non-physical entity that is not subject to physical laws and cannot be reduced to physical processes; body and mind are separate entities

8. ___ monism
    h. the philosophical position that mental events are reducible to physical events in the brain, so that "mind" and body are one and the same

9. ___ natural selection
    i. any inheritable characteristic that increases the likelihood that survival will be maintained in the species

10. ___ perspective
    j. a theoretical vantage point from which to analyze behaviour and its causes

11. ___ sociobiology
    k. an evolutionary theory of social behaviour that emphasizes the role of adaptive behaviour in maintaining one's genes in the species' gene pool

12. ___ psychology
    l. the scientific study of behaviour and its causes

The Cognitive / Psychodynamic Perspectives

1. ___ artificial intelligence
    a. research involving the application of scientific knowledge to solve practical problems

2. ___ cognitive perspective
    b. a psychological perspective that views humans as rational information processors and problem solvers, and focuses on the mental processes that influence behaviour

3. ___ functionalism
    c. an early school of American psychology that focused on the functions of consciousness and behaviour in helping organisms adapt to their environment and satisfy their needs

4. ___ Gestalt psychology
    d. a German school of psychology that emphasized the natural organization of perceptual elements into wholes, or patterns, as well as the role of insight in problem solving

5. ___ hysteria
    e. a psychological disorder studied and treated by Freud in which physical symptoms appear without any apparent underlying organic cause

6. ___ insight

   f. in Gestalt psychology, the sudden perception of a useful relationship or solution to a problem; in psychoanalysis, the conscious awareness of unconscious dynamics that underlie psychological problems

7. ___ introspection

   g. the method of "looking within" and verbally reporting on immediate experience; used by the structuralists to study the contents of the mind

8. ___ psychodynamic perspective

   h. a psychological perspective that focuses on inner personality dynamics, including the role of unconscious impulses and defences, in understanding behaviour

9. ___ repression

   i. the basic defence mechanism that actively keeps anxiety-arousing material in the unconscious

10. ___ social constructivism

   j. the position that people construct their reality and beliefs through their cognitions

11. ___ structuralism

   k. an early German school of psychology established by Wilhelm Wundt that attempted to study the structure of the mind by breaking it down into its basic components, thought to be sensations

The Behavioural / Humanistic Perspectives

1. ___ behaviour modification

   a. therapeutic procedures based on operant conditioning principles, such as positive reinforcement, operant extinction, and punishment

2. ___ behavioural perspective

   b. a view that emphasizes the manner in which the environment and the learning experiences it provides shape and control behaviour

3. ___ behaviourism

   c. a school of psychology that emphasizes the role of learning and environmental control over behaviour, and maintains that the proper subject matter of psychology is observable behaviour; John Watson and B. F. Skinner were major figures in behaviourism

4. ___ British empiricism

   d. a 17th-century school of philosophy championed by John Locke, according to which all the contents of the mind are gained experientially through the senses; this notion was later a cornerstone for the behaviourists' position that we are shaped through our experiences

5. ___ cognitive behaviourism

   e. a behavioural approach that incorporates cognitive concepts, suggesting that the environment influences our behaviour by affecting our thoughts and giving us information; these cognitive processes allow us to control our behaviour and the environment

6. ___ humanistic perspective

   f. a psychological perspective that emphasizes personal freedom, choice, and self-actualization

7. ___ self-actualization

   g. in humanistic theories, an inborn tendency to strive toward the realization of one's full potential

8. _h_ terror management theory

   h. a theory that focuses on the ways people defend against the fear of death

The Sociocultural Perspective / Historical Context / Integrating the Perspectives

1. _a_ collectivism   a. a cultural factor that emphasizes the achievement of group rather than individual goals and in which personal identity is largely defined by ties to the larger social group (see individualism)

2. ___ culture   b. the enduring values, beliefs, behaviours, and traditions that are shared by a large group of people and passed from one generation to the next

3. _c_ individualism   c. a cultural characteristic that favours the achievement of individual over group goals and which is characteristic of many Western nations; self-identity is based primarily on one's own attributes and achievements (see collectivism)

4. ___ interaction   d. in analyzing causal factors, the influence that the presence or strength of one factor can have on other causal factors

5. _f_ levels of analysis   e. an approach to analyzing behavioural phenomena and their causal factors in terms of biological, psychological, and environmental factors

6. _b_ norms   f. test scores derived from a relevant sample used to evaluate individuals' scores; behavioural "rules"

7. _g_ sociocultural perspective   g. a perspective that emphasizes the role of culture and the social environment in understanding commonalties and differences in human behaviour

Key People: *Write the letter of the ideas associated with the person in the space provided*

1. _e_ Eliot Aronson   a. developed psychoanalysis
2. _j_ Albert Bandura   b. proposed idea of natural selection
3. _b_ Charles Darwin   c. leading humanistic theorist
4. _a_ Sigmund Freud   d. leader of Gestalt psychology
5. _h_ Luigi Galvani   e. jigsaw program
6. _d_ Wolfgang Kohler   f. believed that the real causes of behaviour are environmental
7. _k_ Donald Hebb   g. discovered stages of cognitive development
8. _g_ Jean Piaget   h. severed leg of frog moved if electrical current applied
9. _c_ Carl Rogers   i. proposed idea of structuralism
10. _f_ B.F. Skinner   j. cognitive behaviourist
11. _i_ Wilhelm Wundt   k. invented the concept of the cell assembly

Review at a Glance: *Write the term that best fits the blank to review what you learned in this chapter.*

The Nature of Psychology

Psychology is the scientific study of (1) _____ and the factors that influence it. Psychologists have a quest for knowledge for its own sake, which is called (2)_ _____ and also pursue knowledge that is designed to solve specific practical problems, a type of research known as (3) _____ _____. The Robber's Cave study by Sherif et al. (1961) showed that hostility between groups could be reduced by having children work together in (4) _____ _____. This basic research was later used by Aronson et al. (1978) in the (5) _____ _____, which required that children had to cooperate in order to achieve a goal that neither could achieve alone. As scientists, psychologists have four basic goals regarding behaviour: to (6) _____, (7) _____, (8) _____, and (9) _____ it.

Perspectives on Behaviour: Guides to Understanding and Discovery

(10) _____ are vantage points for analyzing behaviour. The six different perspectives used by psychologists are the (11) _____, (12) _____, (13) _____, (14) _____, (15) _____, and (16) _____ perspectives. The ancient Greek belief that the mind is a spiritual entity not subject to the physical laws that govern the body is called (17) _____ _____ _____. The alternative view that mind and body are one is called (18) _____. The biological perspective emphasizes the roles of the brain, biochemical processes, and (19) _____ _____ _____. According to Darwin's evolutionary theory, any inheritable characteristic that increases the likelihood of survival will be maintained in the species because individuals having the characteristic will be likely to survive and reproduce. This process is known as (20) _____ _____. Psychologists in the field of (21) _____ _____ stress the ideas that an organism's biology determines its behavioural capacities and its behaviour determines whether or not it will survive. Thus, behaviours may well be products of evolution. Similarly, (22) _____ suggest that complex social behaviours are also built into the human species as products of evolution. Another area within the biological perspective is (23) _____ _____, which is the study of how behavioural tendencies are influenced by genetic factors. The cognitive perspective views people as problem solvers and (24) _____ _____. Today's cognitive perspective has roots in the debate between the structuralist, functionalist, and Gestalt camps. The structuralists, who believed that sensations are the basic elements of consciousnness, attempted to study consciousness through the technique of (25) _____. In contrast, the approach that held that psychology should study the "whys" of consciousness, or (26) _____, was influenced by evolutionary theory. The study of how elements of experience are organized into wholes, or (27) _____ _____, suggested that the whole was greater than the sum of its parts. Modern cognitive psychologists study cognitive processes involved in things like decision-making and problem-solving. (28) _____ _____ was one of the most prominent

theorists in the study of childhood cognitive development. A modern offshoot of the cognitive perspective studies complex human thought, reasoning, and problem-solving by developing computer models and is known as   (29) _____ _____. Theorists who maintain that "reality" is in large part our own mental creation are known as (30) _____ _____. The perspective emphasizing the role of unconscious processes and unresolved past conflicts is known as the (31) _____ perspective and is most associated with (32) _____ _____. The behavioural perspective developed from (33) _____ _____, which held that all ideas and knowledge are gained empirically. Today, behaviourists emphasize the (34) _____ determinants of behaviour. An attempt to bridge the gap between the behavioural and cognitive perspectives popularized by Albert Bandura, among others, is called (35) _____ _____. Humanistic psychologists stress the importance of conscious motives and free will and believe that we are motivated to reach our full potentials, a state called (36) _____. According to (37) _____ _____ _____, an innate desire for life despite the realized inevitability of death creates an anxiety called existential terror. The enduring beliefs, values, behaviours, and traditions shared by a large group of people, or (38) _____, also influences our behaviour. The rules that society establishes to indicate what behaviour is acceptable are known as (39) _____.

Integrating the Perspectives: Three Levels of Analysis

The three main levels of analysis that can be used to understand behaviour are the (40) _____, (41) _____, and (42) _____ levels. These levels are usually combined to explain behaviour. Indeed, the presence of one factor can influence the effects of other factors, a process called (43) _____.

Fields Within Psychology

There are a number of specialty fields within the larger field of psychology. For instance, (44) _____ psychologists are involved with the diagnosis and treatment of emotional disorders and abnormal behaviour while (45) _____ psychologists study the biological foundations of behaviour.

Internet Scavenger Hunt

1. Here's your chance to learn more about the diversity of psychology by engaging in an Internet scavenger hunt. Study Sheet 1.3 gives a list of questions to which you can find the answers on the WWW.

Apply What You Know

1. Explain each perspective's view of human nature and focus of study by using Study Sheet 1.1. The exercise should take about 20 minutes and it is well worth the effort.

2. Think of a self-help book that you've read recently. Which of the perspectives that you learned about in Chapter 1 does the book use? Give some examples of how the book uses those perspectives.

3. Choose one of the following (obesity, alcohol use, drug use, juvenile delinquency) and analyze the possible causes of the behaviour by using each of the three levels of analysis (biological, psychological, and environmental). Use Study Sheet 1.2.

Practice Test   22/30

<u>Multiple Choice Items</u>: *Please write the letter corresponding to your answer in the space to the left of each item.*

b   1. According to the text, psychology is defined as the _b_ .

    a. study of people's subjective mental lives.
    b. scientific study of behaviour and its causes.
    c. examination of unconscious factors.
    d. study of personality

b   2. Dr. Adams is a psychologist who works in the area of animal behaviour. She has a particular interest in crows and her research is primarily aimed at gaining more information about the behaviours of these birds, such as their mating habits, eating rituals, and so on. Dr. Adams research is <u>best categorized</u> as _a_ research.

    a. applied
    b. basic
    c. insight
    d. interaction

_C_   3. The jigsaw program (Aronson et al., 1978) worked in reducing inter-group conflict because _C_ .

    a.   working together on jigsaw puzzles created more cooperation
    b.   cooperative experiences only increase inter-group conflict
    c.   the children were required to cooperate in order to reach a goal that neither group could reach alone
    d.   groups almost always prefer to cooperate than to fight each other

_a_   4. Dr. Smith is a psychologist who is interested in studying aggression in sports. For her research, she attends high school basketball games and records the number of aggressive acts that she observes. Dr. Smith's research is <u>best viewed</u> as meeting the _a_ goal of psychology.

    a.   description
    b.   understanding
    c.   prediction
    d.   control

_d_   5. Two psychologists are arguing over the causes of depression. One firmly believes that the disorder has a biological basis and that research should focus on identifying and treating these biological factors. In contrast, the other acknowledges the likely contribution of biology, but asserts that cognitions and thoughts are stronger causes of the disorder and believes that research should instead focus on identifying the key thoughts associated with depression and on effectively changing these thoughts. This difference in opinion can <u>most likely be attributed</u> to the psychologists' different _d_ .

    a.   personalities
    b.   educational backgrounds
    c.   family histories
    d.   psychological perspectives on behaviour

_b_   6. In attempting to explain the violent behaviour of Charles Whitman, some psychologists focused on the potentially important causal role of Whitman's unusual and irrational thoughts. These psychologists are attempting to explain Whitman's behaviour in terms of the _b_ level of analysis.

    a.   structural
    b.   psychological
    c.   environmental
    d.   biological

_c_   7. Monists believed that _a_ .

    a.   the mind is a spiritual entity not subject to physical laws
    b.   the biological perspective was wrong
    c.   mental events are a product of physical events
    d.   the love of money was the root of all evil

_d_ 8. Karl Lashley investigated the brain mechanisms involved in learning by _d_.

    a. severing the leg of a frog and finding that the leg moved when he applied electrical current to it
    b. studying the neurological differences between smart and dumb mice
    c. measuring the EEG activity in trained an untrained animals
    d. damaging specific brain areas of animals and observing how this impacted learning and memory

_c_ 9. The idea that any inheritable characteristic that increases the likelihood of survival will be maintained in the species because individuals having the characteristic will be more likely to survive and reproduce is known as _c_.

    a. evolution
    b. sociobiology
    c. natural selection
    d. behavioural genetics

_b_ 10. Occasionally parents will sacrifice their lives in order to ensure the survival of their children. Someone associated with sociobiology would argue that these instances _c_.

    a. are due to innate altruistic drives within every human being
    b. occur because genetic survival (of people who share your genes) is more important than individual survival
    c. are due to the conflict between unconscious psychological forces and psychological defences
    d. occur because of the reinforcement of altruistic behaviour by culture and society

_a_ 11. The study of both identical and fraternal twins in an attempt to understand behaviour is used most by _a_.

    a. behaviour genetics
    b. evolutionary psychology
    c. sociobiology
    d. the cognitive perspective

_b_ 12. The approach known as _b_ attempted to analyze the mind in terms of its basic elements.

    a. functionalism
    b. structuralism
    c. Gestalt psychology
    d. insight psychology

_c_ 13. Gestalt psychology is concerned with _c_.

    a. the biological influences on behaviour
    b. the environmental determinants of behaviour
    c. how elements of experience are organized into meaningful wholes
    d. artificial intelligence

_d_ 14. Psychologists who study artificial intelligence are most interested in studying _d_ .

    a.   the environmental determinants of behaviour
    b.   the biological influences on behaviour
    c.   intelligence in nonhuman primates
    d.   computer models of complex human thought

_d_ 15. A cognitive psychologist attempts to explain the long-term conflict between the Catholics and Protestants in Ireland in terms of the different "mental realities" that people in each group have created for themselves. This psychologist most likely adheres to the _d_ cognitive viewpoint.

    a.   artificial intelligence
    b.   cognitive neuroscience
    c.   introspection
    d.   social constructivism

_b_ 16. As a young Viennese medical student in the 1880's, Freud began to focus on the disorder called _b_ , in which physical disorders such as blindness develop without any organic cause.

    a.   repression
    b.   hysteria
    c.   psychodynamism
    d.   monism

_d_ 17. The psychological defence mechanism of _d_ is thought to protect people from anxiety by keeping anxiety-producing thoughts, feelings, memories, and impulses in the unconscious.

    a.   insight
    b.   psychoanalysis
    c.   hysteria
    d.   repression

_b_ 18. Donald Hebb, a Canadian psychologist, invented a hypothetical brain structure called a "cell assembly" which proved to be a very important contribution to _c_

    a.   developmental psychology.
    b.   artificial intelligence.
    c.   gestalt psychology.
    d.   cognitive behaviourism.

_a_ 19. People associated with the philosophical perspective of British empiricism _a_ .

    a.   view observation as a more valid approach to knowledge than reasoning
    b.   view reasoning as a more valid approach to knowledge than observation
    c.   believe that internal factors are the major determinants of human behaviour
    d.   assume that most human behaviour is motivated by unconscious forces

_d_ 20. A psychologist is being interviewed on a local news program regarding the recent problems with school violence. The psychologist proposes that we need to significantly change the environments in which our children are being raised by more heavily reinforcing the behaviours we would like to see in our kids. This psychologist is most likely associated with the _a_ psychological perspective.

a. humanistic
b. psychodynamic
c. cognitive
d. behavioural

_a_ 21. Which area of Canada has the most clinical psychologists per capita? c

a. Quebec
b. Western Canada
c. Ontario
d. Maritimes

_d_ 22. Susan is having trouble with anxiety and is working with a psychologist to address this problem. As part of her treatment, the psychologist teaches Susan 1) how to change her anxiety-provoking thoughts and 2) how to change her environment so that it reinforces the new behaviours she wants to learn. Susan's therapist is most likely associated with the _C_ area of psychology.

a. humanistic
b. psychodynamic
c. sociocultural
d. cognitive-behavioural

_d_ 23. Of the following famous psychologists, who was born in Canada?. d

a. Piaget
b. Freud
c. Wundt
d. Bandura

_c_ 24. Nguyen is working with a psychologist who pays a great deal of attention to how he finds personal meaning in his life. The psychologist also focuses on the power of choice and free will. This psychologist most likely adheres to the _c_ psychological perspective.

a. behavioural
b. psychodynamic
c. humanistic
d. biological

_a̶ C_ 25. The "cognitive revolution", where there was renewed interest in mental events, took place in the C

   a. late 1800's.
   b. the 1920's
   c. the 1960's
   d. the 1990's

_a_ 26. Humanistic theorists believe that people are motivated to reach their full potential, a state called _a_ .

   a. self-actualization
   b. terror management
   c. existential anxiety
   d. existential bliss

_c_ 27. Gabriella was raised in a family where individual achievement and accomplishment were stressed by both of her parents. She was constantly encouraged to set personal goals for her self and to strive to achieve them. The values emphasized by Gabriella's family are <u>most consistent</u> with _C_ .

   a. collectivism
   b. structuralism
   c. individualism
   d. functionalism

_a_ 28. In developed countries such as Canada and the United States _a_

   a. women are about twice as likely as men to report being depressed.
   b. women are about ten times as likely as men to report being depressed.
   c. the incidence of depression is the same for both sexes.
   d. men are about five times as likely as women to report being depressed.

_d_ 29. After scoring the game-winning penalty kick in the 1999 World Cup, U.S. player Brandy Chastain took off her jersey in her excitement and revealed her sports bra. Some people took offence to this, probably because Chastain violated _d_ .

   a. reciprocity
   b. the principles of individualism
   c. the principles of collectivism
   d. cultural norms

_b_ 30. Of the following, the one which is <u>not</u> a level of analysis for understanding the causes of behaviour is the _C_ level.

   a. biological
   b. unconscious
   c. psychological
   d. environmental

True/False Items: *Write T or F in the space provided to the left of each item.*

_____ 1. The goal of basic research is to solve practical problems.

_____ 2. Psychologists are interested in controlling behaviour.

_____ 3. Natural selection is a process that selects behaviours that have survival value, according to evolutionary psychology.

_____ 4. According to the biological perspective, evolution has not played a role in the development of modern human behaviour.

_____ 5. Gestalt psychology is concerned with how elements of experience are organized into wholes.

_____ 6. According to the social constructivist view, there is a single "reality."

_____ 7. The perspective that emphasizes unconscious processes is the psychodynamic perspective.

_____ 8. An attempt to bridge the gap between the behavioural and cognitive perspectives is called cognitive behaviourism.

_____ 9. Individual goals are subordinated to those of the group in individualistic cultures.

_____ 10. In an interaction, the presence or strength of one factor can influence the effects of other factors.

Short Answer Questions

1. How do monism and dualism differ?

2. What are the basic principles of evolutionary psychology?

3. What kinds of factors do biological psychologists use to explain human behaviour?

4. What kinds of factors do humanistic psychologists use to explain human behaviour?

5. How do sociocultural factors affect behaviour?

Essay Questions

1. Why would biological factors influence human behaviour?

2. Why would environmental factors such as culture influence human behaviour?

3. If we believe that behaviour is affected by environmental factors, does that mean that people don't have personal control over their behaviour? Explain your answer.

4. Although both biological and environmental factors are likely to affect behaviour, would one set of factors be more likely to affect behaviour than the other?

5. Why would evolutionary factors affect behaviour?

Study Sheet 1.1 Psychological Perspectives on Behaviour

Perspective	View of Human Nature	Focus of Study
Biological		
Cognitive		
Psychodynamic		
Behavioural		
Humanistic		
Sociocultural		

Study Sheet 1.2 Integrating the Perspectives

Behaviour to be explained _____

Biological explanation for behaviour

Psychological explanation for behaviour

Environmental explanation for behaviour

Study Sheet 1.3: Internet Scavenger Hunt

1. Who was the first woman to be elected president of the Canadian Psychological Association?

2. In what year was she elected?

3. What percentage of doctorates in psychology are currently awarded to women?

4. What percentage of doctorates in psychology are currently awarded to African Americans?

5. What percentage of doctorates in psychology are currently awarded to French Canadians?

6. What percentage of doctorates in psychology are currently awarded to Asian Canadians?

7. What percentage of doctorates in psychology are currently awarded to Native Canadians?

8. Who was the first Canadian woman to be awarded a doctorate in psychology?

9. Who was the first African American male to be awarded a doctorate in psychology?

10. Who became the American Psychological Association's first African American president?

Answer Keys

Answer Key for Key Terms

1. s	11. y	21. dd	31. g
2. j	12. z	22. cc	32. d
3. l	13. q	23. o	33. b
4. ii	14. hh	24. bb	34. ee
5. i	15. a	25. u	35. t
6. f	16. e	26. c	36. ff
7. n	17. k	27. m	37. h
8. ll	18. kk	28. r	38. gg
9. w	19. x	29. aa	
10. jj	20. p	30. v	

Answer Key for Key People

1.	e	7.	k
2.	j	8.	g
3.	b	9.	c
4.	a	10.	f
5.	h	11.	i
6.	d		

Answer Key for Review at a Glance

1. behaviour	16. sociocultural	31. psychodynamic
2. basic research	17. mind-body dualism	32. Sigmund Freud
3. applied research	18. monism	33. British empiricism
4. cooperative experiences	19. genetic factors	34. environmental
5. jigsaw program	20. natural selection	35. cognitive behaviourism
6. describe	21. evolutionary psychology	36. self-actualization
7. understand	22. sociobiologists	37. terror management theory
8. predict	23. behaviour genetics	38. culture
9. control	24. information processors	39. norms
10. perspectives	25. introspection	40. biological
11. biological	26. functionalism	41. psychological
12. cognitive	27. Gestalt psychology	42. environmental
13. psychodynamic	28. Jean Piaget	43. interaction
14. behavioural	29. artificial intelligence	44. clinical
15. humanistic	30. social constructivists	45. physiological

Answer Key for Practice Test Multiple Choice Questions

1.	b	16.	b
2.	b	17.	d
3.	c	18.	b
4.	a	19.	a
5.	d	20.	d
6.	b	21.	a
7.	c	22.	d
8.	d	23.	d
9.	c	24.	c
10.	b	25.	c
11.	a	26.	a
12.	b	27.	c
13.	c	28.	a
14.	d	29.	d
15.	d	30.	b

Answer Key for Practice Test True/False Questions

1.	F	6.	F
2.	T	7.	T
3.	T	8.	T
4.	F	9.	F
5.	T	10.	T

Answer Key for Practice Test Short Answer Questions

1. Monists (in the material form) believed that the mind is not a separate spiritual entity from the body and thus is subject to the same physical forces as the body is. Mind-body dualists, on the other hand, believed that the mind is a separate spiritual entity from the body and thus is not governed by physical laws. Most modern biological psychologists would agree with the monist position.

2. Evolutionary psychologists believe that evolution has played an important role in the development of human behaviour. Behaviours that enhanced the abilities of individuals to adapt to their environment in turn increased the likelihood of survival of these individuals and their ability to reproduce. These behaviours were then selected through natural selection.

3. Psychologists using the biological perspective rely on four major factors in explaining human behaviour. First, they study the structures and processes of the brain. Second, they study genetic factors through twin and adoption studies in the field of behaviour genetics. Third, they study biochemical factors. Fourth, they study the influence of evolution on the development of modern human behaviours.

4. Humanistic psychologists emphasize a number of tendencies in their explanations of human behaviour. They believe that people have free will, innate tendencies toward growth and self-actualization, and attempt to find meaning from their existence. This is a positive view of human nature, as it suggests that people will grow to their full potential if the environment is benign.

5. The sociocultural perspective emphasizes the roles of culture (enduring values, beliefs, behaviours and traditions shared by a group of people) and norms. Norms are rules that specify proper behaviour for a particular culture or society.

Answer Key for Practice Test Essay Questions

1. Biological factors would likely influence human behaviour for a number of reasons:
   a. We are biological creatures just as dogs, birds, and dolphins are, and we believe that biological factors affect the behaviours of members of those species
   b. Our brains control various behaviours, and the brain is a biological structure.
   c. Like other species, we are subject to evolutionary forces
   d. Genes and biochemical factors influence the development of our bodies, and we use our bodies to engage in behaviour.

2. Environmental factors such as culture likely influence human behaviour for a number of reasons:
   a. According to the ideas of British empiricism, we gain knowledge through our senses.
   b. The basic principles of learning apply to animal and human species.
   c. We are products of our culture and societies and thus behave in different ways from people in different cultures and societies.
   d. The nature of our environment determines what behaviours we need to engage in to adapt and survive

3. Even if we believe that environmental factors have a great deal of influence over our behaviour, that does not mean that no other factors influence them. For instance, a person can learn to control biological factors through procedures like biofeedback. We can also alter many environmental factors. For instance, we may work to change cultural norms and other aspects of culture that influence our behaviours.

4. It is highly likely that both biological factors and environmental factors influence behaviour. It is difficult to determine which would be a more important factor. They likely interact with one another in complex ways to produce complex human behaviours and interact as well with various psychological factors, such as cognition and personality.

5. Evolutionary factors likely affect human behaviour because of two main reasons:
   a. First, we are biological creatures. There is a great deal of evidence that evolution has affected plants and other animals over millions of years through natural selection. Psychologists using the biological perspective have good reason to think similar procedures have applied to human behaviour over millions of years.
   b. Second, all of the perspectives mentioned in the textbook stress the adaptability of human beings to their environment. As evolution works through the natural selection of traits and behaviours that promote survival, it is likely that evolutionary factors have affected the development of human behaviour.

Chapter 2. Studying Behaviour Scientifically

Learning Objectives

2.1 Describe the three primary attitudes associated with scientific inquiry.

2.2 Using Darley and Latané's research, illustrate the six steps of the scientific process.

2.3 Describe the difference between a hypothesis and a theory.

2.4 Describe the two approaches to understanding behaviour and explain which approach scientists prefer.

2.5 Describe the characteristics of a good theory.

2.6 Describe the importance of operational definitions and recognize examples of them.

2.7 Describe the most common methods psychologists use to measure behaviour, and a limitation of each.

2.8 Describe and identify the advantages and disadvantages of the case study method, naturalistic observation, and survey research.

2.9 Explain the importance of random sampling for conducting survey research.

2.10 Describe the purpose and methods of correlational research.

2.11 Explain why scientists cannot draw causal conclusions from correlational research.

2.12 Describe and interpret correlation coefficients and scatterplots and explain how correlational research can be used to predict behaviour.

2.13 Describe the characteristics of an experiment and explain how experiments can investigate causal relations among variables.

2.14 Define and differentiate independent and dependent variables.

2.15 Describe experimental and control groups in an experiment.

2.16 Describe how random assignment and counterbalancing assist in designing an experiment.

2.17 Describe how experimental research has assisted in our understanding of environmental stimulation and brain development and understanding the effects of alcohol on sexual arousal.

2.18 Recognize the various research methods and contrast their primary advantages and disadvantages.

2.19 Define internal validity and explain how the following factors threaten it: confounding variables, demand characteristics, the placebo effect, and experimenter expectancy.

2.20 Define the double blind procedure and describe why it is used.

2.21 Differentiate between internal and external validity.

2.22 Identify the major ethical issues in human research.

2.23 Describe the debate regarding the ethics of research using animals.

2.24 Describe how critical thinking skills can be used to evaluate claims made in everyday life.

Chapter Overview

This chapter will help you to understand how to evaluate psychological research. The chapter opens with some basic steps in the scientific process, which apply to all scientific research, not just that in psychology. Once you start with an initial observation or question, you then form a hypothesis, or a tentative prediction or explanation about the phenomenon you are studying. Then you test the hypothesis by conducting research, analyzing the data, and determining if your hypothesis is correct or should be rejected. Further research on the phenomenon then helps to build theory, a set of formal statements about how and why certain events are related. New hypotheses are then derived from the theory and tested. There are two major approaches to understanding behaviour: hindsight understanding (after-the-fact explanations) and understanding through prediction, control, and theory building (the scientific approach). Psychologists study and measure variables, operationally defining them in terms of the procedures used to measure them. Psychologists rely on self-reports, reports by others, physiological measures, and behavioural responses to measure variables.

Psychologists use several methods of doing research. Descriptive research identifies how humans and animals behave. Case studies, which are in-depth analyses of individuals, groups, or events, are a type of descriptive research. Studies of animals or humans in natural settings are examples of naturalistic observation. Questionnaires or interviews are administered to people in survey research. It is important that the characteristics of the sample represent the population so that the researchers can make accurate conclusions about the population. This is often accomplished through random sampling. Associations between variables are measured through correlational research. If two variables are correlated, that does not necessarily mean that one variable <u>causes</u> the other variable. The correlation coefficient is a statistic that measures the association between the variables. A positive correlation occurs when higher scores on one variable are associated with higher scores on another variable. A negative correlation occurs when higher scores on one variable are associated with <u>lower</u> scores on another variable. The plus or minus sign of a correlation coefficient tells you the direction of the relationship, while the absolute value of the statistic tells you the strength of the relationship.

Correlations help researchers examine the relationships between variables. Experiments are used to determine cause-and-effect relationships. When performing experiments, researchers <u>manipulate</u> one or more variables (the independent variable[s]) and measure whether this manipulation produces changes in a second variable or variables (the dependent variable[s]). The researcher attempts to control for other factors (extraneous or confounding variables) that might influence the outcome. In many experiments, participants are randomly assigned to either an experimental group (receives the treatment) or a control group (does not receive the treatment). The two groups are then compared statistically to see if there is any difference between them. Another way to design an experiment is to expose each participant to all conditions of the experiment.

Psychologists are particularly interested in assuring others that their research is valid. Internal validity represents the degree to which an experiment supports clear causal conclusions. It is important to try to rule out other factors that may have influenced the results so that the researcher can conclude that it was the manipulation of the independent variable, rather than some other factor, that produced changes in the dependent variable. If the researcher cannot do that, he or she has a problem with the confounding of variables. Some problems that researchers try to control are demand characteristics, or cues that participants pick up about how they are "supposed" to behave, placebo effects, in which participants' expectancies affect their behaviour, and experimenter expectancy effects, by which researchers subtly and unintentionally influence the behaviour of their participants through their actions. External validity refers to the extent to which the results of a particular study can be generalized to other people, settings, and conditions. Researchers rely on replication, or the ability of a study to be repeated with the same results, to determine the external validity of the findings.

Ethical standards are very important in psychological research. The Canadian Psychological Association (CPA) guideline of informed consent states that participants should be given a full description of the procedures to be followed, and should be told that they have the right to withdraw from the study without penalty. Sometimes, psychologists use deception studies, in which participants are misled about the nature of the study. These experiments are controversial but may be necessary to obtain natural, spontaneous responses from people. Ethical standards are also applied to research with animals. Research with animals is controversial, but many scientists would argue that research with animals is necessary for both practical and theoretical reasons. The Canadian Council on Animal Care has published extensive guidelines on animal research.

Chapter Outline

Scientific Principles in Psychology
    Scientific Attitudes
    Gathering Evidence: Steps in the Scientific Process
    Two Approaches to Understanding Behaviour
    Defining and Measuring Variables

Methods of Research
    Descriptive Research: Recording Events
        Research Foundations: Studies of Bullying in Canadian Schools
    Correlational Research: Measuring Associations Between Events
    Experiments: Examining Cause and Effect
    Experimental Versus Descriptive/Correlational Approaches

Threats to the Validity of Research
    Confounding of Variables
    Demand Characteristics
    Placebo Effects
    Experimenter Expectancy Effects
    Replicating and Generalizing the Findings
        Research Frontiers: Science, Psychics and the Paranormal

Ethical Principles in Human and Animal Research
    Ethical Standards in Human Research
    Ethical Standards in Animal Research

Critical Thinking in Science and Everyday Life
        Psychological Applications: Evaluating Claims in Research and Everyday Life

Problem-Based Learning

EMDR

http://www.trauma-pages.com/emdr-2001.htm
A bibliography of journal articles on EMDR that have been published between 1989 and 2001.

http://www.theness.com/articles/emdr-nejs0401.html
An article by Bunmi Olatunji from the New England Journal of Skepticism criticizing EMDR.

Research

http://psych.hanover.edu/research/exponnet.html
Part of the American Psychological Society website. Contains a large number of online experiments that students can participate in.

http://www.psychwww.com/resource/journals.htm
An index of over 1,500 psychology and social science journals.

http://psychexps.olemiss.edu
PsychExperiments-This site offers students the chance to participate in a large number of lab experiments on perception and cognition.

General

www.psychologicalscience.org
American Psychological Society-This site is the home page for the American Psychological Society and it contains a wealth of information including student tips, teaching resources, journal articles, news and events and links to many areas of psychology. This site also has links to online experiments.

http://www.psychwww.com
PsychWeb-A comprehensive website containing links to all areas of psychology, information about careers, student tips, psychology departments and other resources.

Key Terms: *Write the letter of the definition next to the term in the space provided.*

1. ___ archival measures
2. ___ case study
3. ___ confounding of variables
4. ___ control group
5. ___ correlation coefficient
6. ___ correlational research
7. ___ demand characteristics
8. ___ dependent variable
9. ___ descriptive research
10. ___ double-blind procedure
11. ___ experiment
12. ___ experimental group
13. ___ experimental expectancy effects
14. ___ external validity
15. ___ hypothesis
16. ___ independent variable
17. ___ informed consent
18. ___ internal validity
19. ___ meta-analysis
20. ___ naturalistic observation
21. ___ negative correlation
22. ___ operational definition
23. ___ placebo

a. every member of the population has an equal probability of being chosen
b. defines a variable in terms of the specific procedures used to produce or measure it
c. the factor that is measured by the experimenter
d. cues that participants pick up about a hypothesis
e. an in-depth analysis of an individual, group, or event
f. the researcher measures two variables and then statistically analyzes whether they are related
g. both experimenter and participant are kept unaware as to which condition the participant is in
h. a tentative explanation or prediction
i. the group that receives a treatment
j. degree to which the results of a study can be generalized to other people, settings, and conditions
k. the observation of behaviour in its natural setting
l. group that does not receive a treatment
m. a statistical procedure for combining the results of different studies that examine the same topic
n. a set of formal statements that explains how and why certain events are related to each other
o. when participants have been given a description of experimental procedures, and have been given freedom of withdrawal
p. a statistic that indicates the direction and strength of the relation between two variables
q. already existing records or documents
r. an inactive or inert substance
s. occurs when higher scores on one variable are associated with lower scores on a second variable
t. a method for examining cause-effect relationships
u. represents the degree to which an experiment supports clear causal conclusions
v. information about a topic is obtained by administering questionnaires or interviews
w. seeks to identify how humans and other animals behave, particularly in natural settings

24. ___ placebo effect

x. each participant has an equal likelihood of being assigned to any one group within an experiment

25. ___ population

y. when people receiving a treatment show a change in behaviour because of their expectations

26. ___ positive correlation

z. individuals about whom we are interested in drawing conclusions

27. ___ random assignment

aa. any characteristic that can vary

28. ___ random sampling

bb. ways that experimenters influence their participants to act in ways that are consistent with the hypothesis

29. ___ replication

cc. the process of repeating a study to determine whether the original findings can be duplicated

30. ___ representative sample

dd. a subset of individuals drawn from the larger population of interest

31. ___ sample

ee. higher scores on one variable are associated with higher scores on a second variable

32. ___ scatterplot

ff. when two variables are intertwined in such a way that we cannot determine which one has influenced a D.V.

33. ___ survey research

gg. sample that reflects characteristics of the population

34. ___ theory

hh. graph that depicts the relationship between variables

35. ___ variable

ii. the factor that is manipulated by the experimenter

Review at a Glance:

Write the term that best fits the blank to review what you learned in this chapter.

Scientific Principles in Psychology

Doing scientific research involves using the scientific process. Once a researcher has observed a phenomenon or formulated an initial question about it, he or she forms a (1) Hypothesis, or tentative explanation or prediction, about it. Researchers then test the idea, analyze the data, and determine if the hypothesis was correct or should be rejected. As additional evidence comes in, researchers attempt to build (2) Theories, which are sets of formal statements that explain how and why events are related. There are two main approaches to understanding behaviour. After-the-fact understanding used to explain a behaviour is known as (3) _____ _____. Scientists, though, typically try to understand a phenomenon through (4) _____, (5) _____, and (6) _____ _____. Psychologists study (7) _____, which are characteristics that vary. Defining a variable in terms of the specific procedures used to measure or produce it is known as an (8) _____ _____. Psychologists measure behaviour in a number of different ways. (9)_____ - _____ _____ ask people to report on their own knowledge, beliefs or feelings. Measures of heart rate, blood pressure etc. are known as (10) _____

_____. Already existing records of people's behaviour that are used for research are known as (11) _____ _____.

Methods of Research

An in-depth analysis of an individual, group, or event is called a (12) _____ _____. Sometimes researchers are interested in describing behaviour that occurs in its natural setting, a type of research called (13) _____ _____. Information about a topic is obtained by administering questionnaires or interviews to many people in (14) _____ _____. In survey research, researchers are interested in making conclusions about a (15) _____, which represents the entire set of individuals about whom we are interested in making conclusions. Because it is often impractical to study an entire population, researchers typically study a subset of that population called a (16) _____. To draw valid conclusions about the population, the sample must accurately reflect the characteristics of the population. Such a sample is known as a (17) _____ _____. When every member of the population has an equal probability of being chosen for the sample, the researcher has created a (18) _____ _____. When researchers are interested in measuring the associations between events, they conduct (19) _____ _____, though such research does not indicate causation. A statistic that measures the direction and strength of the relationship between two variables is called a (20) _____ _____. When higher scores on one variable are associated with lower scores on a second variable, the researcher has discovered a (21) _____ correlation. When higher scores on one variable are associated with higher scores on a second variable, the researcher has discovered a (22) _____ correlation. A type of research method that is used to determine cause-and-effect relationships is known as an (23) _____. In an experiment, the variable that is manipulated by the experimenter is known as the (24) _____ variable, whereas the variable that is measured by the experimenter is known as the (25) _____ _____ variable. Through (26) _____ _____ , participants in an experiment are often assigned to groups. The (27) _____ group is the group that receives a treatment, while the (28) _____ group does not.

Threats to the Validity of Research

It is important for researchers to establish that their research is valid. (29) _____ _____ represents the degree to which an experiment supports clear causal conclusions. A problem with internal validity exists when two variables are intertwined in such a way that we cannot determine which one has influenced a dependent variable, a condition known as (30) _____ _____ _____. Cues that participants pick up about the hypothesis of a study are known as (31) _____ _____. Inactive or inert substances known as (32) _____ are often used to control for participant expectancy effects. When an experimenter subtly and unintentionally influences the behaviour of participants so that it is consistent with the hypothesis of the study, the effects are called (33) _____ _____ effects. Researchers are interested in establishing not only internal validity but also in establishing (34) _____ _____ , which is the degree to which the results of a study can be generalized to other people, settings, and conditions. To determine whether a tentative conclusion reached in one study is valid, the results of the study must be (35) _____. Research designed to statistically combine the results of

many studies involves a statistical procedure known as (36) _____
_____.

Ethical Principles in Human and Animal Research

When research participants are given a full description of the research, and are told that they are free to withdraw from the study without penalty, the participants have received (37) _____ _____. Studies in which participants are misled as to the nature of the study are known as (38) _____ studies.

Apply What You Know

1. Remember that operational definitions define a variable in terms of the specific procedures used to produce or measure it. Use Study Sheet 2.1 to write operational definitions for each of the following concepts: intelligence, "good memory," aggression, love, and happiness.

2. Dr. Lena Onmee hypothesizes that stress and anger cause depression. However, having been out of school too long, Dr. Onmee has forgotten the basics of experimentation, so she turns to you, ace psychology student, for help in designing her experiment. Describe how you would advise her to set up the experiment by using Study Sheet 2.2.

3. Use Study Sheet 2.3 to find seven problems with the following study:

Space psychologist Spiff lands on the dreaded planet Zorg. Nothing much is known of the Zorgian people, but they are rumoured to be vicious and dangerous to humans. To determine if this is the case, Spiff decides to do an experiment. He hypothesizes that the Zorgians are only likely to be vicious and dangerous when they are angered, so he defines anger as his dependent variable. A group of southern Zorgians, who are known to be quite different from the northern Zorgians, volunteer to participate in Spiff's study. He lets the angry Zorgians be in his control group and the non-angry Zorgians be in his experimental group and tells them the hypothesis of the study before it begins. He then measures the viciousness and dangerousness of both groups and compares them by using meta-analysis.

Internet Scavenger Hunt

1. Access the Statistics Canada website (http://www.statcan.ca) and determine the percentages of males and females, racial groups, and age groups in the county in which your college or high school is located in the 2001 census. Describe how you, as a researcher, would draw a representative sample from that population.

Practice Test

<u>**Multiple Choice Items**</u>: *Please write the letter corresponding to your answer in the space to the left of each item.*

_C_ 1. A tentative explanation or prediction about some phenomenon is called a _C_.

  a. theory
  b. thesis
  c. hypothesis
  d. variable

_b_ 2. Theories are _a_ _b_

  a. tentative explanations or predictions about some phenomenon
  b. formal statements that explain how and why events are related
  c. characteristics that vary
  d. definitions of variables in terms that they are produced or measured

_a_ 3. One of the problems of after-the-fact or "hindsight" explanations is that _a_.

  a. there are many ways of explaining past events and there is usually no way to know which of these ways is correct
  b. they fail to provide a foundation on which further scientific study can occur
  c. they are usually too theoretically complex and sophisticated
  d. they overemphasize the importance of external validity

_d_ 4. Bored with a life of fighting supercriminals and trying to stay resistant to the charms of Lois Lane, Superman tries to find a way to occupy his time. Deciding to study superhuman powers, he defines such powers as being "faster than a speeding bullet, more powerful than a locomotive, and able to leap tall buildings in a single bound." Superman has created a(n) _d_ of the variable.

  a. hypothesis
  b. self-report measure
  c. physiological measure
  d. operational definition

_d_ 5. A researcher is interested in studying factors that influence interpersonal attraction. In a study designed to explore this variable, the researcher uses a very attractive person for an assistant. Interpersonal attraction is then assessed by whether or not the people participating in the study call the attractive assistant to ask the person on a date. In this example, calling the attractive assistant represents a(n) _d_ of interpersonal attraction.

  a. correlational study
  b. hypothesis
  c. case study
  d. operational definition

_c_ 6. A social psychologist is interested in studying aggression in sports fans. He goes to various sporting events and keeps track of the number of aggressive acts that occur between fans using a well-defined coding system. This psychologist is using _c_ to measure behaviour.

    a. self-report measures
    b. physiological measures
    c. behavioural observations
    d. the double-blind method

_d_ 7. Trying to determine why men cheat on their wives, a research psychologist studies Bill Clinton in an in-depth analysis. This psychologist is using the _d_ method of study.

    a. correlational
    b. experimental
    c. archival
    d. case study

_a_ 8. In order to learn about the social behaviour of children, a developmental psychologist goes to an elementary school, finds a seat near one of the windows in a classroom, and watches the children playing on the playground outside during recess. This psychologist is engaged in _a_.

    a. naturalistic observation
    b. correlational research
    c. a case study
    d. experimental research

_d_ 9. Putting his research plan to work, Superman decides to study Batman, Robin, Aquaman, and Spiderman, and apply his results to all superheroes. In this case "all superheroes" is how Superman is defining his _d_.

    a. sample
    b. random sample
    c. representative sample
    d. population

_a_ 10. Dringenberg and his colleagues at Queens University examined the effects of alcohol on prenatal development. Because of ethical concerns they used guinea pigs rather than humans. In this experiment, prenatal development was the _a_ variable.

    a. dependent
    b. independent
    c. random
    d. confounding

_____ 11. Dr. Chang is interested in conducting a survey of all the college students at her university. She is careful when conducting her research to make sure that each student on campus has an equal chance of participating in her survey. To create her survey sample, Dr. Chang is using random _a_.

a. sampling
b. assignment
c. preference
d. appointment

_____ 12. The use of a _C_ sample best establishes _____ validity.

a. non-random; internal
b. representative; external
c. representative; internal
d. non-random; external

_____ 13. When it is not clear whether variable X caused variable Y or vice-versa, there is a(n) _b_.

a. demand characteristic
b. bidirectional causality problem
c. third-variable problem
d. experimenter expectancy effect

_____ 14. Dr. Little has heard that people tend to become more politically conservative as they get older and decides to conduct a study to see if this is true. She conducts a telephone survey where she asks participants how old they are and their political identification. She then uses statistics to see if there is a relationship between age and political identification. The design that **best describes** Dr. Little's research is _b_.

a. experimental research
b. correlational research
c. naturalistic observation
d. behavioural observation

_____ 15. Dr. Gonzalez has just completed a correlational study where he found a strong association between parental expectations and child academic achievement. In other words, children who perform well in school tend to have parents who have high expectations for their children. However, Dr. Gonzalez can't tell which variable causes the other. It may be that high expectations cause children to perform better but it may be that children who perform better in school cause their parents to have higher expectations. This particular problem is known as _a_

a. the bidirectional causality problem
b. the third variable problem
c. poor external validity
d. the experimenter expectancy effect

_____ 16. After years of experience, super researcher Dr. Yo G. Bear finds that the more food from stolen picnic baskets in Jellystone Park that bears eat, the sicker they get. Dr. Bear has observed a ___*a*___ relationship between the variables.

a. negative correlational
b. positive correlational
c. zero correlational
d. cause-and-effect

_____ 17. A "Survivor" contestant notices that the more worms a member caught for his or her tribe to eat, the less votes to be voted off the island he or she received in Tribal Council. This contestant has observed a ___*a*___ relationship between the variables.

a. negative correlational
b. positive correlational
c. zero correlational
d. cause-and-effect

_____ 18. For psychologists, the most direct method for testing cause-and-effect relationships is ___*d*___.

a. correlational studies
b. archival studies
c. surveys
d. experiments

_____ 19. In its simplest form, an experiment has three essential characteristics. Of the following, the one which is <u>not</u> a characteristic of experiments is ___*b*___ .

a. an experimental manipulation of an independent variable
b. an experimental manipulation of a dependent variable
c. a measurement of a dependent variable
d. attempts to control for extraneous factors

_____ 20. Dr. Mangat conducted an experiment on the effects of alcohol on driving performance. The subjects were assigned to one of three groups. Group 1 received no alcohol, group 2 had a .05 level of intoxication and group 3 had a .08 level of intoxication. In this experiment driving performance was a ___*a*___ variable.

a. dependent
b. independent
c. control
d. confounding

_____ 21. Pepler and her colleagues at York University asked children their views about bullying at school. In a later study, they video recorded children in bullying situations during recess and found that, contrary to the earlier study, children were not only less helpful to the victim but that they frequently participated with the bully. The first study was __c__ and the second study was _____.

a. a survey; an experiment
b. naturalistic observation; an experiment
c. a survey; naturalistic observation
d. naturalistic observation; a descriptive method

_____ 22. A clinical psychologist has developed a new form of psychotherapy to treat a particular personality disorder. In order to test its effectiveness, a group of people with the personality disorder is selected to receive the therapy for 8 weeks. A second group of people with the disorder is also created but this group receives no therapy at all. At the end of the 8 weeks, the mental health of the people in both groups is assessed to evaluate the new psychotherapy. In this study, the people who did **not** receive any therapy would be in the __b__ group.

a. experimental
b. control
c. random
d. sample

_____ 23. Bored with life on Gilligan's island, the Professor decides to study the effects of rubbing coconut oil on people's skulls. He randomly assigns three castaways to his experimental group and the other three to his control group and measures the mean intelligence level of both groups. The rubbin of coconut oil on people's skulls is the __c__ variable.

a. dependent
b. confounding
c. independent
d. correlational

_____ 24. In survey research, random _____ is typically used to insure that a sample is representative, while in experiments, random __a__ is used to balance differences between participants across the various experimental groups.

a. sampling; assignment
b. assignment; sampling
c. sampling; appointment
d. appointment; assignment

_____ 25. Random assignment controls for important differences between individual participants by _b_ . This is in contrast to designs where each participant is exposed to each condition or group in an experiment. These designs control for individual differences by ____ .

a. balancing them; randomly sampling them
b. holding them constant; balancing them
c. balancing them; holding them constant
d. randomly sampling them; holding them constant

_____ 26. A researcher is interested in interpersonal attraction and the factors that affect it. She designs a study where she looks at the effect of similarity and social warmth on interpersonal attraction. Participants in her study meet a target person who either is or is not similar to the participant (the similarity variable) and who is either friendly or is aloof (the social warmth variable). After interacting with the target person under these conditions, participants are then asked to rate how attractive they think the target person is. In this study, similarity and social warmth are the _a_ variables and interpersonal attraction is the ____ variable.

a. independent; dependent
b. dependent; independent
c. confounding; dependent
d. independent; confounding

_____ 27. Sally has been suffering from depression and finally decides to seek help from a clinical psychologist. After a couple of months of therapy, Sally's depression starts to lift. However, her improvement really isn't due to any of the therapy she has received from her therapist but instead is a product of Sally's expectation that psychotherapy is supposed to be effective and therefore she should be getting better. This example is **best considered** an example of _c_ or (a)

a. experimenter expectancy effects
b. the double-blind effect
c. the placebo effect
d. a study with high external validity

_____ 28. In a famous experiment by Rosenthal and Jacobson (1968), teachers at an elementary school were told at the beginning of the year that certain students were "late bloomers" and most likely these particular students were going to become strong students during the school-year ahead. Sure enough, by the end of the year, the identified students were doing much better in school. Interestingly, the researchers had selected these children randomly at the beginning of the year. The findings in this study are **most similar or analogous** to the problem of _a_ .

a. demand characteristics
b. experimenter expectancy effects
c. the placebo effect
d. random sampling

_____ 29. Which of the following is **NOT** one of the Canadian Psychological Association's four basic ethical principles? *b*

✓ a. responsibility to society
✓ b. integrity in relationships
✓ c. respect for the dignity of persons
 d. avoid animal research that is harmful to animals

_____ 30. Goodale and his colleagues at the University of Western Ontario examined the relationship between perception and action by studying a patient, who because of asphyxiation, had suffered partial brain damage. The method of research they used was

a. a case study.
b. experimental.
c. naturalistic observation
d. a survey.

True/False Items: *Write T or F in the space provided to the left of each item.*

_____ 1. A hypothesis is a tentative explanation or prediction about some phenomenon.

_____ 2. An operational definition is defined as any characteristic that can vary.

_____ 3. The tendency to respond in a socially acceptable manner rather than according to how one truly feels or behaves is called a demand characteristic.

_____ 4. Already existing records or documents used to study some behavioural phenomenon are called archival measures.

_____ 5. When every member of the population has an equal probability of being chosen for the sample, the sample is called a representative sample.

_____ 6. If I predict that the more questions from this study guide you get correct, the higher the score you will get on your next exam, I am predicting a positive correlation between the variables.

_____ 7. The variable that is manipulated by an experimenter is called the independent variable.

_____ 8. The degree to which an experiment supports a clear causal conclusion is known as the study's external validity.

_____ 9. Cues that participants pick up about the hypothesis of the study or about how they are supposed to behave are known as placebo effects.

_____ 10. The process of repeating a study to determine whether the original findings can be duplicated is known as meta-analysis.

Short Answer Questions

1. What types of physiological measures are used by psychologists to study behaviour, and why are they subject to interpretive problems?

2. Describe what correlational research is used to study and what correlation coefficients mean.

3. How are independent and dependent variables and experimental and control groups used in experiments?

4. Distinguish between random sampling and random assignment.

5. What are some of the basic ethical standards used in human research?

Essay Questions

1. Why is it better to study behaviour through prediction, control, and theory building than through hindsight understanding?

2. Describe the four types of measurements used by psychologists to measure variables.

3. Describe three major types of descriptive research.

4. Explain the logic of experimentation.

5. Describe three major threats to the internal validity of an experiment.

Study Sheet 2.1 Operational Definitions

<u>Intelligence</u>

<u>"Good memory"</u>

<u>Aggression</u>

<u>Love</u>

<u>Happiness</u>

Study Sheet 2.2   Designing an Experiment

Hypothesis: Stress and anger cause depression

Independent variables:

Dependent variable:

Operational definition of dependent variable:

Diagram the experimental design (experimental and control groups, random assignment etc.)

Study Sheet 2.3   Problems with the design

1.

2.

3.

4.

5.

6.

7.

Answer Keys

Answer Key for Key Terms

1. q	13. bb	25. z
2. e	14. j	26. ee
3. ff	15. h	27. x
4. l	16. ii	28. a
5. p	17. o	29. cc
6. f	18. u	30. gg
7. d	19. m	31. dd
8. c	20. k	32. hh
9. w	21. s	33. v
10. g	22. b	34. n
11. t	23. r	35. aa
12. I	24. y	

Answer Key for Review at a Glance

1. hypothesis	11. archival records	21. negative	31. demand characteristics
2. theories	12. case study	22. positive	32. placebos
3. hindsight understanding	13. naturalistic observation	23. experiment	33. experimenter expectancy
4. prediction	14. survey research	24. independent	34. external validity
5. control	15. population	25. dependent	35. replicated
6. theory building	16. sample	26. random assignment	36. meta-analysis
7. variables	17. representative sample	27. experimental	37. informed consent
8. operational definition	18. random sample	28. control	38. deception
9. self-report measures	19. correlational research	29. internal validity	
10. physiological measures	20. correlation coefficient	30. confounding of variables	

Answer Key for Practice Test Multiple Choice Questions

1.	c	16.	b
2.	b	17.	a
3.	a	18.	d
4.	d	19.	b
5.	d	20.	a
6.	c	21.	c
7.	d	22.	b
8.	a	23.	c
9.	d	24.	a
10.	a	25.	c

11. a	26. a
12. b	27. c
13. b	28. b
14. b	29. a
15. a	30. d

Answer Key for Practice Test True/False Questions

1. T	6. T
2. F	7. T
3. F	8. F
4. T	9. F
5. F	10. F

Answer Key for Practice Test Short Answer Questions

1. Psychologists use several different types of physiological measurements of behaviour. Heart rate, blood pressure, respiration rate, and hormonal secretions are often studied. Electrical and biochemical processes in the brain are also studied. The problem in interpreting these measures is that it is often unclear how these physiological measures are linked to specific patterns of behaviour.

2. Correlational research is used to study the relationships between variables. Two variables (X and Y) are measured and then are statistically analyzed to determine whether they are related. The statistic that is used to measure the association is called a correlation coefficient. The sign of the coefficient indicates if the variables are positively or negative correlated. A positive correlation means that as one variable increases the other also increases, while a negative correlation means that as one variable increases the other decreases. The absolute value of the correlation coefficient indicates the strength of the relationship.

3. In the simplest kind of experiment, participants are first randomly assigned to either an experimental group or a control group. The experimental group receives the treatment or active level of the independent variable while the control group does not. The independent variable is manipulated by the experimenter. The dependent variable is then measured by the experimenter for each group, and the groups are statistically compared to determine if there is a difference between them.

4. In random sampling, every member of the population has an equal probability of being included in the sample. Random samples are used to try to make the sample representative of the population and to increase the study's external validity. Random assignment is used in experiments to assign people to the various conditions of the experiment. Random assignment helps to increase the internal validity of the experiment.

5. According to CPA's guidelines regarding informed consent, research participants should be given a full description of the procedures to be followed, and should be told that they are free to withdraw from the study at any time without penalty. Researchers are also concerned with a participant's right to privacy, the psychological risk (e.g. emotional stress) to the participant, and the social risk (e.g. whether information about the individual might become known by others, and have detrimental effects) to the participant.

Answer Key for Practice Test Essay Questions

1. Hindsight understanding is problematic when used to explain human and animal behaviour because past events can usually be explained in many ways such that it is not clear which explanation might be the correct one. It is better to use the scientific process to study behaviour. Under controlled conditions, researchers can test their understanding of what causes a certain behaviour by formulating hypotheses and determining whether those predictions are borne out in the lab. When research results support the hypotheses, researchers can create an integrated network of predictions in the process of theory construction.

2. Psychologists rely on four types of measurements to measure variables. Self-report measures are reports by people about their own knowledge, beliefs, feelings, experiences or behaviour. Such measures are often used in survey research. Researchers can also ask other people to report on the behaviour of the individuals under study (reports by others). Physiological measures such as heart rate, blood pressure, respiration rate, hormonal secretions, electrical and biochemical processes in the brain are also studied. A fourth measurement approach is to observe people's overt behaviours in laboratory or naturalistic settings. Finally, psychologists sometimes use archival measures, or already existing records or documents to study human behaviour.

3. Case studies are in-depth analyses of individuals, groups, or events. The case study method enables intensive study of a particular case and the collection of a large amount of data. In naturalistic observation, the researcher observes behaviour as it occurs in its natural setting. Survey research involves administering questionnaires or interviews to many people. Survey questions typically ask about people's attitudes, opinions, and behaviours.

4. In an experiment, there are three essential characteristics. First, the experimenter manipulates one variable. This is known as the independent. Second, the experimenter measures whether this manipulation produces changes in a second variable, known as the dependent variable. Third, the researcher attempts to control for extraneous or confounding variables that might influence the outcome of the experiment. Random assignment to groups is important to make sure that the experiment starts out with equivalent groups of people.

5. One major threat to the internal validity of an experiment is a demand characteristic. Demand characteristics are cues that participants pick up about the hypothesis of a study or about how they are supposed to behave. Placebo effects occur when a participant's expectancies about a treatment influence their behaviour. Experimenter expectancy effects occur when experimenter's subtly and unintentionally influence their participants to respond in a manner that is consistent with the hypothesis of the study.

Chapter 3. Biological Foundations of Behaviour

Learning Objectives

3.1 Name the main parts of a neuron and describe the function of each part.

3.2 Describe the structural components that allow communication between neurons.

3.3 Describe the structure and functions of glial cells.

3.4 Describe the resting membrane potential.

3.5 Describe how electrical potentials in the neuron assist in neural transmission.

3.6 Describe how graded potential and action potentials differ.

3.7 Define myelin and describe how it affects neural transmission.

3.8 Describe the roles of neurotransmitters, the synapse, and receptor sites in nervous system activity.

3.9 Describe how neurotransmitters have excitatory or inhibitory effects.

3.10 Describe how molecules of neurotransmitter are deactivated at the synapse.

3.11 Describe the primary functions of acetylcholine, dopamine, serotonin, and endorphins and disorders associated with their malfunctioning.

3.12 List and describe the three major types of neurons.

3.13 Differentiate between the central nervous system and the peripheral nervous system.

3.14 Describe the two divisions of the peripheral nervous system and their functions.

3.15 Name the two divisions of the autonomic nervous system and describe how they help to maintain homeostasis.

3.16 Describe the role of the spinal cord in reflexes.

3.17 Describe the methods used by scientists to study the brain, and brain-behaviour relations.

3.18 Name and describe the function of the structures in the hindbrain, midbrain, and forebrain.

3.19 Describe the functions of the ascending and descending reticular formation, and how these functions have earned it the name "the brain's gatekeeper".

3.20 Describe the role of the thalamus in sensation and perception.

3.21 Describe the major functions of the lobes of the cerebral cortex and identify their location on a diagram of the brain.

3.22 How are somatic sensory and motor cortexes organized?

3.23 Describe the role of the frontal cortex in higher mental functions.

3.24 Describe the role of the corpus callosum in lateralization of the cerebral hemispheres.

3.25 Describe the split brain studies.

3.26 Describe neural plasticity in relation to brain development and recovery from brain damage.

3.27 Describe how the brain interacts with the endocrine and immune systems.

Chapter Overview

After reading this chapter, you should have a better idea of the biological influences on human and animal behaviour. The chapter covers the neural bases of behaviour, the nervous system (including the structures and functions of the brain), nervous system interactions with the endocrine and immune systems, and genetic influences on behaviour. Specialized cells called neurons are the building blocks of the nervous system. Each neuron has three main parts: the cell body, which contains the biochemical structures that keep the neuron alive, the dendrites, which collect information from neighbouring neurons and send it on to the cell body, and the axon, which conducts electrical impulses away from the cell body to other neurons, muscles, and glands. Glial cells support neurons by holding them in place, manufacturing nutrient chemicals, and absorbing toxins and waste materials. An action potential is a sudden reversal in the neuron's membrane voltage. The shift from negative to positive voltage is called depolarization. The depolarization process occurs when the dendrites of the cell are stimulated, resulting in small shifts in the cell membrane's electrical potential, a shift called a graded potential. If the graded potential is large enough to reach the action potential threshold, an action potential occurs. Either an action potential occurs or it does not, according to the all-or-none law. When a neuron is stimulated, tiny protein structures called ion channels are activated. Sodium ion channels allow positively charged sodium ions to enter the interior of the cell, leading to the process of depolarization. Immediately after an impulse passes any point on the axon, a time period called a refractory period occurs, during which another action potential cannot occur. The myelin sheath is a tubelike insulating substance covering some axons in the brain and spinal cord.

Neurons communicate through synaptic transmission. The synapse is a tiny gap between the axon terminal and the next neuron. Chemical substances called neurotransmitters, which are stored in synaptic vesicles, carry messages across the synapse and bind to receptor sites. Once a neurotransmitter molecule binds to its receptor, it continues to activate or inhibit the neuron until deactivation occurs. One method of deactivation is reuptake, in which the transmitter molecules are taken back into the presynaptic neuron. There are many types of neurotransmitters. One involved in memory and muscle activity is acetylcholine. Blockage of dopamine by antipsychotic drugs has been found to be effective in the treatment of schizophrenia. A class of neurotransmitter that is involved in reducing pain and increasing feelings of well-being are called endorphins. Serotonin may be involved in mood, eating, sleep, and sexual behaviour.

There are three major types of neurons in the nervous system. Sensory neurons input messages from the sense organs to the spinal cord and brain, motor neurons carry impulses from the brain and spinal cord to the muscles and organs, and interneurons perform connective or associative functions within the nervous system. The division of the nervous system containing the brain and spinal cord is called the central nervous system. The division that consists of all neurons connecting the CNS with the muscles, glands, and sensory receptors is called the peripheral nervous system. In turn, the PNS is divided into two systems. The somatic nervous system consists of sensory and motor neurons while the autonomic nervous system regulates the body's glands and involuntary functions such as breathing, circulation, and digestion. The autonomic nervous system consists of two branches. The sympathetic branch activates or arouses bodily organs while the parasympathetic branch slows down body processes. Most nerves enter and leave the CNS via the spinal cord. Some simple stimulus-response sequences such as pulling away from a hot stove typically don't involve the brain and are known as spinal reflexes.

Psychologists have used a number of methods of studying the brain. Neuropsychological tests measure verbal and nonverbal behaviours affected by brain damage. Sometimes researchers destroy neurons under controlled conditions or stimulate them with electrical current or with chemicals. The activity of large groups of neurons is often studied via an electroencephalogram (EEG). The newest tools of discovery involve brain imaging. X-ray technology used to study brain structures is called computerized axial tomography (CAT) scanning. Pictures of brain activity involve the use of positron emission tomography (PET) scans. A technique to measure both brain structures and functions is called magnetic resonance imaging.
The brain historically has been divided into three main divisions. The hindbrain consists of the brain stem and cerebellum. The brain stem is involved in life support. The medulla plays a major role in vital body functions such as heart rate and respiration is the. The pons is a bridge carrying nerve impulses between higher and lower levels of the nervous system. The cerebellum is concerned primarily with muscular coordination, learning, and memory. An important relay centre for the visual and auditory systems is contained in the midbrain. Within the midbrain is the reticular formation, which is involved in brain arousal, sleep, and attention. The size and complexity of the forebrain separates humans from lower animals. An important sensory relay station in the forebrain is the thalamus, while the hypothalamus plays a major role in motivational and emotional behaviour. The limbic system helps to coordinate behaviours needed to satisfy emotional and motivational urges. Within the limbic system are the hippocampus, which is involved in the formation and storage of memories and the amygdala, which is linked to aggression and fear. The outermost layer of the brain is called the cerebral cortex. Each hemisphere of the cortex is divided into the frontal, parietal, occipital, and temporal lobes, each of which is associated with particular sensory and motor functions. Lying at the rear of the frontal lobe is the motor cortex, which is involved in controlling muscles. The somatic sensory cortex receives sensory input. Two specific speech areas are also located in the cortex. Wernicke's area is involved in speech comprehension while Broca's area is involved in the production of speech. The association cortex is involved in the highest levels of mental functions. People who suffer from agnosia, the inability to identify familiar objects often have suffered damage to their association cortex. Executive functions, such as, goal setting, judgement, and planning may be controlled by the prefrontal cortex. The brain is typically also divided into two hemispheres: the left and the right. The corpus callosum is a bridge that helps the two hemispheres communicate and work together. When a function is located more in one hemisphere than the other, it is known as lateralization. "Split-brain" research designed to look at the relative functions of the hemispheres involves studying the roles of the corpus callosum and the optic chiasma. The brain as a structure develops over time. The ability of neurons to change in structure and function is known as neural plasticity.

The endocrine system consists of numerous glands distributed throughout the body. The system conveys information via hormones, which are chemical messengers secreted by the glands into the bloodstream. The adrenal glands secrete stress hormones, which mobilize the body's immune system. When foreign substances known as antigens invade the body, the immune system produces antibodies to destroy them. Problems arise with both an underactive and an overactive immune system. An overactive response, known as an autoimmune reaction, results when the immune system incorrectly identifies part of the body as an enemy and attacks it. A relatively new field called psychoneuroimmunology studies how psychological factors affect health and illness.

Chapter Outline

The Neural Bases of Behaviour
    Neurons
    Nerve Conduction: An Electrochemical Process
        The Action Potential
        The Myelin Sheath
    How Neurons Communicate: Synaptic Transmission
        Neurotransmitters
        Excitation, Inhibition, and Deactivation
        Specialized Transmitter Systems

The Nervous System
    The Peripheral Nervous System
        The Somatic Nervous System
        The Autonomic Nervous System
    The Central Nervous System
        The Spinal Cord
        The Brain
        Unlocking the Secrets of the Brain
            Research Foundations: Wilder Penfield and a Cortical Map
    The Hierarchical Brain: Structures and Behavioural Functions
        The Hindbrain
        The Midbrain
        The Forebrain
        The Cerebral Cortex: Crown of the Brain
        Hemispheric Lateralization: The Left and Right Brains
        Plasticity in the Brain: The Role of Experience and the Recovery of Function
            Psychological Applicatiions: Healing the Nervous System

Nervous System Interactions With the Endocrine and Immune Systems
    Interactions with the Endocrine System
    Interactions Involving the Immune System
            Research Frontiers: How Psychological Factors Affect the Immune System

Problem-Based Learning

http://www.ninds.nih.gov/index.htm
National Institute of Neurological Disorders and Stroke-Contains information about many disorders including Agnosia.

http://www.cortex-online.org
Cortex-Website for the journal Cortex which contains articles on the brain. It contains many articles on the effects of brain lesions on cognitive functions and hemispheric specialization.

http://www.neuroguide.com
Neurosciences on the Internet-A large searchable database of neuroscience resources on the internet.

http://faculty.washington.edu/chudler/neurok.html
Neuroscience for Kids-Although it is listed for kids it contains information about the brain and many interesting experiments and activities.

http://www.med.harvard.edu/AANLIB/home.html
The Whole Brain Atlas-Contains numerous images of various parts of the brain under normal and abnormal conditions.

Key Terms: *Write the letter of the definition next to the term in the space provided.*

The Neural Basis of Behaviour

1. ___ acetylcholine

2. ___ action potential

3. ___ action potential threshold

4. ___ all-or-none law

5. ___ axon

6. ___ cell body

7. ___ dendrites

8. ___ depolarization

9. ___ dopamine

10. ___ endorphins

11. ___ glial cells

12. ___ graded potential

a. a sudden reversal in the cell membrane's voltage

b. an insulation layer covering the axons in the brain and spinal cord

c. a neurotransmitter involved in memory and muscle activity

d. collect messages from other neurons and send them to the cell body

e. a neurotransmitter found in excess in the brains of schizophrenics

f. a shift from negative to positive voltage inside the neuron

g. a neurotransmitter involved in mood, eating, sleep, and sexual behaviour

h. cells that are the basic building blocks of the nervous system

i. small shifts occurring in the cell membrane's electrical potential

j. a time period during which the membrane is not excitable and cannot discharge an action potential

k. chemical substances that carry messages across the synapse

l. contains the biochemical structures to keep

13. ___ ion channels

14. ___ myelin sheath

15. ___ neurons

16. ___ neurotransmitters

17. ___ receptor sites

18. ___ refractory period

19. ___ reuptake

20. ___ serotonin
21. ___ synaptic cleft
22. ___ synaptic vesicles

the neuron alive

m. where neurotransmitters bind themselves in the postsynaptic neuron

n. the required level of intensity needed to fire the neuron

o. action potential occurs with maximum intensity or does not occur at all

p. neurotransmitters are taken back into the presynaptic axon terminal

q. conducts electrical impulses away from the cell body to neurons, muscles, and glands

r. a tiny gap between the axon terminal and the next neuron

s. neurotransmitters involved in reducing pain and increasing well-being

t. support cells that hold neurons in place
u. where neurotransmitters are stored
v. allow specific ions to flow back and forth across the cell membrane

The Nervous System

1. ___ agnosia

2. ___ amygdala

3. ___ association cortex

4. ___ autonomic nervous system

5. ___ Broca's area

6. ___ central nervous system

7. ___ cerebral cortex

8. ___ computerized axial tomography

9. ___ corpus callosum

10. ___ electroencephalogram

11. ___ forebrain

12. ___ frontal lobe

13. ___ hippocampus
14. ___ hypothalamus

15. ___ interneurons

a. simple stimulus-response sequences that do not involve the brain

b. plays a major role in hunger, thirst and sexual and emotional behaviour

c. a sheet of unmyelinated cells that form the outermost layer of the brain

d. part of the ANS that has an activation or arousal function

e. a test that measures verbal and nonverbal behaviours that are affected by particular types of brain damage

f. a structure in the brain stem that plays an important role in heart rate and respiration

g. comprises all the neurons that connect the central nervous system with the muscles, glands, and senses

h. a measurement of the activity of large groups of neurons

i. part of the cortex that controls muscles involved in voluntary body movements

j. carries input messages from the sense organs to the brain and spinal cord

k. helps to coordinate behaviours needed to satisfy motivational and emotional urges

l. an area in the frontal lobe involved in the production of speech

m. uses X-ray technology to study brain structures

n. the lobe in which the area governing body sensations is located

o. transmits messages from the sense organs to the spinal

16. ___ lateralization
17. ___ limbic system

18. ___ magnetic resonance imaging
19. ___ medulla

20. ___ midbrain
21. ___ motor cortex

22. ___ motor neuron
23. ___ neural plasticity

24. ___ neuropsychological test
25. ___ occipital lobe

26. ___ optic chiasma

27. ___ parasympathetic nervous system
28. ___ parietal lobe
29. ___ peripheral nervous system

30. ___ pons

31. ___ positron emission tomography
32. ___ prefrontal cortex

33. ___ prefrontal lobotomy

34. ___ reticular formation

35. ___ sensory neuron
36. ___ somatic nervous system
37. ___ somatic sensory cortex
38. _α_ spinal reflex

39. ___ sympathetic nervous system
40. ___ temporal lobe

41. ___ thalamus
42. ___ Wernicke's area

cord and brain

p. involved in the formation and storage of memories

q. a structure that carries impulses between the lower and higher levels of the nervous system

r. part of the ANS that slows down body processes

s. part of the cortex that receives sensory input that give rise to sensations of heat, touch, and cold

t. the inability to identify familiar objects

u. perform connective or associative functions within the nervous system

v. the seat of the so-called "executive functions"

w. a neural bridge acting as a communication link between the two hemispheres

x. organizes emotional response patterns

y. consists of the sensory neurons that are specialized to transmit messages from sensory receptors and motor neurons to the muscles

z. contains clusters of sensory and motor neurons connecting higher and lower portions of the nervous system

aa. the lobe where the brain's visual area is located

bb. scans that measure brain activity

cc. when a function is located more in one hemisphere than in the other

dd. the ability of neurons to change in structure and function

ee. consists of all the neurons in the brain and spinal cord

ff. an area in the temporal lobe involved in speech comprehension

gg. can be used to measure both brain structure and activity

hh. the lobe where messages from the auditory system are sent

ii. involved in brain arousal, sleep, and attention

jj. the lobe where speech production is located

kk. a sensory relay station

ll. an area of the cortex involved in the highest mental functions, including perception, language, and thought

mm. controls the glands and the smooth muscles of several organs

nn. consists of two large cerebral hemispheres that wrap around the brain stem

oo. where fibers from the optic nerve cross over

pp. a procedure that severs the nerve tracts that connect the frontal lobe with the subcortical regions involved in emotion

Nervous System Interactions with the Immune System

1. __b__ adrenal glands
2. __d__ antigens
3. __e__ autoimmune response
4. __a__ endocrine system

5. __c__ hormones

6. __f__ psychoneuroimmunology

a. consists of numerous glands distributed throughout the body
b. secrete hormones regulating many metabolic processes
c. chemical messengers secreted from the glands into the bloodstream
d. foreign substances that trigger a biochemical response by the immune system
e. an overactive response occurring when the immune system mistakenly identifies part of the body as an enemy and attacks it
f. a discipline that studies how psychological factors affect health and illness

Key People: *Write the letter of the ideas associated with the person in the space provided.*

c
1. __b__ Carl Wernicke
2. __h__ Wilder Penfield
3. __e__ Phineas Gage
4. ___ Oliver Sacks
5. ___ Roger Sperry
6. ___ Egas Moniz
7. ___ James Olds and Peter Milner
8. ___ Otto Loewi
9. __f__ D. O. Hebb
10. __d__ Paul Broca

a. "reward and punishment areas" in hypothalamus
b. agnosia case study
c. language comprehension area in the brain
d. language production area in the brain
e. dramatic personality change after brain injury
f. model of changes in neurons resulting from learning
g. Nobel prize: prefrontal lobotomy
h. Stimulation of the brain to map functions
i. Nobel prize: chemical neurotransmission
j. Nobel prize: split-brain research

Review at a Glance: *Write the term that best fits the blank to review what you learned in this chapter.*

The Neural Bases of Behaviour

Specialized cells called (1) _____ are the building blocks of the nervous system. Each neuron has three main parts. The (2) _____ _____ contains the biochemical structures that keep the neuron alive, and the genetic information that controls cell development and function is in its nucleus. (3) _____ collect information from neighbouring neurons and send it on to the cell body. The part of the neuron that conducts electrical impulses away from the cell body to other neurons, muscles, and glands is called the (4) _____. Cells known as (5) _____ _____ support neurons by holding them in place, manufacturing nutrient chemicals, and absorbing toxins and waste materials. A sudden reversal in the neuron's membrane voltage is called an (6) _____ _____ and the shift from negative to positive voltage is called (7) _____. The depolarization process occurs when the dendrites of the cell are stimulated, resulting in small shifts in the cell membrane's electrical potential, a shift called a (8) _____ _____. If the graded potential is large enough to reach the (9) _____ _____ , an action potential occurs. Either an action potential occurs or its does not, according to the (10) _____ _____ _____ _____. When a neuron is stimulated, tiny protein structures called (11) _____ are activated. Sodium ion channels allow positively charged sodium ions to enter the interior of the cell, leading to the process of depolarization. Immediately after an impulse passes any point on the axon, a time period called an (12) _____ period occurs, during which another action potential cannot occur. A tubelike substance covering some axons in the brain and spinal cord is known as the (13) _____ _____. Neurons communicate through synaptic transmission. Chemical substances called (14) _____ carry messages across the synaptic cleft and bind to (15) _____ _____. Once a neurotransmitter molecule binds to its receptor, it continues to activate or inhibit the neuron until deactivation occurs. One method of deactivation is (16) _____, in which the transmitter molecules are taken back into the presynaptic neuron. There are many types of neurotransmitters. One involved in memory and muscle activity is (17) _____. Blockage of _____ by antipsychotic drugs has been found to be effective in treating symptoms of schizophrenia. A class of neurotransmitter that is involved in reducing pain and increasing feelings of well-being are (19) _____.

The Nervous System

There are three major types of neurons in the nervous system. (20) _____ neurons input messages from the sense organs to the spinal cord and brain, (21) _____ neurons carry impulses from the brain and spinal cord to the muscles and organs, and   (22) _____ perform connective or associative functions within the nervous system. The division of the nervous system containing the brain and spinal cord is called the (23) _____ nervous system. The division that consists of all neurons connecting the CNS with the muscles, glands, and sensory receptors is called the (24) _____ nervous system. In turn, the PNS is divided into two systems. The (25) _____ nervous system consists of sensory and motor neurons while the (26) _____ nervous system regulates the body's glands and involuntary functions such as breathing, circulation, and digestion. The autonomic nervous system consists of two branches. The (27) _____ branch activates or arouses bodily organs while the (28) _____ branch slows down body processes. Most nerves enter and leave the CNS via the spinal cord. Some simple stimulus-response sequences such as pulling away from a hot stove typically don't involve the brain and are known as (29) _____ _____. Psychologists have used a number of methods of studying the brain. (30) _____ tests measure verbal and nonverbal behaviours that are known to be affected by brain damage. Sometimes researchers destroy neurons under controlled conditions or stimulate them with electrical current or with chemicals. Such techniques are known as (31) _____ _____ _____ techniques. The activity of large groups of neurons is often studied via an (32) _____. The newest tools of discovery involve brain imaging. X-ray technology used to study brain structures are called   (33) _____ _____ _____ scans. Pictures of brain activity involve the use of (34) _____ _____ _____. A technique to measure both brain structures and function is called (35) _____ _____

_____. The brain historically has been divided into three main divisions. The hindbrain consists of the brain stem and cerebellum. The brain stem is involved in life support. A structure that plays a major role in vital body functions such as heart rate and respiration is the (36) _____. The (37) _____ is a bridge carrying nerve impulses between higher and lower levels of the nervous system. The cerebellum is concerned primarily with muscular coordination, learning, and memory. An important relay centre for the visual and auditory systems is contained in the (38) _____. Within the midbrain is the (39) _____ _____, which is involved in brain arousal, sleep, and attention. The size and complexity of the (40) _____ separates humans from lower animals. An important sensory relay station in the forebrain is the (41) _____, while the (42) _____ plays a major role in motivational and emotional behaviour. The (43) _____ system helps to coordinate behaviours needed to satisfy emotional and motivational urges. Within the limbic system are the (44) _____, which is involved in the formation and storage of memories and the (45) _____, which is linked to aggression and fear. The outermost layer of the brain is called the (46) _____ _____. Each hemisphere of the cortex is divided into four lobes, the (47) _____, (48) _____, (49) _____, and (50) _____ lobes, each of which is associated with particular sensory and motor functions. Lying at the rear of the frontal lobe is the (51) _____ cortex, which is involved in controlling muscles. The (52) _____ sensory cortex receives sensory input. Two specific speech areas are also located in the cortex. (53) _____ area is involved in speech comprehension while (54) _____ area is involved in the production of speech. The (55) _____ is involved in the highest levels of mental functions. People who suffer from (56) _____, the inability to identify familiar objects often have suffered damage to their association cortex. Executive functions such as goal setting, judgement, and planning may be controlled by the (57) _____ cortex. The brain is typically also divided into two hemispheres: the left and the right. The (58) _____ _____ is a bridge that helps the two hemispheres communicate and work together. When a function is located more in one hemisphere than the other, it is known as (59) _____. "Split-brain" research designed to look at the relative functions of the hemispheres involves studying the roles of the corpus callosum and the (60) _____ _____. The brain as a structure develops over time. The ability of neurons to change in structure and function is known as (61) _____ _____.

Nervous System Interactions with the Endocrine and Immune Systems

The (62) _____ system consists of numerous glands distributed throughout the body. The system conveys information via (63) _____, which are chemical messengers secreted by the glands into the bloodstream. The (64) _____ glands secrete stress hormones, which mobilize the body's immune system. When foreign substances known as (65) _____ invade the body, the immune system produces antibodies to destroy them. Problems arise with both an underactive and an overactive immune system. An overactive response known as an (66) _____ reaction results when the immune system incorrectly identifies part of the body as an enemy and attacks it.

Apply What You Know

1. Describe what is occurring in the diagram on Study Sheet 3.1.

2. Label the parts of the neuron shown on Study Sheet 3.2. (The myelin sheath is already indicated for you!)

3. Label the parts of the brain shown on Study Sheet 3.3.

Internet Scavenger Hunt

1. Do males and females have different brain structures? Do they use their brains in different ways? Do some library research to determine what researchers have found regarding sex differences in brain structures and functions. What differences do you find?

27/30

Practice Test

<u>**Multiple Choice Items:**</u> *Please write the letter corresponding to your answer in the space to the left of each item.*

_c_ 1. Specialized cells that are the basic building blocks of the nervous system are called _c_.

    a. axons
    b. dendrites
    c. neurons
    d. glial cells

_d_ 2. A sudden reversal in the cell membrane's voltage, during which the membrane voltage moves from −70mv to +40mv is called _d_.

    a. the action potential threshold
    b. the all-or-none law
    c. a graded potential
    d. an action potential

_c_ 3. The changes in the electrical potential of a neuron that are proportional to the amount of incoming stimulation from other neurons are called _c_ potentials.

    a. resting
    b. action
    c. graded
    d. polarized

_a_ 4. When a neuron is stimulated, tiny protein structures on the cell membrane called _a_ are activated.

    a. ion channels
    b. neurotransmitters
    c. synaptic vesicles
    d. myelin sheaths

_c_ 5. Multiple sclerosis occurs when a person's own immune system specifically attacks _c_.

    a. the dendrites
    b. the glial cells
    c. the myelin sheath
    d. the ion channels

_a___ 6. A tiny gap between the axon terminal and the next neuron through which the neurotransmitters pass is called the _a_.

a. synaptic cleft
b. synaptic vesicle
c. myelin sheath
d. ion channel

_c___ 7. After binding to a receptor, _b____ mimic the naturally occurring neurotransmitter whereas _____ denies the neurotransmitter access to its'receptor.

a. antidepressants; cocaine
b. stimulants; morphine
c. opiates; caffeine
d. antipsychotics; Valium

_d___ 8. The ability of people to continue to function despite a severe injury is due in large part to the release of _d____ which can act as an analgesic.

a. acetylcholine
b. dopamine
c. glutamate
d. endorphins

_d___ 9. The _d_ nervous system consists of all the neurons of the brain and spinal cord.

a. sympathetic
b. parasympathetic
c. peripheral
d. central

_b___ 10. The sympathetic and parasympathetic nervous systems play complementary roles in maintaining _b_, which refers to a balanced or constant internal state.

a. homeosynthesis
b. homeostasis
c. neural plasticity
d. a resting potential

_b_ 11. During brain surgery, Dr. Penfield placed a small electrode on various portions of a patient's exposed cerebral cortex. Though the patient had a local anesthetic applied to his scalp, he was still conscious and Dr. Penfield asked him to report what he experienced when different parts of his brain were electrically activated. Dr. Penfield was using _b__ to study the relation between the brain and behaviour.

a. neuropsychological tests
b. stimulation techniques
c. brain imaging
d. electrical recording

_c_ 12. CAT scans, PET scans, and MRIs are all examples of _C_.

   a. electrical recording
   b. destruction and stimulation techniques
   c. brain imaging
   d. neuropsychological tests

_d_ 13. A new born baby is having trouble regulating her breathing and heart rate and doctors are forced to place her on life support. Given her symptoms, it is **most likely** that this infant may have some abnormalities in or damage to her _b_.

   a. thalamus
   b. hypothalamus
   c. cerebellum
   d. medulla

_a_ 14. Parkinson's Disease results from a deficiency of _a_ in the _____.

   a. dopamine; basal ganglia
   b. serotonin; cerebellum
   c. serotonin; medulla
   d. dopamine; cerebrum

_d_ 15. Until recently, researchers believed the hypothalamus was responsible for reward and motivation. However research at Concordia and McGill universities has demonstrated that it is actually the _d_ that is important for reward and motivation

   a. basal ganglia
   b. superior colliculus
   c. Wernicke's area
   d. nucleus accumbens

_b_ 16. Control of voluntary body movements is localized in the _b_.

   a. temporal lobe
   b. motor cortex
   c. association cortex
   d. occipital lobe

_c_ 17. The sensory cortex _C_.

   a. is not involved in sensation
   b. contains the association cortex
   c. receives input from our sensory receptors and gives rise to sensations of heat, touch, cold, and our senses of body movement and balance
   d. performs the same functions as the motor cortex

_a_ 18. As a result of a head trauma, a man loses his ability to create speech and talk but can still understand what people say to him. He has **most likely** suffered damage to _a_.

    a. Broca's area
    b. the amygdala
    c. the cerebellum
    d. Wernicke's area

_d_ 19. Scientists have suggested that the entire period of human evolution could be labelled "the age of the _d_ lobe."

    a. occipital
    b. temporal
    c. parietal
    d. frontal

_b_ 20. The neural link between the two hemispheres that allows them to act as a single unit is called the _b_.

    a. Broca's area
    b. corpus callosum
    c. reticular formation
    d. basal ganglia

_a_ 21. Research on hemispheric lateralization has demonstrated that the left hemisphere is more specialized for _a_ and the right hemisphere is more specialized for _____.

    a. language; music
    b. negative emotion; music
    c. face recognition; language
    d. music; positive emotion

_a_ 22. Research demonstrating that rat pups raised in stimulating environments had larger neurons with more dendritic branches and that musicians who do complex string work with their left hands tend to have larger corresponding somatosensory areas were both discussed as examples of _b_.

    a. neural plasticity
    b. split-brain research
    c. what happens when the corpus callosum is cut
    d. functions influenced by Wernicke's area

_b_ 23. Immature, "uncommitted" cells that can mature into any type of neuron or glial cell needed by the brain are called _b_.

    a. neural plastic cells
    b. neural stem cells
    c. interneurons
    d. motor neurons

_a_   24. The _a_ system consists of numerous glands distributed throughout the body.

    a.   endocrine
    b.   immune
    c.   central
    d.   parasympathetic

_b_   25. Hormones are the primary method of communication for the _b_.

    a.   nervous system
    b.   endocrine system
    c.   immune system
    d.   cerebral cortex

_c_   26. When an _c_ invades the body, the _____ system creates _____ to destroy it.

    a.   antibody; endocrine; antigen
    b.   antigen; endocrine; antibody
    c.   antigen; immune; antibody
    d.   antibody; immune; antigen

_b_   27. The specialized barrier that prevents many substances from entering the brain is:
                                                  b

    a.   neural barrier
    b.   blood-brain barrier
    c.   barrier reef
    d.   neural-brain barrier

_c_   28. Glial cells have been found to be able to communicate: _c_

    a.   only with other glial cells
    b.   only with neurons
    c.   with both glial cells and neurons
    d.   with both neurons and endocrines

_d_   29. A bite by a Black Widow spider produces: _d_

    a.   an increase in seretonin
    b.   a decrease in dopamine
    c.   an increase in dopamine
    d.   an increase in acetylcholine

_b_   30. The graceful movements of a cat and the uncoordinated movements of an intoxicated person are both associated with this part of the brain: _b_

    a.   cerebrum
    b.   cerebellum
    c.   frontal lobe
    d.   occipital lobe

True/False Items: *Write T or F in the space provided to the left of each item.*

☑ F 1. The basic building blocks of the nervous system are dendrites.

✓ T 2. Positively charged sodium ions flow into the interior of the neuron, creating a state of partial depolarization, when the ion channels are activated.

✗ T 3. Neurons communicate via neurotransmitters.

✓ F 4. The two divisions of the central nervous system are the parasympathetic and sympathetic.

✗ T 5. PET scans measure brain structure.

✗ F 6. The cerebellum is concerned primarily with muscular movement coordination, but it also plays a role in learning and memory.

✗ T 7. The hypothalamus acts as a sensory relay station in the brain and is known as the "switchboard" of the brain.

✓ T 8. The association cortex is involved in the highest levels of mental functions, including perception, language, and thought.

✓ T 9. Hormones are secreted by glands in the endocrine system.

✗ F 10. The fight-or-flight response results from activation of the parasympathetic nervous system.

Short Answer Questions

1. Describe the functions of the different parts of neurons.

2. Describe the divisions of the peripheral nervous system and their functions.

3. Describe four methods of study that attempt to unlock the secrets of the brain.

4. Describe how Broca's and Wernicke's areas are involved in speech comprehension and speech production.

Essay Questions

1. Describe the process that occurs to create an action potential.

2. Describe the process by which neurons communicate with each other.

3. Describe the functions associated with the different areas of cerebral cortex.

4. Describe how split-brain research is used to study the lateralization of function.

5. What evidence indicates that the nervous, endocrine, and immune systems interact with each other?

Study Sheet 3.1   Neural Firing

Polarized membrane

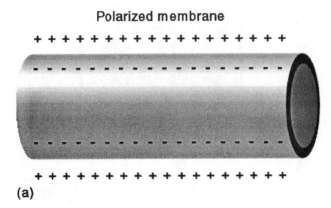

(a)

Depolarization
(sodium ions flow in)

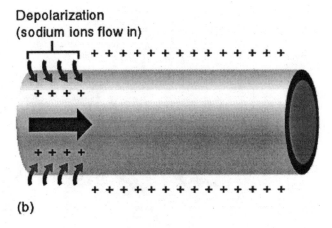

(b)

Sodium ions pumped
out of neuron
Depolarization

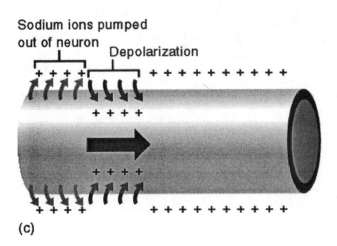

(c)

Flow of depolarization

Direction of
depolarization
wave

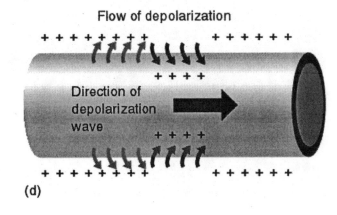

(d)

Study Sheet 3.2 Parts of the Neuron

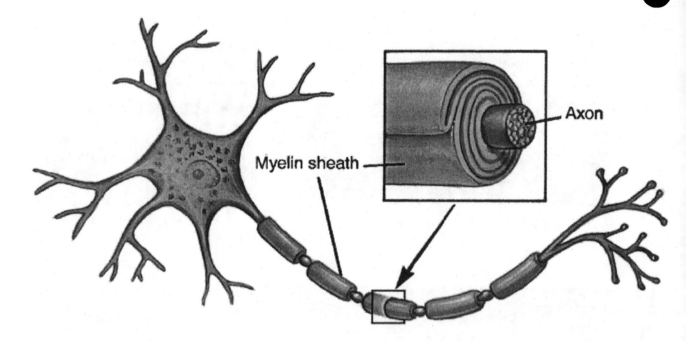

Study Sheet 3.3 Parts of the Brain

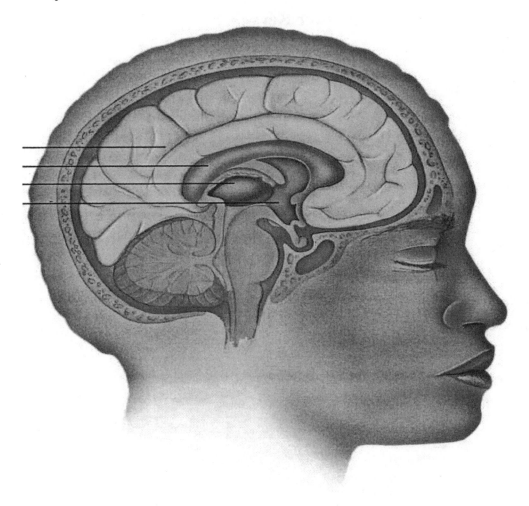

Answer Keys

Answer Key for Key Terms

The Neural Bases of Behaviour

1.	c	12.	i
2.	a	13.	v
3.	n	14.	b
4.	o	15.	h
5.	q	16.	k
6.	l	17.	m
7.	d	18.	j
8.	f	19.	p
9.	e	20.	g
10.	s	21.	r
11.	t	22.	u

The Nervous System

1.	t	15.	u	29.	g
2.	x	16.	cc	30.	q
3.	ll	17.	k	31.	bb
4.	mm	18.	gg	32.	v
5.	l	19.	f	33.	pp
6.	ee	20.	z	34.	ii
7.	c	21.	i	35.	j
8.	m	22.	o	36.	y
9.	w	23.	dd	37.	s
10.	h	24.	e	38.	a
11.	nn	25.	aa	39.	d
12.	jj	26.	oo	40.	hh
13.	p	27.	r	41.	kk
14.	b	28.	n	42.	ff

Nervous System Interactions with the Endocrine and Immune Systems

1.	b	4.	a
2.	d	5.	c
3.	e	6.	f

Answer Key for Key People

1.	c	5.	j	9.	f
2.	h	6.	g	10.	d
3.	e	7.	a		
4.	b	8.	i		

Answer Key for Review at a Glance

1. neurons
2. cell body
3. dendrites
4. axon
5. glial cells
6. action potential
7. depolarization
8. graded potential
9. action potential threshold
10. all-or-none law
11. ion channels
12. refractory
13. myelin sheath
14. neurotransmitters
15. receptor sites
16. reuptake
17. acetylcholine
18. dopamine
19. endorphins
20. sensory
21. motor
22. interneurons
23. central
24. peripheral
25. somatic

26. autonomic
27. sympathetic
28. parasympathetic
29. spinal reflexes
30. neuropsychological
31. destruction and stimulation
32. electroencephalogram
33. computerized axial tomography
34. positron emission tomography
35. magnetic resonance imaging
36. medulla
37. pons
38. midbrain
39. reticular formation
40. forebrain
41. thalamus
42. hypothalamus
43. limbic
44. hippocampus
45. amygdala
46. cerebral cortex
47. frontal
48. parietal
49. occipital
50. temporal

51. motor
52. somatic
53. Wernicke's
54. Broca's
55. association
56. agnosia
57. prefrontal
58. corpus callosum
59. lateralization
60. optic chiasma
61. neural plasticity
62. endocrine
63. hormones
64. adrenal
65. antigens
66. autoimmune

Answer Key for Practice Test Multiple Choice Questions

1. c
2. d
3. c
4. a
5. c
6. a
7. c
8. d
9. d
10. b
11. b
12. c
13. d
14. a
15. d

16. b
17. c
18. a
19. d
20. b
21. a
22. a
23. b
24. a
25. b
26. c
27. b
28. c
29. d
30. b

Answer Key for Practice Test True/False Questions

1.	F	6.	T
2.	T	7.	F
3.	T	8.	T
4.	F	9.	T
5.	F	10.	F

Answer Key for Practice Test Short Answer Questions

1. The neuron has three main parts: the axon, dendrites, and a cell body. The cell body contains the biochemical structures needed to keep the neuron alive. Its nucleus contains the genetic information that determines how the cell develops. The dendrites collect messages from neighbouring neurons and send the messages to the cell body. The axon conducts electrical impulses away from the cell body to other neurons, muscles, and glands.

2. The main divisions of the peripheral nervous system are the somatic and autonomic nervous systems. The somatic nervous system consists of the sensory neurons that are specialized to transmit messages from the body's sense organs and the motor neurons that send messages from the brain and spinal cord to the muscles. The autonomic nervous system controls the glands and smooth involuntary muscles of the heart and other organs and controls involuntary functions such as respiration and digestion. The autonomic nervous system is divided into two branches: the sympathetic and parasympathetic. The sympathetic activates or arouses behaviour, while the parasympathetic branch slows down body processes. The interaction between the two branches generally creates a state of homeostasis, a balanced internal state.

3. Neuropsychological tests measure verbal and nonverbal behaviours that are affected by brain damage. Destruction and stimulation techniques are used to destroy brain structures and stimulate them via electrical or chemical measures respectively to determine the functions of the structures. Electrical recordings such as EEGs are used to measure the activity of large groups of neurons. Finally, brain-imaging techniques such as CT and PET scans as well as MRIs are used to study both the structure and activities of the brain.

4. Broca's area in the frontal lobe is involved in the production of speech through its connections with the motor cortex areas that control the muscles used in speech. Wernicke's area in the temporal lobe is involved in speech comprehension.

Answer Key for Practice Test Essay Questions

1. An action potential is a sudden shift in the neuron's membrane voltage from –70mv to +40mv, a shift called depolarization. When the dendrites of one neuron are stimulated, small shifts in the cell's electrical potential called graded potentials occur. If the graded potential is large enough to reach the action potential threshold, the neuron fires according to the all-or-none law. The depolarization of the membrane is due to an influx of sodium ions through the ion channels when the neuron is stimulated. The influx of sodium ions creates a state of partial depolarization, which can generally reach the action potential threshold of –55mv.

2. Neurons communicate with each other via synaptic transmission. Neurotransmitters such as serotonin and dopamine formed inside the neuron are stored in synaptic vesicles in the axon terminals. When an action potential comes down an axon, neurotransmitters are released into the synaptic cleft. They then bind with postsynaptic receptors on the next neuron and either excite or inhibit the postsynaptic neuron.

3. The motor cortex controls 600 or more muscles involved in voluntary body movements. The somatic sensory cortex receives sensory input that gives rise to sensations of heat, touch, cold, and our senses of balance and body movement. The association cortex is involved in higher level mental functions such as perception, language, and thought.

4. Lateralization refers to the relatively greater localization of a function in one hemisphere or the other. Split-brain studies involve studying patients whose corpus callosum has been severed. Because the corpus callosum has been cut, visual information can be restricted to either side of the brain (right visual field to left hemisphere and left visual field to right hemisphere). The patient's perceptions and behaviour are then measured to determine the functions of the hemispheres.

5. The immune, endocrine, and nervous systems are all part of a communication network. Studies of interactions between the immune and nervous systems have shown that stimulation or destruction of the hypothalamus and cerebral cortex affect immune system functioning. Activation of the immune system results in increased brain activity. Additionally, the action of immune system cells are influenced by neurotransmitters. Studies of the interaction of the immune and endocrine systems have found that immune cells can produce hormones, allowing them to directly influence glands.

Chapter 4. Genes, Evolution, and Behaviour

Learning Objectives

When you have mastered the material in this chapter, you will be able to:

4.1   Differentiate between phenotype and genotype.

4.2   Explain how genetic transmission occurs from parents to offspring.

4.3   Describe dominant, recessive, or polygenetic modes of transmission.

4.4   Describe the methods used in recombinant DNA research.

4.5   Describe the gene knockout procedure and how it is used to study behaviour. Describe the limitations of this approach.

4.6   Define heritability and explain why it is important to the field of behavioural genetics.

4.7   Describe how adoption and twin studies are used behavioural genetics.

4.8   Describe the influence of genes on intelligence, including how much variation in intelligence test scores can be accounted for by heredity.

4.9   Describe how the concept of reaction range illustrates the interaction between heredity and the environment.

4.10   Describe the major findings of the Minnesota Twin Study.

4.11   Define evolution and describe Darwin's principle of natural selection.

4.12   Describe the importance of adaptations, explaining how bipedal locomotion and enhanced brain development were adaptive in human evolution.

4.13   Describe how evolutionary psychologists use both remote and proximate factors to explain behavioural phenomena.

4.14   Describe the origin of basic personality traits according to evolutionary theorists.

4.15   Describe what is meant by parental investment and how parental investment influences mating systems.

4.16   Describe how the idea of parental investment explains differences in physical size between the sexes.

4.17   Describe the differences and similarities between male and female mate preferences.

4.18   Describe how an evolutionary analysis explains the finding that women in all cultures tend to marry older males.

4.19   Explain the difference between altruism and cooperation.

4.20   Explain the kin selection and reciprocity theories of altruism.

4.21   Describe the functions of aggression from an evolutionary perspective.

4.22   Explain which members of a group are usually the most aggressive, and why this makes sense from an evolutionary perspective.

4.23   Explain what is meant by genetic determinism, and explain why genes do not always have an effect.

4.24   Explain why Social Darwinism, the idea that some members of society are genetically better than others, does not make sense from an evolutionary perspective.

4.25   Explain how an evolutionary analysis may suggest social or political changes, and provide an example.

Chapter Overview

This chapter covers genetic influences on behaviour and the relationship between evolutionary theories and behaviour.

Hereditary potential is carried within the DNA portion of the 23 pairs of chromosomes in units called genes, whose commands trigger the production of proteins that control body structures and processes. Genotype (genetic structure) and phenotype (outward appearance) are not identical, in part because some genes are dominant while others are recessive. Many characteristics are influenced by the interactions of multiple genes. Behaviour geneticists study the contributions of genetic and environmental factors to psychological traits and behaviours. Adoption and twin studies are the major research methods used in an attempt to disentangle hereditary and environmental factors. Especially useful is the study of identical (monozygotic) and fraternal (dizygotic) twins who were separated early in life and raised in different environments. These studies suggest that many psychological characteristics have appreciable genetic contributions. Genetic engineering allows scientists to duplicate and alter genetic material or, potentially, to repair dysfunctional genes. These procedures promise groundbreaking advances in treatment of diseases, but they also raise momentous ethical and moral issues.

Evolutionary psychology focuses on biologically-based mechanisms that evolved as solutions to a species' problems of adaptation. Evolution is a change over time in the frequency with which particular genes occur within an interbreeding population. The cornerstone of Darwin's theory of evolution is the principle of natural selection, which posits that biologically-based characteristics that contribute to survival and reproductive success increase in the population over time because those who lack the characteristic are less likely to pass on their genes. Mating behaviours, parental behaviours, and mate preferences are behaviours which may have been selected, because they ensure not only our own survival but also the survival of the species. As a social species, humans depend on interactive strategies such as, cooperation, altruism, and aggression to work together to benefit the group members and to distribute resources.

Biological factors allow a range of effects, depending on the environment in which they function. Thus, cultural factors, learning experiences, interpersonal relations, and other environmental factors combine with biological factors to influence behaviour. One might think that if the heritability of a particular trait is high, then society can have little effect on the trait. In actuality, however, if a particular society were to put pressure on everyone to conform to a particular behaviour, then environmental influences would be similar for everyone; consequently, the causal weight for that behaviour would shift toward biological factors.

Chapter Outline

GENETIC INFLUENCES
>   Chromosomes and Genes
>   >   Dominant, Recessive, and Polygenic Effects
>   >   Mapping the Genetic Code
>   >   Genetic Engineering: The Edge of Creation
>   Behaviour Genetics Techniques

GENETIC INFLUENCES ON BEHAVIOUR
>   Heredity, Environment, and Intelligence
>   Biological Reaction Range, Environment, and Intelligence
>   >   Behaviour Genetics and Personality
>   >   *Psychological Applications: Genetic Counselling*

EVOLUTION AND BEHAVIOUR
>   Evolution of Adaptive Mechanisms
>   >   Evolution
>   >   Natural Selection
>   >   Adaptations
>   >   An Evolutionary Snapshot of Human Nature
>   Evolutionary Psychology
>   >   Personality
>   >   Mating Systems and Parental Investment
>   >   Mate Preference
>   >   >   *Research Foundations: Gender Differences in the Ideal Mate*
>   >   Altruism
>   >   Aggression
>   >   >   *Research Frontiers: Inequality, Competition and Murder*

HOW NOT TO THINK ABOUT BEHAVIOUR GENETICS AND EVOLUTIONARY PSYCHOLOGY
>   Genetic Determinism
>   Social Darwinism
>   Defending the Status Quo

Problem-Based Learning

"What is the Human Genome Project?"

http://www.ornl.gov/sci/techresources/Human_Genome/project/about.shtml
This website will describe the Human Genome Project. The goals of this project, which began in 1990, included the identification of the genes in human DNA are discussed at this site. "Sequence and analysis of the human genome working draft was published in February 2001 and April 2003 issues of *Nature* and *Science*"

"Evolutionary Psychology: A Primer" by Leda Cosmides and John Tooby.

http://www.psych.ucsb.edu/research/cep/primer.html
The authors of this website describe the goals of research in evolutionary psychology. "Evolutionary psychology is an *approach* to psychology, in which knowledge and principles from evolutionary biology are put to use in research on the structure of the human mind."

Still have questions?
Visit this site for answers to Frequently Asked Questions about Evolutionary Psychology.

http://www.anth.ucsb.edu/projects/human/evpsychfaq.html
This site was written and is maintained by Edward Hagen who answers questions frequently raised when discussing the theoretical position of evolutionary psychology.

Key Terms: *Write the letter of the definition next to the term in the space provided.*

1. ___ adaptations

2. ___ adoption studies

3. ___ altruism

4. ___ biologically based mechanisms

5. ___ chromosomes

6. ___ concordance

7. ___ cooperation

8. ___ domain-specific adaptation

a. a behaviour genetics method in which identical (monozygotic) and fraternal (dizygotic) twins are compared on some characteristic; this method is particularly informative if the twins have been raised in different environments

b. a change over time in the frequency with which particular genes, and the characteristics they produce, occur within an interbreeding population.

c. a number of genes working together to create a particular phenotypic characteristic

d. a numerical estimate of the percentage of group variability in a particular characteristic that can be attributed to genetic factors

e. a research method in behaviour genetics in which adopted people are compared on some characteristic with both their biological and adoptive parents in an attempt to determine how strong a genetic component the characteristic might have

f. biological and behavioural changes that allow organisms to meet recurring environmental challenges to their survival, thereby increasing their reproductive ability

g. evolved biological structures that receive input from the environment, process the information, and respond to it

h. gene-splicing procedure that can be used to produce new life forms, such as bacteria that can produce scarce chemical materials like human growth hormone

9. ___ dominant gene	i.	the biological units of heredity, located on the chromosomes
10. ___ evolution	j.	the evolutionary process through which characteristics that increase the likelihood of survival and reproduction are preserved in the gene pool and thereby become more common in a species over time
11. ___ Evolutionary personality theory	k.	a procedure in which a specific gene is altered in a way that prevents it from carrying out its normal function
12. ___ genes	l.	the observable characteristics produced by one's genetic endowment
13. ___ gene knockout	m.	the likelihood that two people share the same characteristic
14. ___ genetic determinism	n.	the specific genetic makeup of the individual, which may or may not be expressed in the observable phenotype
15. ___ genotype	o.	tightly coiled strands of DNA and protein that contain genes
16. ___ heritability coefficient	p.	one of a gene pair that needs another gene just like it in order for the trait/characteristic to show up in the phenotype
17. ___ kin selection	q.	the range of possibilities that the genetic code allows
18. ___ monogamy	r.	one of a gene pair that controls whether a trait/characteristic will be displayed
19. ___ natural selection	s.	an approach that asks: Where did the traits come from in the first place?"
20. ___ parental investment	t.	refers to the time, effort, energy, and risk associated with caring successfully for each offspring
21. ___ phenotype	u.	a mating system in which one male may mate with many females
22. ___ polyandry	v.	a mating system in which one female may mate with many males
23. ___ polygenic transmission	w.	a mating system in which all members of the group may mate with all other members of the group
24. ___ polygynandry	x.	a mating system in which one male may mate with one female
25. ___ polygyny	y.	refers to situations in which one individual helps another and in so doing also gains some advantage themselves
26. ___ reaction range	z.	occurs when on individual helps another and in doing so they accrue some cost
27. ___ recessive gene	aa.	theory that argues that altruism is in essence long-term cooperation (cost of helping will eventually be repaid)
28. ___ recombinant DNA procedure	bb.	theory that argues that altruism developed to increase the survival of relatives
29. ___ Social Darwinism	cc.	erroneous view that genes have invariant and unavoidable effects
30. ___ theory of reciprocal altruism	dd.	theory that argues that if the more fit are more successful, then those at top of social and economic ladder must be the most fit of all
31. ___ twin studies	ee.	evolutionary adaptations designed to solve a particular problem, such as selecting a suitable mate, choosing safe foods to eat, or avoiding certain environmental hazards

Key People: *Write the letter of the ideas associated with the person in the space provided.*

1. ___ Charles Darwin	a.	parental investment
2. ___ David Buss	b.	biological basis for major personality traits
3. ___ Hans Eysenck	c.	survival of the fittest

4. ___ Robert Trivers   d. Evolutionary Personality Theory
5. _e_ Gregor Mendel   e. genetic experiments on garden peas
6. ___ Martin Daly and   f. natural selection
      Margo Wilson
7. _c_ Herbert Spencer   g. evolutionary analysis of aggressive behaviours

Review at a Glance: *Write the term that best fits the blank to review what you learned in this chapter.*

Genetic Influences

Hereditary potential is carried in units called genes, which are found within the (1) _____ portion of the 23 pairs of (2) _____. The specific makeup of the individual is known as the (3) _____, while the observable characteristics produced by that genetic endowment is known as the person's (4) _____. Some genes are dominant and some are recessive. If a gene in the pair received from both the mother and the father is (5) _____, then the characteristic it controls will be displayed in the phenotype. If the gene received from one parent is (6) _____, then the characteristic will not show up unless the gene received from the other parent is also (14) _____. When many gene pairs combine to create a single phenotypic trait, the process is called (7) _____ _____. The study of how the genetic and environmental factors affect human behaviour is called (8) _____ _____. Studies of individuals who are genetically related but raised apart, known as (9) _____ studies, are useful in determining the importance of genetic versus environmental factors in a given trait. Especially useful are studies of twins, both identical, or (10) _____, and fraternal, or (11) _____. In (12) _____ engineering, scientists duplicate or alter genetic material; they may also repair (13) _____ genes.

Genetic Influences on Behaviour

All of our behaviours reflect the (14) _____ between genes and environment. Two extensively researched areas on the influence of genes and environment are (15) _____ and (16)_____ . In general, as genetic similarity between individuals increases, their similarity in terms of a variety of psychological characteristics (17) _____. The Minnesota Twin Study assessed more than (18) _____ pairs of twins. Surprisingly, these studies showed an absence of important effects of the (19) _____ environment. Rather, experiences such as (20) _____ social interactions, and (21) _____ were found to be important. These experiences are referred to as (22) _____ experiences of each individual. Research at UBC and Western Ontario has demonstrated a genetic basis for a variety of attitudes, such as attitudes towards (23) _____ , (24) _____, playing organized sports, riding roller coasters, and (25) _____.

Evolution and Behaviour

The cornerstone of Darwin's theory of (26) _____ is the principle of (27) _____ _____. According to this principle, biologically based characteristics that help a species (28) _____ will increase in the population over time because members of the species who lack that characteristic will be less likely to pass on their (29) _____. The modern study of biologically based mechanisms that evolved as solutions to a species' problems of (30) _____ is known as (31) _____ psychology. Genetically based (32) _____ often occur in "packages," which can mean that a trait that impairs (33) _____ may persist if another trait in the same package is more important for survival.

Evolutionary Psychology

According to David Buss, there are a limited number of basic dimensions to human (34) _____ which he argues are found (35)_____ across all humans. These traits are consistently found because according to Buss, they help us to (36) _____ and to (37) _____ . In an effort to ensure not only our own survival but also survival of the species, humans have to invest considerable time, effort, energy, and risk in caring for their offspring. This is referred to as (38)_____ and varies across species. Trivers argued that various mating strategies will be adopted based on the investment required to successfully raise offspring. If both male and female investment is high, he predicts a (39)_____ mating system. Other mating systems include (40)_____ in which one female may mate with many males, and polgyny in which one male may mate with several females. When all members may mate with all others, a system found among some primates, the system is called (41)_____ and is thought to be one possible way to (42)_____ competition and may account for the (43)_____ that is associated with it. In studies of preferences for mates, women prefer men who (44)_____ whereas, men state a preference for females who show signs of (45)_____. In one study, females rated as most attractive a male when he was shown interacting positively with a (46) _____, possibly indicating male attractiveness to women is enhanced by signs of parental investment. Many benefits of our being a social species are based on our ability to (47)_____ with others. This strategy allows the group to achieve more than each member could individually. Altruism is different in that helping another accrues a (48) _____ to the self. Two theories of altruism are the (49)_____that argues that altruistic acts developed to promote the survival of relatives; and (50) _____ that argues that altruism is in essence long-term cooperation. Many species, including chimpanzees and humans have evolved mechanisms to support (51)_____ behaviours that may function to divide limited resources among a group.

Genetic Determinism

An error made by many people is to assume that if something is genetic, it cannot be (52) _____. The idea that genes have invariant and unavoidable effects is called (53) _____. Evolutionary psychologists would argue strongly (54) _____ such a view. It is important to keep in mind that genes work through an (55) _____. They may set the (56) _____ range for a characteristic, but it is the (57) _____ that determines the actual development within the range. Another misunderstanding is that Darwin proposed (58) _____, a term coined by Herbert Spencer. The ideas associated with this distortion of Darwin's theory became know as (59) _____Darwinism. The argument that if genetics has resulted in a trait or behaviour , that the trait or behaviour is 'natural' and 'right' ignores the fact that genes operate in (60) _____, which we have the ability to change.

Apply what you know

Chapter 1 of your textbook begins by presenting these four basic steps in the critical thinking process:

- *"What exactly are you asking me to believe?"*
- *"How do you know? What is the evidence?"*
- *"Are there other possible explanations?"*
- *"What is the most reasonable conclusion?"*

You might picture this as a four-step analysis to help you decide whether to accept a given theory or assertion. Now it's your turn to put your textbook to this test.

Review the section on adoption and twin studies. You will find a discussion of the ways in which these studies are useful in behaviour genetics. If someone told you that adoption studies of non-twins are more conclusive than studies of twins raised together, would you agree? Analyze that assertion in the space below. When you have finished, consider using this four-step analysis to evaluate other assertions you encounter.

"What exactly are you asking me to believe?"

"How do you know? What is the evidence?"

"Are there other possible explanations?"

"What is the most reasonable conclusion?"

Internet Scavenger Hunt: *Here's a chance to explore the multi-faceted field of psychology in the context of the World Wide Web. As with any Internet research, it is important to consider how legitimate a given source is before you rely on the information it presents. Your instructor or librarian may give you some specific guidelines for distinguishing which kinds of websites tend to be reputable.*

A. Take another look at the Key Terms and Key People for this chapter. In the space below, make a list of any whose definitions or associations of which you are not yet confident, and any you'd like to learn more about. Try entering the terms on your list into your search engine. Make notes of any helpful information you find.

Key Term or Key Person / Information Found

B. What can you find on the Internet about the latest advances in personality research? In addition to running "personality" through your search engine, examine the online Psychological Abstracts (available in most college libraries) and visit additional sites where you can test your personality such as www.personalitytest.org. Consider the question of the extent to which your most outstanding major personality trait has been influenced by genetics, environment, and your own selection of friends and activities that may have supported or modified this trait. Summarize your findings, citing any articles, books, or other publications that would particularly useful for further research.

Practice Test

Multiple Choice Items: *Write the letter corresponding to your answer in the space to the left of each item.*

_____ 1. The principle stating that a biologically based characteristic that contributes to survival will increase in a population over time because those who lack the characteristic are less likely to pass on their genes is known as _____.

    a. a genetically-based disease
    b. behaviour genetics
    c. natural selection
    d. inheritance

_____ 2. The study of biologically based mechanisms that evolved as solutions to a species' problems of adaptation is called _____.

    a. survival
    b. behaviourism
    c. the theory of evolution
    d. behaviour genetics

_____ 3. Hereditary potential is carried within the _____ portion of the 23 pairs of _____.

    a. dominant; twins
    b. evolutionary; chromosomes
    c. DNA; chromosomes
    d. DNA; genes

_____ 4. A dominant gene is one that _____.

    a. interacts with multiple gene pairs to determine a single phenotype
    b. determines the expression of the trait it controls only if its gene partner is also dominant
    c. determines the expression of the trait it controls only if its gene partner is recessive
    d. directly determines the expression of the trait it controls

_____ 5. Both of Perry's parents have blue eyes and Perry himself also has the gene for blue eyes, yet Perry's eyes are brown. This indicates that the gene for blue eyes is _____.

    a. polygenic
    b. phenotypic
    c. recessive
    d. dominant

_C_ 6. The probability of a child sharing any particular gene with his or her parents is _a_.

    a. .05
    b. .25
    c. .50
    d. 1.0

_b_ 7. Identical twins are known as _b_.

    a. dizygotic because they developed from two zygotes
    b. monozygotic because they developed from a single zygote
    c. monozygotic because each twin has only one zygote
    d. genotypic

_b_ 8. Evolutionary psychologists would predict _a_ in human traits across _____ cultures.

    a. similarities, similar
    b. similarities, different
    c. differences, similar
    d. differences, different

_C_ 9. According to the findings of the cross-cultural study on mate preferences, males rated the most important characteristic in the selection of female mates as: _a/b_

    a. youthfulness
    b. beauty
    c. mutual attraction
    d. good health

_C_ 10. According to the findings of the cross-cultural study on mate preferences, females rated the most important feature in the selection of male mates as: _a_

    a. good health
    b. social status
    c. mutual attraction
    d. good financial prospect

_b_ 11. According to Buss, when it comes to mate preferences across cultures: _b_

    a. regardless of culture, men are the same
    b. most women rated 'good financial prospect' in their top ten characteristics
    c. men and women do not agree on the top 3 – 4 most important characteristics
    d. both men and women rated good health higher than good looks

_b_ 12. The adaptive value of cooperation is:

    a. controversial
    b. clear
    c. inconsistent with evolutionary psychology
    d. consistent with survival of the fittest

_c_ 13. Altruism is defined as helping another, and is: C

    a. the same as cooperating
    b. consistent with social Darwinism
    c. dependent upon accruing a cost to self
    d. often an act of cowardice

_a_ 14. According to Trivers, men are likely more muscular and larger because they have _____ investment in raising their offspring. a

    a. less
    b. more
    c. equal
    d. no

_b_ 15. You are most likely to share personality traits with your sibling is you are: b

    a. identical twins, living apart
    b. identical twins, living together
    c. fraternal twins, living apart
    d. fraternal twins, living together

_a_ 16. If you were adopted the characteristics you would be <u>least</u> likely to share with your adoptive parents are: a

    a. personality traits
    b. religious views
    c. moral beliefs
    d. attitudes towards child rearing

_a_ 17. The approach of behaviour geneticists is to compare the correlations or concordance rates of people who vary in: a

    a. genetic relatedness
    b. the culture they were raised in
    c. age and gender
    d. intelligence

_c_ 18. When it comes to personality, the influence of being raised in a particular family is: *c*

    a. crucial
    b. if not crucial, extremely important
    c. of minimal importance
    d. dependent upon the SES of the family

_____ 19. Behaviour geneticists have conducted a great deal of research in the two areas of: *d*

    a. intelligence and sociability
    b. sociability and personality
    c. personality and intelligence
    d. gender and intelligence

_a_ 20. If the effect the environment has on a trait depends on the genetic makeup of the individual, we conclude the two factors: *c*

    a. interact
    b. are correlated
    c. have a high concordance
    d. similar

_b_ 21. The Theory of Reciprocal Altruism argues that: *d*

    a. altruism is a rare and inexplicable phenomenon
    b. altruism is really cooperation in disguise
    c. altruism makes sense only if you have no memory of events
    d. altruism and cooperation are mutually exclusive

_c_ 22. Kin Selection is: *c*

    a. a theory that predicts we will be more likely to help those who help us
    b. a theory that predicts helping will not occur unless we know who our relatives are
    c. a theory that predicts we will be more likely to help our relatives
    d. a theory about mate selection

_d_ 23. Aggression is thought to have been selected naturally in order to: *d*

    a. obtain a mate
    b. protect a mate
    c. protect offspring
    d. all of the above

_c_ 24. Parental investment refers to: *c*

    a. the amount of money you have put aside to help support your aging parents
    b. the amount of money your parents have set aside to support your education
    c. the time, effort, energy, and risk expended by your parents to ensure your survival
    d. the time, effort, energy, and resources you have invested in your parents' survival

_b_   25. Polygyny is a mating system in which one _____ may mate with many _____. It is common when parental investment is_____.

     a.   female, males, equal
     b.   male, females, unequal
     c.   female, males, unequal
     d.   male, females, equal

_c_   26. Polyandry is a mating system in which one _____ may mate with many _____. It is a common mating system when parental investment is _____.

     a.   female, males, equal
     b.   male, females, unequal
     c.   female, males, unequal
     d.   male, females, equal

_a_   27. Polygynandry is a mating system in which _____ males may mate with _____ females. It is a common mating system, which may _____ aggression and _____ peaceful social groups.

     a.   all, all, decrease, foster
     b.   some, some, decrease, disrupt
     c.   all, all, decrease, disrupt
     d.   some, some, increase, disrupt

_d_   28. Monogamy is a mating system common when parental investment is _____ for the male and _____ for the female.

     a.   low, high
     b.   high, low
     c.   low, low
     d.   high, high

_c_   29. The view that genes always have the same effect on those carrying them is called:

     a.   genetic correlations
     b.   genetic concordance
     c.   genetic determinism
     d.   genetic multiplicity

_b_   30. The view that ignores the important role of successful reproduction, and views evolution as solely about survival of the fittest is called:

     a.   Darwin's theory of Evolution
     b.   Social Darwinism
     c.   Spencer's theory of Evolution
     d.   Evolutionary psychology

True/False Items: *Write T or F in the space provided to the left of each item.*

_____ 1. According to Darwin's theory of evolution, a trait persists in a species when individuals possessing that trait kill off individuals who lack it, thereby dominating the gene pool.

_____ 2. Evolution can be defined as a change over time in the frequency with which particular genes occur within an interbreeding population.

_____ 3. The reaction range for IQ scores could be as high as 15 – 20 points.

_____ 4. When a number of gene pairs combine their influences to create a single phenotypic trait, that process is known as a recombinant DNA procedure.

_____ 5. Darwin coined the term 'survival of the fittest'.

_____ 6. Cooperation in humans makes sense from an evolutionary perspective.

_____ 7. Genetically-based traits natural and therefore are not modifiable.

_____ 8. Once established, a dominance hierarchy decreases aggression.

_____ 9. For humans, the monogamous mating system fits with the level of parental investment required by males and females.

_____ 10. With regard to mate preferences, both males and females rated mutual attraction, dependability, and emotional stability as the three most important characteristics.

Short Answer Questions

1. Explain what psychology has to do with evolution.

2. How do dominant and recessive genes interact to produce phenotypic traits?

3. Distinguish between kin selection and reciprocal altruism theories of altruistic behaviour.

4. Describe the four types of mating systems.

5. Describe how intelligence is a product of both genes and experience.

Essay Questions

1. Describe the behavioural tendencies of two people you know who are closely related to each other. (One of the people may be you, if you wish.) Do these two people have any striking behavioural similarities? Any striking behavioural differences? Now choose two people who are not related to each other and describe their behavioural tendencies. What, if anything, do your observations of their behavioural tendencies suggest about genetic influences on behaviour?

2. Discuss the concept of mate preference and its relation to explaining the status quo (e.g., most women state a preference for men who are slightly older, and marriage statistics reflect this preference). Are the findings regarding mate preferences convincing evidence of a biological basis for mate selection? Can you think of a different possible explanation for the findings of Buss's cross cultural studies of mate preferences?

Answer Keys

Answer Key for Key Terms

1.	f	16.	d
2.	e	17.	bb
3.	z	18.	x
4.	g	19.	j
5.	o	20.	t
6.	m	21.	l
7.	y	22.	v
8.	ee	23.	c
9.	r	24.	w
10.	b	25.	u
11.	s	26.	q
12.	I	27.	p
13.	k	28.	h
14.	cc	29.	dd
15.	n	30.	aa
		31.	a

Answer Key for Key People

1.	f	5.	e
2.	d	6.	g
3.	b	7.	c
4.	a		

Answer Key for Review at a Glance

1.	DNA	31.	evolutionary
2.	chromosomes	32.	traits
3.	genotype	33.	survival
4.	phenotype	34.	personality
5.	dominant	35.	universally
6.	recessive	36.	survive
7.	polygenic transmission	37.	reproduce
8.	behaviour genetics	38.	parental investment
9.	adoption	39.	monogamous
10.	monozygotic	40.	polyandry
11.	dizygotic	41.	polygynandry
12.	genetic	42.	decrease
13.	dysfunctional	43.	peacefulness
14.	interaction	44.	slightly older
15.	intelligence	45.	youthfulness
16.	personality	46.	child
17.	increases	47.	cooperate

18. 400
19. family
20. school experiences
21. individual learning
   experiences
22. unique

23. reading books
24. unrestricted abortion
25. death penalty
26. evolution
27. natural selection
28. surive
29. gene
30. adaptation

48. cost
49. kin selection
50. reciprocal altruism
51. aggressive

52. changed
53. genetic determinism
54. against
55. environment
56. reaction
57. environment
58. survival of the fittest
59. social
60. environment

Answer Key for Practice Test Multiple Choice Items

1. c		16. a	
2. d		17. a	
3. c		18. c	
4. d		19. c	
5. c		20. a	
6. c		21. b	
7. b		22. c	
8. b		23. d	
9. c		24. c	
10. c		25. b	
11. d		26. c	
12. b		27. a	
13. c		28. d	
14. a		29. c	
15. b		30. b	

Answer Key for Practice Test True/False Items

1. F		6. T	
2. T		7. F	
3. T		8. T	
4. F		9. F	
5. F		10. T	

Answer Key for Practice Test Short Answer Questions

1. Psychology is the study of thinking and behaviour, and genetic factors influence many of the ways in which we think and behave. An understanding of how various traits may have evolved helps psychologists to understand how the brain and the rest of the nervous system function. Evolution is one of the ways in which science unravels the complex influences of genes and environment.

2. The phenotype is the observable characteristic produced by a gene. If a gene in the pair received from the mother and father is dominant, the particular characteristic that it controls will be displayed. However, if the gene is recessive, the characteristic will not show up unless the gene inherited from the other parent is also recessive.

3. Kin Selection and the Theory of Reciprocal Altruism both view altruism as an act of cooperation intended to serve the self in the long term. The Kin Selection theory argues that we will be more likely to help those who share our genes, thereby increasing the likelihood that the carriers of our genes will survive and promote the further proliferation of our genes. The Theory of Reciprocal Altruism argues that we will help others even if they are not our relatives, because we expect that the assistance will be reciprocated in the future. The theories are not incompatible. They explain why we are more likely to help as genetic relatedness increases, and why in fewer cases, we will help those who are not related.

4. The four types of mating systems are polygyny in which one male may mate with several females. This is a mating practice predicted to occur when parental investment is unequal; that is, one parent has the lions share of investment in terms of length of pregnancy, length of time until maturity of offspring, energy, risk, and effort, required to raise offspring. The parent with the highest investment will be more selective than the parent who is less invested. Polyandry is a second type of mating system in which one female may mate with several males. As with polygyny, it is common when parental investment of parents is unequal. Polygynandry is a mating system in which all people may mate with all other members of the group. It decreases competition for mates and may foster social harmony. Monogamy is a mating system in which members pair bond. It is common when parental investment is approximately equal.

5. Evidence from twin and adoption studies show that as genetic relatedness increases, the similarities in intelligence scores also increases. Consequently, those with the most similar scores are identical twins. The role of the environment is also evident however, because the correlations between identical twins raised together are higher than those for identical twins reared apart, indicating that shared environmental experiences play a role. The concept of reaction range indicates that although genes may set the limits of intellectual capacity, environment will determine where within those limits one's actual score may fall. This is evident in studies comparing development in impoverished or enriched environments.

Answer Key for Practice Test Essay Questions

As you may have guessed, there are no right or wrong answers to the essay questions in this practice test. That does not mean, however, that all essays are equally good. To get maximum learning benefit from the essay questions, do the following:

- Review each essay a day or two after you wrote it, noting any necessary corrections and any additional support for your points that you can think of.
- Review the section in your textbook that pertains to the topic of each essay. Annotate your essay with any corrections or additional support for your points that you find in the text.
- Spend a few minutes researching the topic of each essay on the Internet. Annotate your essay further with any additional (reliable) information you find.
- Finally, reread each essay with the annotations you have added.

Chapter 5. Sensation and Perception

Learning Objectives

5.1   Differentiate sensation and perception.

5.2   Define psychophysics and describe the absolute threshold and signal detection methods of detecting stimuli.

5.3   Describe research on the effect of subliminal stimuli on attitudes and behaviour.

5.4   Differentiate absolute and difference thresholds.

5.5   Describe how Weber's law assists in determining the difference threshold.

5.6   Define sensory adaptation and describe its importance in detecting stimuli.

5.7   Identify and describe the function of the structures of the human eye involved in the sense of vision.

5.8   Describe visual transduction and how it explains brightness vision and dark adaptation.

5.9   Explain colour vision and colour-deficient vision using the trichromatic, opponent-process, and dual-process theories.

5.10   Describe the process of perception in the visual cortex, including a description of feature-detectors.

5.11   Describe the components of energy that are involved in the sense of audition.

5.12   Identify and describe the function of the structures of the ear involved in the sense of hearing.

5.13   Explain audition using the frequency and place theories of pitch perception.

5.14   Describe sound localization.

5.15   Identify the different types of deafness and explain the source of the problem.

5.16   Identify the structures involved in gustation and describe important functions of the sense of taste.

5.17   Identify the structures involved in olfaction and describe how social and sexual behaviour is regulated by olfaction.

5.18   Identify and describe the structures involved in the tactile and body senses.

5.19   Describe recent innovations in sensory prosthetics for patients with damage to specific sense systems.

5.20   Contrast bottom-up and top-down processing in perception.

5.21   Define selective attention and explain why it is important in perception.

5.22   Describe and recognize examples of Gestalt principles of perceptual organization.

5.23   Describe the role of perceptual schemas, perceptual sets, and perceptual constancies in detecting stimuli.

5.24   Describe and recognize monocular and binocular depth cues and cues for movement.

5.25   Identify the depth cues involved in creating visual illusions.

5.26   Describe the purpose, methods, and results of Kraft's research examining visual illusions causing pilot error.

5.27   Describe the biological development of perceptual skills and explain how it is affected by experience, critical periods, and cross-cultural factors.

Chapter Overview

This chapter covers the basic processes of sensation and perception and is divided into sections on sensory processes, the sensory systems, perception, illusions, pain, and critical periods. The scientific area that studies relations between the physical characteristics of stimuli and sensory capabilities is called psychophysics. Psychophysicists are interested in studying both the absolute limits of sensitivity and the sensitivity to distinguish between different stimuli. The lowest intensity at which a stimulus can be detected fifty percent of the time is called the absolute threshold of the stimulus. Signal detection theorists study the factors that influence such sensory judgements. There has been a lot of study of subliminal stimuli, stimuli so weak or brief that it cannot be perceived consciously, since the 1950's. Such studies have indicated that behaviour cannot be controlled subliminally, but subliminal stimuli can affect attitudes, at least in the laboratory. The difference threshold (also known as the just noticeable difference or jnd) is defined as the smallest difference between two stimuli that can be perceived fifty percent of the time. Weber's law states that the jnd is directly proportional to the magnitude of the stimulus with which the comparison is being made. For instance, the jnd for weight is 1/50, so if one object weighs 50g, then a second object would have to weight at least 51g for you to notice a difference in weight (or if one object weighs 100g, then a second object would have to weigh 102g for you to notice it). People must be attuned to changes in their environmental stimulation. Diminishing sensitivity to an unchanging stimulus is called sensory adaptation.

Psychologists study a number of sensory systems. For example, psychologists study the processes of vision, audition, gustation, olfaction, and the tactile senses. The eye consists of several important structures such as the lens and retina. Nearsightedness, or myopia, occurs when the lens focuses the visual image in front of the retina, while farsightedness, or hyperopia, occurs when the image is focused behind the retina. Rods are black-and-white brightness receptors in the eye, while cones are colour receptors. Bipolar cells have synaptic connections with rods and cones and also connect to ganglion cells, whose axons bundle to form the optic nerve, which sends visual information to the thalamus, which in turn sends information to the primary visual cortex in the brain. Groups of neurons within the primary visual cortex called feature detectors are organized to receive and translate nerve impulses coming from the retina. Visual association cortex is where the final processes of constructing a visual representation occur. Transduction is the process by which the characteristics of a stimulus are converted into nerve impulses. People must adapt to both bright and dark conditions. The progressive improvement in brightness sensitivity that occurs over time under conditions of low illumination (like in a movie theatre) is called dark adaptation. There are several theories of colour vision. The trichromatic theory developed by Young and Helmholtz suggests that there are three types of colour receptors in the retina that are sensitive to blue, green, or red. The opponent-process theory suggests that each of the three different cone types responds to *two* different wavelengths: one to red or green, a second to blue or yellow, and a third to black or white. Dual-process theory combines both theories, as evidence has been found for both. Some people are colour blind. Dichromats are colour blind in only one of the systems, while monochromats are sensitive only to black and white.

The stimuli for hearing are sound waves, which are measured in terms of their frequency (measured in hertz [Hz]) and amplitude (measured in decibels [db]). The transduction system for audition occurs in the inner ear. Vibrating activity of inner ear bones amplifies sound waves. When sound waves strike the eardrum, pressure created by the inner ear bones sets the fluid inside the cochlea into motion. The fluid waves that result vibrate the basilar membrane causing a bending of the hair cells in the organ of Corti. This bending triggers a release of neurotransmitters into the synapse between the hair cells and neurons of the auditory nerve, and nerve impulses are then sent to the brain. To use sound, we must code both pitch and loudness. Loudness is coded by a greater bend by the hair cells, resulting in the release of more neurotransmitters and a higher rate of firing in the auditory nerve. The frequency theory of pitch suggests that nerve impulses sent to the brain match the frequency of the sound wave, while the place theory of pitch suggests that the specific point in the cochlea where the fluid wave peaks and most strongly bends the hair cells serves as a frequency coding cue. Sounds are localized because we have two ears (thus we have binaural ability). Sounds arrive first and loudest at the ear closest to the sound, allowing us to figure out where it is coming from. Almost 3 million people in Canada suffer from hearing loss. Conduction deafness occurs when there is a problem in the system that sends sound waves to the cochlea while nerve deafness occurs when there are damaged receptors in the inner ear or damage to the auditory nerve.

Gustation refers to our sense of taste. The four types of taste receptors found along the tongue create a "taste," which results from neural activity. Olfaction refers to our sense of smell. Humans have about 40 million olfactory receptors. Pheromones, chemical signals found in natural body scents, may affect human behaviour. For instance, some studies show that women who live together or are close friends develop similar menstrual cycles, a phenomenon called menstrual synchrony.

The tactile senses are important to us too. Humans are sensitive to at least touch, pain, warmth, and cold. The sense of kinesthesis provides us with feedback about the positions of our muscles and joints, allowing us to coordinate body movements. Our vestibular sense is the sense of body orientation or equilibrium.

Perception also affects the way that we experience the world. Perception is an active, creative process, which can cause different people to experience exactly the same stimulus in very different ways. To create perceptions the brain uses both bottom-up and top-down processing. In bottom-up processing, a stimulus is broken down into its constituent parts and then combined and interpreted as a whole. In top-down processing, expectations and existing knowledge are used to interpret new information. Because there are so many stimuli impinging on our senses, we can only pay attention to a small fraction of them. These processes are studied experimentally through a technique called shadowing. Attention is affected by both the nature of the stimulus and by personal factors. People are especially attentive to stimuli that might represent a threat to their well-being. People tend to organize the world to make it simpler to understand. Gestalt theorists suggested that people use top-down processing to organize their worlds. For instance, we tend to organize stimuli into a foreground and background, a process called figure-ground relations. People group and interpret stimuli according to the four Gestalt laws of perceptual organization: similarity, proximity, closure, and continuity. Recognizing an image requires that we have a perceptual schema (a representation of the image in memory) to compare it with. We make interpretations of stimulus input and sensory information based on our knowledge and experience. For instance, you can recognize what you're sitting on right now as a chair or sofa based on your experience with such objects in the past. Perceptual sets are sets of expectations that affect our perceptions. Perceptual constancies allow us to recognize familiar stimuli under varying conditions, allowing us to enter into different environments and be able to function. Without perceptual constancies, we would have to relearn what stimuli are in each environment we enter.

We perceive depth through both monocular (one-eye) and binocular (two-eye) cues. For instance, light and shadow (a monocular cue) helps us to see "depth" in paintings. Each eye sees a slightly different image (binocular disparity), and the resulting disparity is analyzed by feature detectors in the brain, which allows us to see depth. The perception of movement requires the brain to perceive various movement cues. Illusions are incorrect perceptions that often result from the inaccurate perception of both monocular and binocular depth cues.

Psychologists also study how pain is perceived by individuals. Endorphins, natural opiates in the body, inhibit the release of neurotransmitters involved in the synaptic transmission of pain impulses. Endorphins are also involved in stress-induced analgesia, a reduction in pain during stressful conditions. Pain is also perceived differently in different cultures, suggesting that psychological factors affect the perception of pain.

Finally, for some kinds of perception, critical periods during which certain kinds of experiences must occur if perceptual abilities and the brain mechanisms that underlie them are to develop suggest that environmental factors also influence the development of sensation and perception.

Chapter Outline

Sensory Processes
> Stimulus Detection: The Absolute Threshold
> Signal Detection Theory
>> *Research Foundations: Subliminal Stimuli: Can They Affect Behaviour?*
> The Difference Threshold
> Sensory Adaptation

The Sensory Systems
> Vision
>> The Human Eye
>> Photoreceptors: The Rods and the Cones
>> Visual Transduction: From Light to Nerve Impulses
>> Brightness Vision and Dark Adaptation
>> Colour Vision
>> Analysis and Reconstruction of Visual Scenes
> Audition
>> Auditory Transduction: From Pressure Waves to Nerve Impulses
>> Coding of Pitch and Loudness
>> Sound Localization
>> Hearing Loss
>>> *Research Frontiers: Sensory Prosthetics: "Eyes" for the Blind, "Ears"*
>>> *for the Hearing Impaired*
> Taste and Smell: The Chemical Senses
>> Gustation: The Sense of Taste
>> Olfaction: The Sense of Smell
> The Skin and Body Senses
>> The Tactile Senses
>> The Body Senses

Perception: The Creation of Experience
> Perception is Selective: The Role of Attention
>> Environmental and Personal Factors in Attention
> Perceptions Have Organization and Structure
>> Gestalt Principles of Perceptual Organization
> Perception Involves Hypothesis Testing
> Perception is Influenced by Expectations: Perceptual Sets
> Stimuli Are Recognizable Under Changing Conditions: Perceptual Constancies

Perception of Depth, Distance, and Movement
> Depth and Distance Perception
>> Monocular Depth Cues
>> Binocular Disparity
> Perception of Movement

Illusions: False Perceptual Hypotheses

Psychological Applications: Stalking a Deadly Illusion

Experience, Critical Periods, and Perceptual Development
    Cross-Cultural Research on Perception
    Critical Periods: The Role of Early Experience
    Restored Sensory Capacity

Problem-Based Learning

Human Factors

http://www.usd.edu/hfnews/index.cfm
The University of South Dakota Psychology Department's Human Factors Program-Contains links to professional organizations, university programs, demonstrations, literature and other resources.

Depth Perception

http://www.stereoscopy.com
Stereoscopy.com-A comprehensive site containing information about 3-D, examples and resources.

http://archive.museophile.sbu.ac.uk/3d
Excellent and comprehensive collection of 3-D pictures, information about 3-D and links to more resources.

http://www.3dcomix.com/about3d
About 3D-Contains many resources, examples of 3-D and general information.

Illusions

http://www.illuweb.supereva.it/indexen.htm?p
A World of Optical Illusions-This site contains many examples of illusions, ambiguous figures, and artwork such as Escher's.

http://www.brl.ntt.co.jp/IllusionForum
IllusionForum-Contains numerous examples of both auditory and visual illusions.

General
http://www.yorku.ca/eye/thejoy.htm
A Canadian web book on visual perception by Peter Kaiser. It contains a general overview that is primarily demonstrations.

Key Terms: *Write the letter of the definition next to the term in the space provided.*

Sensory Processes

1. _D_ absolute threshold
2. _E_ decision criterion

3. _H_ difference threshold

4. _C_ perception

5. _K_ psychophysics

6. _B_ sensation

7. _J_ sensory adaptation

8. _F_ signal detection theory

9. _G_ subliminal stimuli

10. _A_ synesthesia
11. _I_ Weber's Law

a. a "mixing of the senses"
b. the stimulus-detection process by which sense organs respond to and translate environmental stimuli into nerve impulses sent to the brain
c. the active process of recognizing stimulus input and giving it meaning
d. the lowest intensity at which a stimulus can be detected 50% of the time
e. a standard of how certain a person must be that a stimulus is present before they will say they detect it
f. concerned with the factors that influence sensory judgements
g. a stimulus that is so weak or brief that it cannot be perceived consciously
h. the smallest difference between two stimuli that people can detect 50% of the time
i. the difference threshold is directly proportional to the magnitude of the stimulus with which the comparison is being made
j. diminishing sensitivity to an unchanging stimulus
k. the study of the relationships between physical characteristics of stimuli and sensory capabilities

The Sensory Systems

1. _I_ amplitude
2. _N_ basilar membrane
3. _D_ bipolar cells
4. _Y_ cochlea

5. _A_ conduction deafness
6. _C_ cones
7. _J_ dark adaptation

8. _N_ decibels

9. _M_ dual-process theory

10. _D_ feature detectors

11. _G_ fovea

12. _Q_ frequency

13. _Y_ frequency theory

a. nearsightedness
b. farsightedness
c. colour receptors
d. cells with synaptic connections to the rods, cones, and ganglion cells
e. cells whose axons are bundled to form the optic nerve
f. black-and-white brightness receptors
g. a small area in the centre of the retina that contains only cones
h. the process by which the characteristics of a stimulus are converted into nerve impulses
i. protein molecules that aid rods and cones in translating light waves into nerve impulses
j. the progressive improvement in brightness sensitivity that occurs over time under conditions of low illumination
k. theory that there are three types of colour receptors in the retina
l. theory that each of the three cone types respond to two different wavelengths
m. theory that combines trichromatic and opponent-process theory

14. __o__ ganglion cells

15. __cc__ gestation

16. __s__ hertz

17. __ii__ hyperopia

18. __hh__ kinesthesis

19. __ii__ lens

20. __gg__ menstrual synchrony

21. __jj__ myopia

22. __aa__ nerve deafness

23. __dd__ olfaction

24. __v__ opponent-process theory

25. __kk__ optic nerve

26. __x__ organ of Corti

27. __p__ parallel processing

28. __ff__ pheromones

29. __I__ photopigments

30. __z__ place theory

31. __n__ primary visual cortex

32. __jj__ retina

33. __ee__ rods

34. __ee__ taste buds

35. __H__ transduction

36. __k__ trichromatic theory

37. __ll__ visual acuity

38. __r__ visual association cortex

n. part of the brain that receives visual information from the thalamus

o. cells that receive and integrate sensory nerve impulses originating in the retina

p. a process by which separate but overlapping modules within the brain are simultaneously analyzed

q. the number of sound waves per second

r. place in the brain where successively more complex features of the visual scene are combined and interpreted

s. the technical measure of cycles per second

t. the vertical size of the sound wave

u. a measure of the physical pressure that occurs at the eardrum

v. a coiled, snail-shaped tube filled with fluid in the inner ear

w. a sheet of tissue within the cochlea that runs its length

x. contains thousands of hair cells

y. theory of pitch perception that states that nerve impulses sent to the brain match the frequency of the sound wave

z. theory of pitch perception that states that the specific point in the cochlea where the fluid wave peaks and most strongly bends the hair cells serves as a frequency coding cue

aa. a type of deafness caused by problems involving the mechanical system that transmits sound waves to the cochlea

bb. a type of deafness that is caused by damaged receptors within the inner ear or damage to the auditory nerve

cc. the taste sense

dd. the smell sense

ee. receptors concentrated along the edges and back surface of the tongue

ff. chemical signals found in natural body scents

gg. the tendency of women who live together or are close friends to become more similar in their menstrual cycles

hh. sense that provides us with feedback about our muscles' and joints' positions and movements

ii. an elastic structure that becomes thinner to focus on distant objects and thicker to focus on nearby objects

jj. a multilayered tissue at the rear of the eyeball

kk. bundle of ganglion cells

ll. ability to see fine detail

Illusions, Pain, and Perceptual Development

1. __H__ binocular cues
2. __M__ binocular disparity
3. __A__ bottom-up processing
4. __N__ convergence
5. __L__ critical periods
6. __J__ endorphins
7. __D__ figure-ground relations
8. __G__ monocular cues
9. __O__ perceptual constancies
10. __E__ perceptual schema
11. __F__ perceptual set
12. __C__ shadowing
13. __K__ stress-induced analgesia
14. __I__ stroboscopic movement
15. __B__ top-down processing

a. a processing function by which the brain takes in individual elements of the stimulus and combines them into a unified perception
b. a process by which sensory information is interpreted in the light of existing knowledge, ideas, and expectations
c. a technique in which participants are asked to repeat one message while listening simultaneously to two messages sent through headphones
d. the tendency to organize stimuli into a foreground and background
e. a mental representation of perceptual phenomenon that we use to compare new stimuli to in the process of recognition
f. a readiness to perceive stimuli in a particular way
g. depth cues that require only one eye
h. depth cues that require both eyes
i. illusory movement produced when a light is flashed and another light is flashed nearby milliseconds later
j. natural opiates that act as pain-killers
k. a reduction in perceived pain that occurs under stressful conditions
l. periods during which certain kinds of experiences must occur if perceptual abilities and the brain mechanisms that underlie them are to develop normally
m. process by which each eye sees a slightly different image
n. a binocular distance cue produced by feedback from the muscles that turn your eyes inward to view a near object
o. allow us to perceive familiar objects under varying conditions

Review at a Glance: *Write the term that best fits the blank to review what you learned in this chapter.*

Sensory Processes

We experience the world through our senses. However, some people suffering from (1) _____ experience sounds as colours or tastes as touch. The study of the relationships between physical characteristics of stimuli and sensory capabilities is called (2) _____. One thing that psychophysicists study is the intensity need to detect a stimulus. The minimal intensity needed to detect a stimulus 50% of the time is called the (3) _____ _____. People are sometimes uncertain about whether they have detected a stimulus and set their own (4) _____ _____ to decide whether they have detected it or not. The theory that is concerned with the factors that influence sensory judgement is called (5) _____ _____ theory. A stimulus so weak or brief that it cannot be perceived consciously is called a (6) _____ stimulus. People must also be able to distinguish between stimuli. The smallest difference between two stimuli that people can perceive 50% of the time is

called the (7) _____ threshold or the (8) _____ _____
_____. (9) _____ _____ states that the jnd is directly
proportional to the magnitude of the stimulus with which the comparison is made.
Sensory systems are attuned to changes in stimulation. The diminishing sensitivity to an
unchanging stimulus is called (10) _____ _____.

The Sensory Systems

(11) _____ _____ results when the (12) _____ focuses an
image in front of the (13) _____ while (14) _____ occurs when the lens
focuses the image behind the retina. The cells in the eye that detect colour are called
(15) _____, while the cells that detect black-and-white and brightness are called
(16) _____. Rods and cones translate light waves into nerve impulses with the
action of protein molecules called (17) _____ in the process of (18) _____.
Rods and cones have synaptic connections with (19) _____ _____,
which in turn have synaptic connections with ganglion cells, the axons of which form the
(20) _____ _____. A small area of the retina containing only cones is
called the (21) _____, where the cones have individual connections to bipolar
cells. Our ability to see fine detail, or our (22) _____ _____, is greatest
when the visual image projects directly onto the fovea. We must adapt to different levels
of illumination. The progressive improvement in brightness sensitivity that occurs over
time in conditions of low illumination like in a movie theatre is called
(23) _____ _____. Several theories suggest how we sense colour.
According to the (24) _____ theory, there are three types of colour receptors in
the retina, while according to the (25) _____ _____ theory, each type
of colour receptor is sensitive to two different wavelengths. The (26) _____
_____ theory is a more modern theory, combining both theories. Feature
detectors in the (27) _____ _____ _____ receive and integrate
various sensory nerve impulses originating in the retina. Visual information is finally
analyzed and recombined in the (28) _____ _____ _____.
Psychologists also study how we detect sound. Sound waves are measured both in the
number of sounds waves, or cycles, per second, which is the (29) _____ of the
sound waves, and in their vertical size, or (30) _____. Sound waves travel into
the auditory canal of the ear and stimulate the three tiny bones of the middle ear, which
amplify the sound wave. The pressure created sets the fluid in the (31) _____ _____
into motion. The fluid waves that result vibrate the (32) _____ membrane and set
the (33) _____ cells into motion. Neurotransmitters are then released and nerve
impulses are sent to the brain. There are two theories of how we code pitch. The
(34) _____ theory suggests that nerve impulses sent to the brain match the
frequency of the sound wave, while the (35) _____ theory suggests that specific
point in the cochlea where the fluid wave peaks and most strongly bends the hair cells
serves as a frequency coding cue. A type of hearing loss called (36) _____
deafness occurs when the system sending sound waves to the cochlea is damaged, while
(37) _____ deafness occurs when inner ear receptors or the auditory nerve is
damaged. (38) _____ is the sense of taste, while (39) _____ refers to
our sense of smell. Receptors called (40) _____ _____ concentrated on
the tongue allow us to taste things. Some researchers believe that (41) _____,
chemical signals found in natural body scents, may affect human and animal behaviour.
Humans are sensitive to at least four tactile senses: touch, pain, warmth, and cold. The
body senses include (42) _____, which provides us with feedback about the

positions of our muscles and joints and the (43) _____ sense, which is the sense of body orientation or equilibrium.

Perception: The Creation of Experience

Perception is an active, creative process. To create perceptions, the brain uses both (44) _____ - _____ processing, which involves taking in individual elements of a stimulus and then combining them into a unified perception, and (45) _____ - _____ processing, which is when the brain uses existing knowledge and expectations to perceive a stimulus. Perceptions have organization and structure. Gestalt theorists discovered many of the basic principles of organization. For example, we tend to organize stimuli into foreground figures and backgrounds, a process called (46) _____ - _____ relations. The four Gestalt principles of organization are (47) _____, (48) _____, (49) _____, and (50) _____. Perception involves hypothesis testing. Recognizing a new stimulus, for example a flying animal with feathers, wings, and a beak as a bird, requires use of a perceptual (51) _____. Readiness to perceive certain stimuli in a certain way is called a perceptual (52) _____. We can recognize familiar stimuli under different environmental conditions because of perceptual (53) _____.

Perception of Depth, Distance, and Movement

To judge depth, the brain relies on both (54) _____ cues, which require one eye, and (55) _____ cues, which require two eyes. Depth cues rely on (56) _____ _____, in which each eye sees a slightly different image. A second binocular distance cue called (57) _____ is produced by feedback from the muscles that turn our eyes inward to view a near object.

Perception as a Psychobiological Process: Understanding Pain

Pain involves a complex set of sensations and perceptions. To help us deal with pain, the brain has its own built-in analgesics called (58) _____. A phenomenon attributed to endorphins is (59) _____ - _____ _____, a reduction in perceived pain during stressful episodes. Culture and early experience can both influence the perception of pain. For some aspects of perception, there are (60) _____ _____, during which certain kinds of experiences must occur if perceptual abilities and the brain mechanisms that underlie them are to develop. If no experience stimulating the development during this time occurs, then it is too late to undo the deficit.

Apply What You Know

1. Describe how visual stimuli are projected to the two hemispheres by referring to the diagram on Study Sheet 5.1.

2. Describe the process shown in the diagram on Study Sheet 5.2.

3. Draw a figure using each of the four Gestalt principles of perceptual organization. Use Study Sheet 5.3.

Internet Scavenger Hunt

1. If perception is a subjective phenomenon, we would expect that people of different cultures would perceive the same objects or events in quite different ways. Using the PsycInfo database or <u>Psychological Abstracts</u> (available in your college library), find two studies that examine such cultural differences and report their findings.

Study #1:

Study #2:

Practice Test

Multiple Choice Items: *Please write the letter corresponding to your answer in the space to the left of each item.*

_____ 1. The lowest intensity at which a stimulus can be detected 50% of the time is known as the ____.

    a. difference threshold
    b. absolute threshold
    c. signal detection
    d. just noticeable difference

_____ 2. A participant in a signal detection study has the tendency to be bolder in her decisions regarding the presence of a target stimulus. As a result, she has more hits but also has more false alarms. This example demonstrates how ____ can affect ____.

    a. situational factors; participant characteristics
    b. situational factors; decision criterion
    c. participant characteristics; situational factors
    d. participant characteristics; decision criterion

_____ 3. Regarding the impact of subliminal messages on attitudes and behaviour, research has found that subliminal messages have ____.

    a. no impact on attitudes and behaviours
    b. an equal impact on attitudes and behaviours
    c. a stronger impact on behaviours than on attitudes
    d. a stronger impact on attitudes than on behaviours

_____ 4. The ____ threshold is defined as the smallest difference between two stimuli that can be perceived 50% of the time.

    a. absolute
    b. sensation
    c. difference
    d. perceptual

_____ 5. According to a Weber fraction, the jnd for weight is 1/50. Therefore, if an object weighed 1kg (1000g), a second object would have to minimally weigh ____ for you to notice a difference between the two objects.

    a. 2kg
    b. 1020g
    c. 1050g
    d. 50g

_____ 6. You have just prepared a bath for yourself and as you are getting in, the water feels very hot, almost too hot. However, you continue to ease yourself into the tub and pretty soon, even though it has remained the same temperature, the water no longer feels so hot. The characteristic of sensory neurons that is responsible for this phenomenon is known as _____.

a. sensory adaptation
b. the refractory period
c. the all-or-none law
d. signal detection

_____ 7. The receptors for black-and-white and brightness are called _____, while the receptors for colour are called _____.

a. rods; cones
b. cones; rods
c. ganglion cells; bipolar cells
d. bipolar cells; ganglion cells

_____ 8. The department of transportation contacts you and asks what colour they should make their road signs so that they will be most visible at night. Given what you have learned in this class about the sensitivity of rods under conditions of low illumination, one colour that you would **not** want to pick is _____.

a. yellow
b. blue
c. green
d. red

_____ 9. The progressive improvement in brightness sensitivity that occurs over time under conditions of low illumination is called _____.

a. transduction
b. dark adaptation
c. visual acuity
d. opponent-process

_____ 10. The current modern theory of colour sensation uses the _____ theory to explain the behaviour of the cones in colour vision while a modified version of the _____ theory that emphasizes the role of ganglion cells is used to explain the presence of afterimages and certain types of colour blindness.

a. trichromatic; additive colour mixture
b. dual process; trichromatic
c. opponent process; dual process
d. trichromatic; opponent process

_____ 11. Groups of neurons within the primary visual cortex that are organized to receive and integrate sensory nerve impulses originating in specific regions of the retina are called _____.

a. ganglion cells
b. bipolar cells
c. feature detectors
d. opponent procesors

_____ 12. According to the Canadian Hearing Society, a safe level to listen to your portable CD player at is _____ .

a. below 85 db
b. below 120 db
c. below 94 db
d. below 10 db

_____ 13. In Canada, approximately _____ percent of the population suffers from some form of hearing loss.

a. 1
b. 2
c. 10
d. 25

_____ 14. The place theory of pitch perception states that pitch is determined by _____.

a. neurons that fire at the same frequency as the incoming stimulus
b. neurons that fire at the same amplitude as the incoming stimulus
c. the specific place in the cochlea where the fluid wave peaks more
d. the way that the eardrum resonates in response to different frequencies

_____ 15. Research on critical periods and experience has demonstrated that kittens raised in a vertically striped chamber

a. did not see horizontal patterns.
b. did not see vertical patterns.
c. were able to see horizontal and vertical patterns equally well.
d. did not see either vertical or horizontal patterns.

_____ 16. The chemical sense of taste is called _____, while the chemical sense of smell is called _____.

a. the vestibular sense; olfaction
b. gustation; olfaction
c. olfaction; the vestibular sense
d. olfaction; kinesthesis

_____ 17. The four qualities that our sense of taste responds to are ___.

a. sweet, sour, salty, bitter
b. sweet, sour, salty, tart
c. sour, salty, biting, tart
d. sweet, sour, salty, sugary

_____ 18. Chemical signals found in natural body scents that may affect human and animal behaviour are called _____.

a. olfactors
b. buds
c. gustators
d. pheromones

_____ 19. Of the following, the one which is <u>not</u> classified as a tactile sensation is _____.

a. pressure
b. touch
c. warmth
d. gustation

_____ 20. Our sense of body orientation or equilibrium is called _____.

a. kinesthesis
b. the vestibular sense
c. olfaction
d. balance

_____ 21. As you are reading this question, feature detectors in your visual system are analyzing the various stimulus components and recombining them into your perception of letters and words. This is an example of _____ processing.

a. figure-ground
b. top-down
c. parallel
d. bottom-up

_____ 22. Perceptual set is an example of _____ processing.

a. figure-ground
b. top-down
c. parallel
d. bottom-up

_____ 23. A new commercial presents its product in a rather novel and intense way, making use of a lot of movement and special effects. If this ad were to capture your attention, it would **best** be viewed as an example of how _____ can affect attention.

a. personal motives
b. sensory adaptation
c. internal factors
d. environmental factors

_____ 24. You would likely recognize the following set of stimuli as the word "cat" due to the Gestalt principle of _____.

C /-\ T

a. similarity
b. figure-ground
c. proximity
d. continuity

_____ 25. In 1950, psychologist Harold Kelley invited a guest lecturer to his class. Half of his students were led to believe that the guest lecturer was a warm person while the other half was told that he was rather cold. When rating the guest lecturer afterwards, students tended to rate him in a way that was consistent with the expectations they had been given ahead of time. This example was presented to demonstrate how _____ can affect _____.

a. perceptual schemas; perceptual sets
b. perceptual schemas; bottom-up processing
c. perceptual sets; social perceptions
d. sensory adaptation; sensory habituation

_____ 26. A binocular distance cue produced by feedback from the muscles that turn your eyes inward to view a near object is called _____.

a. stroboscopic movement
b. convergence
c. monocularism
d. perceptual constancy

_____ 27. Stroboscopic movement refers to _____.

a. the movement of a visual image to an area outside of the fovea
b. instances where a light appears to move between two adjacent flashing lights
c. illusory movements that are due to binocular depth cues
d. illusory movements that are due to perceptual constancies

_____ 28. Compelling but incorrect perceptions of stimuli are called ____.

a. illusions
b. perceptual schemas
c. perceptual sets
d. stroboscopic movements

_____ 29. Endorphins are thought to exert their painkilling effects by ____.

a. enhancing the release of neurotransmitters involved in pain impulses
b. deadening or numbing the part of the frontal cortex that processes pain
c. inhibiting the release of neurotransmitters involved in pain impulses
d. facilitating the process of sensory adaptation

_____ 30. Longitudinal research on the Sonicguide has found that.

a. children above 10 years of age have difficulty learning how to use the device.
b. young infants require lengthy training sessions in order to use the device effectively.
c. the device cannot be learned effectively by any age group.
d. female children learn to use the device more quickly than male children.

True/False Items: *Write T or F in the space provided to the left of each item.*

_____ 1. People who experience sounds as colours or tastes suffer from synesthesia.

_____ 2. A standard of how certain people must be that a stimulus is present before they will say they detect it is called the absolute threshold of the stimulus.

_____ 3. For people who suffer from myopia, the lens focuses the visual image behind the retina.

_____ 4. Transduction is the process whereby the characteristics of a stimulus are converted into nerve impulses.

_____ 5. Opponent-process theory proposed that each of the three cone types responds to two different wavelengths.

_____ 6. Amplitude is a measure of the loudness of sound and is measured in decibels.

_____ 7. There is no evidence for the hypothesis of menstrual synchrony.

_____ 8. Perceptual constancies allow us to recognize familiar objects under varying conditions.

_____ 9. People of all cultures perceive pain in the same way, suggesting that it is purely a biological function.

_____ 10. If particular patterns of perception do not develop during critical periods, they never will.

Short Answer Questions

1. What is sensory adaptation?

2. Describe the differences between the Young-Helmholtz trichromatic theory and the opponent-process theory.

3. What is the difference between frequency and amplitude?

4. What is the difference between bottom-up and top-down processing?

5. How do perceptual schemas and perceptual set affect perception?

Essay Questions

1. Describe how the absolute threshold, decision criteria, the difference threshold, and Weber's Law affect the process of stimulus detection.

2. Describe how rods and cones send their messages to the brain.

3. Describe the process of auditory transduction.

4. Describe the four Gestalt laws of perceptual organization.

5. How do we perceive depth and distance?

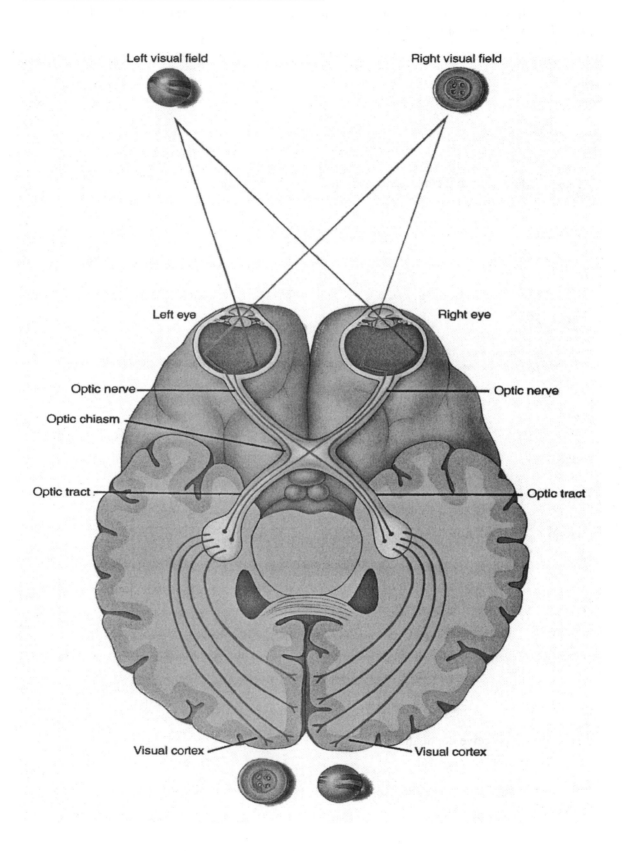

Left visual field

Right visual field

Left eye

Right eye

Optic nerve

Optic nerve

Optic chiasm

Optic tract

Optic tract

Visual cortex

Visual cortex

Study Sheet 5.2 Theories of Colour Vision

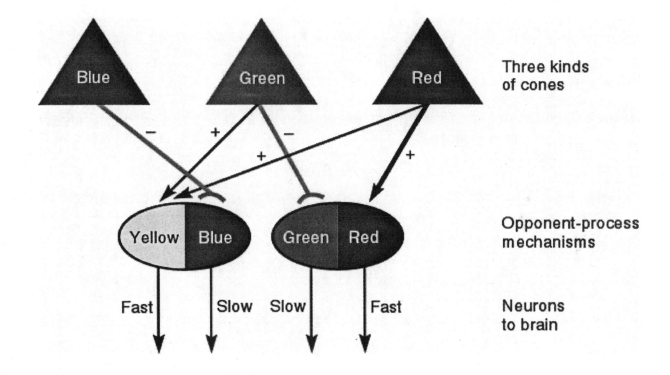

Study Sheet 5.3 Gestalt Principles of Perceptual Organization

1. Similarity

2. Proximity

3. Closure

4. Continuity

Answer Keys

Answer Key for Key Terms

Sensory Processes

1.	d		7.	j
2.	e		8.	f
3.	h		9.	g
4.	c		10.	a
5.	k		11.	i
6.	b			

The Sensory Systems

1.	t		20.	gg
2.	w		21.	a
3.	d		22.	bb
4.	v		23.	dd
5.	aa		24.	l
6.	c		25.	kk
7.	j		26.	x
8.	u		27.	p
9.	m		28.	ff
10.	o		29.	I
11.	g		30.	z
12.	q		31.	n
13.	y		32.	jj
14.	e		33.	f
15.	cc		34.	ee
16.	s		35.	h
17.	b		36.	k
18.	hh		37.	ll
19.	ii		38.	r

Perception and Illusions

1.	h		9.	o
2.	m		10.	e
3.	s		11.	f
4.	n		12.	c
5.	l		13.	k
6.	j		14.	i
7.	d		15.	b
8.	g			

Answer Key for Review at a Glance

1. synesthesia
2. psychophysics
3. absolute threshold
4. decision criterion
5. sensory detection
6. subliminal
7. difference
8. just noticeable difference (jnd)
9. Weber's Law
10. Sensory adaptation
11. myopia
12. lens
13. retina
14. hyperopia
15. cones
16. rods
17. photopigments
18. transduction
19. bipolar cells
20. optic nerve
21. fovea
22. visual acuity
23. dark adaptation
24. trichromatic
25. opponent process
26. dual process
27. primary visual cortex
28. visual association cortex
29. frequency
30. amplitude
31. cochlea
32. basilar
33. hair
34. frequency
35. place
36. conduction
37. nerve
38. Gustation
39. olfaction
40. taste buds
41. pheromones
42. kinesthesis
43. vestibular
44. bottom-up
45. top-down
46. figure-ground
47. similarity
48. proximity
49. closure
50. continuity
51. schema
52. set
53. constancies
54. monocular
55. binocular
56. binocular disparity
57. convergence
58. endorphins
59. stress-induced analgesia
60. critical periods

Answer Key for Practice Test Multiple Choice Questions

1.	b	16.	b
2.	d	17.	a
3.	d	18.	d
4.	c	19.	d
5.	b	20.	b
6.	a	21.	d
7.	a	22.	b
8.	d	23.	d
9.	b	24.	d
10.	d	25.	c
11.	c	26.	b
12.	a	27.	b
13.	c	28.	a
14.	c	29.	c
15.	a	30.	b

Answer Key for Practice Test True/False Questions

1.	T	6.	T
2.	F	7.	F
3.	F	8.	T
4.	T	9.	F
5.	T	10.	T

Answer Key for Practice Test Short Answer Questions

1. Sensory adaptation refers to the diminishing sensitivity to an unchanging stimulus. This type of adaptation is sometimes called habituation. Sensory adaptation helps us to get used to stimuli.

2. Trichromatic theory argued that there are three types of colour receptors, one sensitive to wavelengths that correspond to blue, another to green, and the third to red. Opponent-process theory argued that each of the three cone types correspond to two wavelengths: the first type to red or green, the second type to blue or yellow, and the third type to black or white.

3. Frequency is the number of sound waves, or cycles, per second and is measured in hertz (Hz). Frequency is a measure of the sound's pitch. Amplitude refers to the vertical size of the sound wave and is measured in decibels (db). Amplitude is a measure of the sound's loudness.

4. In bottom-up processing, feature detectors break down stimuli into their constituent parts, and the system then combines them into a unified perception. In top-down processing, existing knowledge and expectations guide the process of the perception of a stimulus.

5. Perceptual schemas are mental representations by which we compare new stimuli in order to recognize them. Perceptual sets are sets of expectancies that influence our perceptions of new stimuli.

Answer Key for Practice Test Essay Questions

1. The absolute threshold is the lowest intensity at which a stimulus can be detected 50% of the time. An example is a candle flame seen at 50 km on a clear, dark night. People's level of sensitivity is different. Each person sets their decision criterion, which is a standard of how sure they must be that they have sensed a stimulus before they will report sensing it. The difference threshold refers to the smallest <u>difference</u> between two stimuli that people can perceive 50% of the time. The difference threshold is also known as the just noticeable difference (jnd). Weber's Law states that the jnd is directly <u>proportional</u> to the magnitude of a stimulus with which the comparison is being made.

2. Rods, black-and-white and brightness receptors, and cones, colour receptors, are in the retina. Both have synaptic connections with bipolar cells. Bipolar cells, in turn, have synaptic connections with ganglion cells, whose axons collect into a bundle to form the optic nerve. The optic nerve sends the messages to the brain. Rods and cones translate light waves into nerve impulses through the action of protein molecules called photopigments. The absorption of light by these photopigments affects the rate of neurotransmitter release at the receptor's synapse with the bipolar cells.

3. Sound waves travel into an auditory canal leading to the eardrum. Beyond the eardrum, in the middle ear, in which three tiny bones, the hammer, anvil, and stirrup, amplify the sound waves. The pressure created sets the fluid inside the cochlea into motion, resulting in the vibration of the basilar membrane and the membrane above it. This vibration causes the bending of the hair cells in the organ of Corti, triggering a release of neurotransmitters into the synaptic space between the hair cells and the neurons of the auditory nerve, resulting in nerve impulses sent to the brain.

4. The law of similarity says that when parts of a configuration are perceived as similar, they will be perceived as belonging together. The law of proximity says that elements that are near each other are likely to be perceived as part of the same configuration. The law of closure states that people tend to close the open edges of a figure or fill in gaps in an incomplete figure. The law of continuity states that people link individual elements together so they form a continuous line or pattern that makes sense.

5. Depth and distance are perceived through both monocular and binocular depth cues. One monocular (one eye) cue is light and shadow. Linear perspective refers to the perception that parallel lines converge as they recede into the distance. An object's height in the horizontal plane, clarity, relative size, and motion parallax are also monocular cues. Binocular cues rely on the brain's feature detectors, which are attuned to depth cues. A second binocular distance cue, convergence, is produced by muscles that turn your eyes inward to view a near object.

Chapter 6. States of Consciousness

Learning Objectives

6.1 ✓ Define the characteristics of consciousness and describe how it is measured.

6.2 ✓ Describe Freud's levels of consciousness: conscious, preconscious, and unconscious.

6.3 ✓ Differentiate the characteristics of cognitive unconscious and emotional unconscious and explain their interaction using a theory of information processing module.

6.4 ✓ Identify and describe the brain structures involved in maintaining circadian rhythms.

6.5 Describe conditions associated with disruptions of circadian rhythms and interventions used to treat them.

6.6 Differentiate patterns of brain waves associated with stages of slow wave and REM sleep.

6.7 Identify brain structures associated with sleep and describe how environmental factors also affect sleep.

6.8 Describe how sleep changes as we age.
   Less REM

6.9 Describe the types of sleep deprivation and their effects on functioning.

6.10 Describe the theories regarding the purpose of sleep, including the restoration model, the evolutionary/circadian model, and the memory consolidation model.

6.11 Identify the symptoms and potential causes of insomnia, narcolepsy, REM-sleep behaviour disorder, sleepwalking, nightmares, night terrors, and sleep apnea.

6.12 Identify which stages of sleep are most closely associated with dreaming.

6.13 Outline findings of research conducted on the content of dreams.

6.14 Describe theories regarding the purpose of dreaming, including wish fulfillment, activation-synthesis theory, problem solving models, and cognitive-process theories.

6.15 Contrast daydreams with dreams we have at night.

6.16 Describe how agonist and antagonist drugs affect neural transmission.

6.17 Define both tolerance and withdrawal and explain how these drug effects are involved in the classification of substance dependence and how they are influenced by classical conditioning.

6.18 Recognize examples and describe the effect upon the nervous system and behaviour of the major classes of drugs: depressants, stimulants, opiates, hallucinogens, and marijuana.

6.19   Describe the purpose, methods, and results of the study on alcohol myopia and driving conducted by MacDonald and colleagues (1995).

6.20   Using the Three Levels model, describe the genetic, psychological, and environmental factors that interact to explain drug use and dependence.

6.21   Define hypnosis and hypnotic susceptibility.

6.22   Describe findings from research studies on hypnosis that have examined engaging in involuntary behaviours, pain tolerance, hypnotic amnesia, and memory enhancement.

6.23   Contrast dissociation and social cognitive theories of hypnosis and explain how each explains research on brain activity during hypnosis.

Chapter Overview

This chapter covers various aspects of consciousness, including what consciousness is thought to be, circadian rhythms, and states of altered consciousness that include sleep and dreaming, drugs, and hypnosis.

Consciousness is defined as our moment-to-moment awareness of ourselves and our environment. It is subjective, meaning that everyone's sense of reality is different (you might remember the term 'subjective reality' from previous chapters). It is also private. Other people don't have direct access to your consciousness. It is dynamic or changing in that we go through different states of awareness at different times. Finally, it is self-reflective. The mind is aware of itself. Thus, consciousness is central to how we define our "selves." Freud was one of the first psychologists to study consciousness, suggesting that we have a conscious mind, which contains everything that we are currently aware of, a preconscious mind, which contains things that can be brought into consciousness, and an unconscious mind, which contains things that ordinarily cannot be brought into conscious awareness. Some modern psychodynamic views suggest that emotional and motivational processes may operate unconsciously. States of consciousness are typically measured via self-report, physiological measures, and behavioural measures. Current cognitive psychologists view conscious and unconscious processes as complementary forms of information processing. People use both voluntary conscious effort, or controlled processing, and little or no conscious effort, or automatic processing, to perform various tasks. Automatic processing facilitates divided attention, enabling us to do several things at once, like watching TV, talking on the phone, and doing homework at the same time. The modular mind approach suggests that various "modules," or information processing subsystems within the brain, interact to help us perform various behavioural tasks.

Circadian rhythms are our daily biological clocks and are controlled by the suprachiasmatic nuclei of the hypothalamus. These rhythmic changes in body temperature, certain hormonal secretions, and other bodily functions like sleep and waking states are on an approximately 24 hour cycle. Various environmental changes such as seasons, jet lag, and night-shift work can alter our circadian rhythms. For example, seasonal affective disorder (SAD) is a cyclic tendency to become psychologically depressed during certain months of the year (particularly fall or winter). Some people's circadian rhythms adjust better to such environmental events than do those of others.

Psychologists have been very interested in the nature of the sleep cycle. EEG recordings of brain waves show that beta waves, which have a high frequency but a low amplitude, occur during active waking states, while alpha waves occur during feelings of relaxation or drowsiness. We go through several stages of sleep. Stage 1 is a stage of light sleep from which we can easily be awakened. As sleep becomes deeper in Stage 2, sleep spindles, periodic bursts of brain wave activity, occur in the EEG patterns. Very slow and large delta waves occur in Stage 3 and in Stage 4 sleep, and then the EEG pattern changes as we go back into Stage 3 and 2 patterns. At this point in the sleep cycle, people enter REM sleep, or rapid-eye-movement sleep. During REM sleep, physiological arousal increases to daytime levels for many people, and dreaming often occurs (although dreaming also occurs in non-REM stages).

Sleep is biologically regulated, but the environment plays a role as well. As we age, we sleep less and the time spent in Stages 3 and 4 declines. REM sleep declines during infancy and early childhood and then remains fairly stable. People have different sleep needs and don't necessarily need eight hours a night. The number of hours of sleep we need seems to be affected by both genetic and various environmental factors. Studies of sleep deprivation have generally showed deficits in mood, and in cognitive and physical performance. It is somewhat unclear exactly why we sleep. The restoration model argues that sleep recharges our rundown bodies. Experimental evidence has been only modestly supportive of this model, though. Evolutionary/circadian sleep models suggest that sleep has developed through evolutionary processes. Early members of the human species may have performed tasks like hunting and food gathering during the day and were more likely to survive predators if they stayed in shelter at night. Thus, the typical human today sleeps at night. There are several types of sleep disorders. Insomnia refers to chronic difficulty in falling or staying asleep. Narcoleptics suffer from extreme daytime sleepiness and sudden, uncontrollable sleep attacks. People with REM-sleep behaviour disorder (REM-BD) don't experience normal REM sleep paralysis and may kick violently or throw punches while asleep! People with sleep apnea repeatedly stop and restart breathing during sleep. Sleepwalkers typically walk during Stage 3 or 4 sleep and seem vaguely aware of their environment, though they are typically unresponsive to other people. Most people have nightmares, and some, typically children, have night terrors.

Dreams are a source of endless curiosity for people, including psychologists, who study when and why we dream. We tend to dream more during REM states and during the last few hours of sleep. We typically dream about familiar people and places. Our cultural backgrounds, life experiences, and current concerns influence the content of our dreams. Freud's psychoanalytic theory argued that dreams serve "wish fulfillment," the gratification of unconscious urges. According to activation-synthesis theory, dreams occur because the cortex is trying to make sense of random neural activity. Problem-solving models suggest that dreams help us find creative solutions to problems. Cognitive-process dream theories argue that both dreaming and waking thought are produced via the same neural processes.

Psychologists study the effects of various drugs on the brain and on behaviour. Agonists are drugs that increase neurotransmitter activity, while antagonists are drugs that decrease neurotransmitter activity. When a drug is used repeatedly, people may develop a tolerance to it and suffer compensatory responses, which are opposite of the drug effects. Discontinued drug use produces withdrawal symptoms, during which more compensatory processes occur. Depressants such as alcohol, barbiturates, and tranquilizers depress nervous system activity. Stimulants such as amphetamines and cocaine increase neural firing, while opiates produce pain relief and a sense of euphoria. Hallucinogens like LSD produce hallucinations. Both genes and culture seem to determine drug effects.

Hypnosis is a state of heightened suggestibility. Hypnotized people subjectively experience their actions to be involuntary, but hypnosis does not seem to involve any unique power that would get people to act against their wills. People under hypnosis sometimes perform what seem to be fantastic physical feats, but the effects may simply be placebo effects. On the other hand, hypnosis seems to increase pain tolerance and is not a placebo effect. Researchers seem to agree that hypnosis can affect amnesia, but they dispute the causes. Whether hypnosis can improve memory is highly debatable. Dissociation theories of memory suggest that hypnosis literally involves a dissociation of consciousness such that a person simultaneously experiences two streams of consciousness. Social-cognitive theories suggest that people are acting out the role of being hypnotized when under a hypnotic trance and thus act in ways that conform to the role of what they believe a hypnotized person can do.

Chapter Outline

The Puzzle of Consciousness
    Measuring States of Consciousness
    Levels of Consciousness: Psychodynamic and Cognitive Perspectives
        The Cognitive Unconscious
        The Emotional Unconscious
        The Modular Mind

Circadian Rhythms: Our Daily Biological Clocks
    Keeping Time: Brain and Environment
        Early Birds and Night Owls
    Environmental Disruptions of Circadian Rhythms
        Psychological Applications: Combating Winter Depression, Jet Lag, and Night Shift Disruptions

Sleep and Dreaming
    Stages of Sleep
        Stage 1 through Stage 4
        REM sleep
    Getting a Night's Sleep: Brain and Environment
    How Much Do We Sleep?
        Short- and Long-Sleepers
        From Genes to Lifestyles
    Sleep Deprivation
    Why Do We Sleep?
    Sleep Disorders
        Insomnia
        Narcolepsy
        REM-Sleep Behaviour Disorder
        Sleep Apnea
        Sleepwalking
        Nightmares and Night Terrors
    The Nature of Dreams
        When Do We Dream?
        What Do We Dream About?
        Why Do We Dream?

Problem-Based Learning

Hypnosis

http://www.hypnosis-research.org/
Provides resources about hypnosis for research and teaching.

Sleep and Dreams

http://psych.ucsc.edu/dreams
The Quantitative Study of Dreams-Provides information about the authors' research, how to conduct research on dreams and relevant resource material.

http://sleepdisorders.about.com/library/weekly/aa121000a.htm
Provides an introductory level approach to sleep disorders and related health issues. Contains a story about sleepwalking and murder.

http://www.sleepquest.com/
Provides information on various aspects of sleep. Dr. William Dement, a leading sleep researcher, is the Chief Scientific Advisor.

Key Terms: *Write the letter of the definition next to the term in the space provided.*

1. ___ activation-synthesis theory
2. ___ alcohol myopia
3. ___ alpha waves
4. ___ amphetamine psychosis
5. ___ automatic processing
6. ___ beta waves
7. ___ blood-brain barrier
8. ___ circadian rhythms
9. ___ cognitive-process dream theory
10. ___ consciousness
11. ___ controlled effortful processing
12. ___ delta waves
13. ___ depressants
14. ___ dissociation theory (of hypnosis)
15. ___ divided attention

a. our moment-to-moment awareness of ourselves and our environment
b. the voluntary use of attention and conscious effort
c. the ability to perform more than one activity at the same time
d. daily biological cycles
e. located in the hypothalamus, regulate circadian rhythms
f. a hormone that has a relaxing effect on the body
g. a cyclic tendency to become psychologically depressed during certain months of the year
h. large waves that regularly appear in Stage 3 and Stage 4 sleep
i. Stages 3 and 4 of sleep together
j. the sleep stage that includes rapid eye movements
k. theory that sleep recharges our run-down bodies and allows us to recover from physical and mental fatigue
l. theories that suggest that sleep's main purpose is to increase a species' chances of survival
m. chronic difficulty in falling asleep, staying asleep, or getting restful sleep
n. extreme daytime sleepiness and sudden, uncontrollable sleep attacks
o. a sleep disorder in which the loss of muscle tone that causes normal REM sleep paralysis is absent
p.

16. ___ evolutionary/circadian sleep models
17. ___ fantasy-prone personalities
18. ___ hallucinogens
19. ___ hypnosis
20. ___ hypnotic suggestibility scale
21. ___ insomnia
22. ___ melatonin
23. ___ narcolepsy
24. ___ night terrors
25. ___ opiates
26. ___ problem-solving dream model
27. ___ REM sleep
28. ___ REM sleep behaviour disorder
29. ___ restoration model
30. ___ seasonal affective disorder
31. ___ sleep apnea
32. ___ slow-wave sleep
33. ___ social-cognitive theory (of hypnosis)
34. ___ stimulants
35. ___ substance dependence
36. ___ suprachiasmatic nuclei
37. ___ THC (tetrahydrocannabinol)
38. ___ tolerance
39. ___ wish fulfillment
40. ___ withdrawal

q. breathing repeatedly stops and restarts during sleep
r. frightening dreams that are more intense than nightmares
s. the gratification of our unconscious desires and needs during dreams
t. theory that during REM sleep the brain stem bombards the higher brain centres with random neural activity, causing the cortex to try to interpret the activity and resulting in dreams
u. theory that dreams can help us find creative solutions to problems
v. theory that proposes that dreaming and waking thought are produced by the same mental systems in the brain
w. people with these types of personality live in a fantasy world that they control
x. a special lining of tightly packed cells that lets vital nutrients pass so that neurons can function
y. decreasing responsivity to a drug
z. occurrence of compensatory responses after discontinued drug use
aa. formal name for drug addiction
bb. drugs that decrease nervous system activity
cc. a "shortsightedness" in thinking suffered by intoxicated people
dd. drugs that increase neural firing and arouse the nervous system
ee. powerful mind-altering drugs that produce hallucinations
ff. a state of heightened suggestibility
gg. contains a standard series of pass/fail suggestions that are read to a subject after hypnotic induction
hh. theory that suggests that hypnosis creates a division of consciousness
ii. theory that suggests that hypnotic experiences result from expectations of people who are motivated to take on the role of being "hypnotized"
jj. brain waves that are indicative of feeling relaxed or drowsy
kk. schizophrenia-like hallucinations and delusions due to drug-induced high levels of dopamine activity
ll. processing that involves little or no conscious effort
mm. brain waves that occur when you are awake and alert
nn. effective pain killers
oo. marijuana's active ingredient

Review at a Glance: *Write the term that best fits the blank to review what you learned in this chapter.*

The Puzzle of Consciousness

(1) _Consciousness_ is defined as our moment-to-moment awareness of ourselves and our environment. It is subjective, private, dynamic, and central to our sense of self. One of the earliest theorists about consciousness was (2) _____, who believed that the mind contains three levels of awareness, the conscious mind, the preconscious mind, and the unconscious. Today, cognitive psychologists believe that both conscious and unconscious thought are complementary forms of information processing. People use both voluntary attention and conscious effort, or (3) _____ processing, and (4) _____ processing, which is performed with little or no conscious effort. Automatic processing facilitates (5) _____ _____, which allows us to do more than one thing simultaneously.

Circadian Rhythms: Our Daily Biological Clocks

The daily biological cycles that we are all subject to are called (6) _____ rhythms. These daily cycles are regulated by the (7) _____ _____ of the hypothalamus. Environmental disruptions such as jet lag, night-shift work, and changes of season can affect circadian rhythms. A disorder called (8) _____ _____ _____ is a cyclic tendency to become psychologically depressed during certain months, which may result from a circadian rhythm disruption.

Sleep and Dreaming

When we are awake and alert, our brains show an EEG pattern of (9) _____ waves, while (10) _____ waves typically occur when we are relaxed or drowsy. Approximately every 90 minutes of sleep, we cycle through different stages of sleep. Stage 1 is a stage of light sleep, while Stage 2 is characterized by (11) _____ _____ in the EEG pattern. Stages 3 and 4 are characterized by (12) _____ waves in the EEG pattern, and, together, they are called (13) _____ - _____ sleep. Rapid eye movements and relaxation of the muscles due to lost muscle tone occur during (14) _____ sleep. It is not exactly clear <u>why</u> we sleep. The (15) _____ model argues that we sleep in order to recover from physical and mental fatigue. (16) _____ / _____ models argue that the main purpose of sleep is to increase a species' chances of survival. Many people suffer from sleep disorders. A chronic difficulty in falling asleep is called (17) _____. Extreme daytime sleepiness and sudden, uncontrollable sleep attacks are characteristic of (18) _____. When the loss of muscle tone that causes normal REM sleep "paralysis" fails to occur, a person experiences (19) _____ - _____ _____ _____. People who repeatedly stop and restart breathing during sleep suffer from (20) _____ _____. Dreams more intense than nightmares, and often suffered by children, are called (21) _____ _____. Freud believed that the main function of dreaming is (22) _____ _____, and distinguished between a dream's manifest content (the surface story) and the (23) _____ content, the disguised psychological meaning of the dream. A more modern theory argues that dreams are the result of the action of the cortex as it tries to make sense of random nerve impulses. This theory is called (24) _____ -

_____ theory. According to (25) _____ - _____ models, dreams can help us find creative solutions to problems. Theories that focus on the process of how we dream and argue that dreams and waking states are governed by the same mental systems in the brain are called (26) _____ - _____ _____ theories. Sometimes people daydream a lot and live in a vivid fantasy world that they control. Such people are said to have a (27) _____ - _____ personality.

Drugs and Altered Consciousness

A special lining of tightly packed cells that screens out many foreign substances but lets vital nutrients and many drugs through is called the (28) _____ - _____ _____. When a drug is used repeatedly the intensity of effects the drug produces tends to decrease over time, a process called (29) _____. Because drugs affect homeostasis, the brain tries to adjust for the imbalance by producing (30) _____ responses. The occurrence of compensatory responses after discontinued drug use is called (31) _____. Drugs that decrease nervous system activity are called (32) _____, while drugs that increase neural firing are called (33) _____. Excessive use of alcohol, a depressant, may result in a "shortsightedness" in thinking that may cause people not to monitor their own actions or think about the long-term consequences of their behaviour, a phenomenon called (34) _____ _____. Powerful mind-altering drugs that produce hallucinations are called (35) _____.

Hypnosis

Hypnosis is a state of heightened suggestibility in which some people are able to experience test suggestions as if they were real. A standard series of pass/fail questions to determine the degree to which a person is subject to hypnotic induction is called a (36) _____ _____ _____. (37) _____ theory proposes that hypnosis involves a division of awareness such that a person simultaneously experiences two streams of consciousness. A second set of theories of hypnosis called (38) _____ - _____ theories suggest that people under hypnosis are simply acting out social roles.

Apply What You Know

1. Keep track of your dreams for one week. The best way to do this is to write down whatever you can remember about your dreams immediately after you wake up. Then, at the end of the week, look back at the content our your dreams and indicate whether you think that the content of your dreams best supports activation-synthesis theory or problem-solving theories. Use Study Sheet 5.1.

2. Not everyone sleeps eight hours per night. Design a survey to examine the mean numbers of hours people sleep per night. Graph your results. What do they show about the average sleeping habits of people at your school? Use Study Sheet 5.2.

Internet Scavenger Hunt

1. Not every culture in the world has similar sleep patterns to those that typically occur in Canada (7-8 hours per night). Do some library research to discover how people in other cultures deal with the universal need for sleep. Describe the research findings.

Practice Test

<u>Multiple Choice Items</u>: *Please write the letter corresponding to your answer in the space to the left of each item.*

_____ 1. Consciousness is _A_ .

    a. subjective
    b. public
    c. static
    d. not central to our sense of self

_____ 2. Looking at a map and deciding what route to take to a new destination would be considered an example of _____.

    a. compensatory processing
    b. controlled processing
    c. automatic processing
    d. preconscious processing

_____ 3. When a person is learning how to type, their behaviour usually involves _____ processing, but someone who can type quickly, efficiently, and accurately is probably utilizing more _____ processing.

    a. automatic; controlled
    b. controlled; automatic
    c. automatic; effortful
    d. effortful; controlled

_____ 4. Healthy _____ neurons were transplanted into the brains of animals whose equivalent neurons had been destroyed. This restored the circadian rhythms in these animals.

    a. cortical
    b. suprachiasmatic nuclei
    c. lateral geniculate nuclei
    d. beta

_____ 5. Katherine is worried about jet lag because she needs to fly from Toronto to Vancouver (return) to visit her aunt. Her body will _____.

    a. likely adjust faster after the Toronto to Vancouver flight.
    b. likely adjust faster after the Vancouver to Toronto flight.
    c. adjust at the same rate for both flights.
    d. not need to adjust because jet lag does not occur for travel between cities that far north of the equator.

_____ 6. The model that suggests that the mind is made up of information-processing subsystems within the brain that perform tasks related to sensation, perception, memory etc. is known as the ____ model.

a. activation-synthesis
b. emotional unconscious
c. circadian rhythm
d. modular

_____ 7. Research on circadian rhythms has found that the shift to Daylight Savings Time results in a temporary increase in:

a. cognitive performance.
b. drug use.
c. self-reported happiness.
d. accidental deaths.

_____ 8. One reason that shiftwork has a detrimental effect on circadian rhythms is that ____.

a. there isn't enough variability in the sleep schedules of shift workers
b. the nature of shiftwork is more physically taxing that other types of work typically done during the day
c. shift workers often get too much sleep
d. shift workers often go home in the morning daylight, which makes it difficult to reset their circadian clocks

_____ 9. EEG recordings of the brain's electrical activity show ____ waves during alert waking states, ____ waves during relaxation and drowsy states, and ____ waves during deep sleep states.

a. alpha; beta; delta
b. alpha; delta; beta
c. beta; alpha; delta
d. delta; alpha; beta

_____ 10. REM is a period of sleep when ____.

a. dreaming does not occur
b. physiological arousal increases to daytime levels
c. dreams are shorter than in non-REM sleep
d. legs and arms typically flail away

_____ 11. Studies examining the sleep habits of identical and fraternal twins have revealed that ____.

a. while genetic factors are significant, environmental factors also account for important sleep differences
b. environmental factors don't really account for any of the sleep differences
c. genetic factors account for essentially all of the sleep differences
d. environmental factors account for essentially all of the sleep differences

_____ 12. Research on REM sleep has found that Christmas examinations resulted in _____ and _____ among university seniors compared to baseline measures of the same students and control subjects.

   a. a decrease in REM sleep; an increase in the number of rapid eye movements during REM sleep
   b. decreased metabolic activity during sleep; an decrease in the number of rapid eye movements during REM sleep
   c. increased metabolic activity during sleep; a decrease in the number of rapid eye movements during sleep
   d. an increase in REM sleep; an increase in the number of rapid eye movements during REM sleep

_____ 13. You awaken in the middle of the night to find your roommate standing in the corner of your room with an aggressive look on his face, punching a pillow, and running in place. Despite this strange behaviour, you realize that your roommate is still asleep and when you wake him he shares with you that he was having this bizarre dream about having been involved in a fight while running on a treadmill. Given what you have learned in introductory psychology, it is **most likely** that your roommate _____.

   a. may have narcolepsy
   b. was sleep walking
   c. experienced the REM rebound effect
   d. may have REM-sleep behaviour disorder (RBD)

_____ 14. A wife is awoken many times during the night by her husband's apparent difficulty breathing. Every few minutes, the husband's airway becomes momentarily obstructed until he gasps and then starts breathing again. It is **most likely** that the husband is suffering from _____.

   a. sleep apnea
   b. airway cataplexy
   c. side effects from the REM rebound effect
   d. nightmares related to drowning

_____ 15. Waking up after who knows how long, Rip Van Winkle decides to experience the new world he has found and runs off to Las Vegas to gamble, see the Strip, and take in a few shows. After 72 straight hours of gambling and boozing, he feels a great deal of physical and mental fatigue and goes back to his hotel suite for another snooze. The model that explains Rip's renewed need to sleep at this point is _____.

   a. evolutionary/circadian theory
   b. the REM sleep model
   c. the restoration model
   d. REM-sleep behaviour disorder

_____ 16. Because of censorship codes in the early years of motion pictures, directors could not show sexual activity on screen. They thus sometimes used metaphors for such activity such as picturing a train going into a tunnel. Freud would argue that if such content appeared in a dream that the content would by symptomatic of _____.

a. problem-solving
b. activation-synthesis
c. the brain's attempt to understand random neural content
d. wish fulfillment

_____ 17. Criticism of the activation-synthesis theory of dreaming has suggested that it overestimates_____ and fails to consider the fact that _____.

a. the role of unconscious desires; dreams occur during REM sleep
b. the problem-solving ability of dreams; dream occur during REM sleep
c. the bizarreness of dreams; dreams also occur during NREM sleep
d. the interpretive capacity of the higher brain; dreams also occur during NREM sleep

_____ 18. The theories that suggest that dreaming and waking thought are produced by the same mental systems in the brain are called _____ theories.

a. problem-solving
b. activation-synthesis
c. wish fulfillment
d. cognitive-process

_____ 19. Beth has a very vivid imagination. Though she has a very ordinary job, she often imagines that she is working on top-secret projects with national security implications. When at home by herself, she is easily able to visualize herself in many exciting and exotic places that she has in fact never actually visited. According to the text, Beth would **best** be classified as having _____.

a. high hypnotic susceptibility
b. a fantasy-prone personality
c. divided attention
d. an hallucinatory personality

_____ 20. Drugs that inhibit or decrease the actions of a neurotransmitter are called _____.

a. stimulants
b. antagonists
c. agonists
d. blood-brain barriers

_____ 21. Opiates such as morphine and codeine both contain molecules that are similar to endorphins, the body's natural painkillers. Opiates like these bind to receptor sites that are keyed to endorphins and trigger similar pain reducing responses. Given these characteristics, both morphine and codeine would be classified as _____.

a. antagonists
b. hallucinogens
c. antigens
d. agonists

_____ 22. In order to stay up late to study for exams, Sara starts drinking sodas with caffeine in them in order to better stay awake. After continuing this practice for several months, Sara notices that she needs to consume more caffeine to achieve the same effect. This decrease in her response to caffeine is **best viewed** as example of what is called _____.

a. withdrawal
b. tolerance
c. placebo effect
d. dependence

_____ 23. If a drug is introduced into the nervous system, the body attempts to maintain its state of optimal physiological balance called _____ by adjusting for this imbalance by producing _____, which are reactions opposite to the effect of the drug.

a. tolerance; compensatory responses
b. withdrawal symptoms; homeostasis
c. compensatory responses; withdrawal symptoms
d. homeostasis; compensatory responses

_____ 24. Alcohol is a(n) _____.

a. depressant
b. stimulant
c. hallucinogen
d. agonist

_____ 25. Ecstasy is classified as a(n) _____ whereas codeine is classified as a(n) _____.

a. stimulant; depressant
b. stimulant; opiate
c. hallucinogen; depressant
d. hallucinogen; stimulant

_____ 26. The most widely used illicit drug in Canada is:

a. cocaine
b. ecstacy
c. marijuana
d. LSD

_____ 27. Research in the area of forensic psychology has found that hypnosis _____ a reliable way to enhance memory and that hypnotized participants typically remember information _____ than nonhypnotized participants who are asked to use imagery or other memory tricks to facilitate recall.

a. is not; no better
b. is; no better
c. is not; better
d. is; better

_____ 28. A state of heightened suggestibility in which some people are able to experience imagined test suggestions as if they were real is called _____.

a. mesmerism
b. animal magnetism
c. hypnosis
d. hypnotic amnesia

_____ 29. Studies of hypnosis have shown that _____.

a. hypnosis can increase pain tolerance
b. hypnosis usually improves one's memory
c. those people under hypnotic induction perform physiological feats significantly greater than those in placebo control groups
d. hypnotized people do not subjectively experience their actions to be involuntary

_____ 30. The theory that argues that hypnotic effects occur because people are acting out a social role is called _____ theory.

a. dissociation
b. divided consciousness
c. social cognitive
d. forensic hypnosis

True/False Items: *Write T or F in the space provided to the left of each item.*

_____ 1. The voluntary use of attention and conscious effort in the performance of tasks is called automatic processing.

_____ 2. Most circadian rhythms are regulated by the brain's suprachiasmatic nuclei.

_____ 3. A pattern of beta waves occur in stage 1 sleep.

_____ 4. Dreams occur only in REM sleep.

_____ 5. It is imperative that all of us get at least eight hours of sleep per night.

_____ 6. People who suffer from narcolepsy have sudden, uncontrollable sleep attacks.

_____ 7. There is a single, agreed-upon model of dreaming.

_____ 8. Decreasing responsivity to a drug is called withdrawal.

_____ 9. Alcohol is a depressant.

_____ 10. Hypnosis can increase one's pain tolerance.

Short Answer Questions

1. Distinguish between controlled and automatic processing.

2. What are circadian rhythms, and how are they controlled by the brain?

3. Describe three different sleep disorders.

4. What is the relationship between drug tolerance, compensatory responses, and withdrawal symptoms?

5. Describe the difference between the dissociation and social cognition theories of hypnosis.

Essay Questions

1. Describe how environmental factors can affect circadian rhythms.

2. Describe the EEG patterns that occur during the various stages of sleep.

3. Describe three theories of dreams.

4. Describe how both genes and culture influence drug effects.

5. What do the studies that compare people under hypnotic induction with those in placebo control groups indicate about the effectiveness of hypnosis?

Study Sheet 6.1 Keeping Track of Dreams

Sunday:

Monday:

Tuesday:

Wednesday:

Thursday:

Friday:

Saturday:

Which theory (or theories) do the content of your dreams support? Explain why!

Study Sheet 6.2 Different Sleep Patterns

N (sample size):

Mean Number Hrs. Sleep:

Graph of Results (Don't forget to label your axes!)

Answer Keys

Answer Key for Key Terms

1.	s	11.	b	21.	m	31.	p
2.	bb	12.	h	22.	f	32.	i
3.	ii	13.	aa	23.	n	33.	hh
4.	jj	14.	gg	24.	q	34.	cc
5.	kk	15.	c	25.	mm	35.	z
6.	ll	16.	l	26.	t	36.	e
7.	w	17.	v	27.	j	37.	nn
8.	d	18.	dd	28.	o	38.	x
9.	u	19.	ee	29.	k	39.	r
10.	a	20.	ff	30.	g	40.	y

Answer Key for Review at a Glance

1. consciousness
2. Freud
3. controlled
4. automatic
5. divided attention
6. circadian
7. suprachiasmatic nuclei
8. seasonal affective disorder
9. beta
10. alpha
11. sleep spindles
12. delta
13. slow-wave
14. REM
15. restoration
16. Evolutionary/circadian
17. insomnia
18. narcolepsy
19. REM-sleep behaviour disorder
20. sleep apnea
21. night terrors
22. wish fulfillment
23. latent
24. activation-synthesis
25. problem-solving
26. cognitive-process dream
27. fantasy-prone
28. blood-brain barrier
29. tolerance
30. compensatory
31. withdrawal
32. depressants
33. stimulants
34. alcohol myopia
35. hallucinogens
36. hypnotic suggestibility scale
37. Dissociation
38. social-cognitive

Answer Key for Practice Test Multiple Choice Questions

1.	a		16.	d
2.	b		17.	c
3.	b		18.	d
4.	b		19.	b
5.	a		20.	b
6.	d		21.	d
7.	d		22.	b
8.	d		23.	d
9.	c		24.	a
10.	b		25.	b
11.	a		26.	c
12.	d		27.	a
13.	d		28.	c
14.	a		29.	a
15.	c		30.	c

Answer Key for Practice Test True/False Questions

1.	F		6.	T
2.	T		7.	F
3.	F		8.	F
4.	F		9.	T
5.	F		10.	T

Answer Key for Practice Test Short Answer Questions

1. Controlled processing involves the voluntary use of attention and conscious effort. Automatic processing occurs when we carry out routine actions or well-learned tasks with little or no conscious effort.

2. Circadian rhythms are daily biological cycles of body temperature, certain hormonal secretions, and other bodily functions. Most circadian rhythms are regulated by the brain's suprachiasmatic nuclei, which are located in the hypothalamus.

3. Insomnia is difficulty in falling asleep, staying asleep, or getting restful sleep. Narcolepsy involves extreme daytime sleepiness and sudden sleep attacks. In REM-sleep behaviour disorder, the normal REM-sleep paralysis is absent. People with sleep apnea stop and restart breathing during sleep. Some people sleepwalk. Some sleepers, particularly children, suffer from night terrors, which are more intense than nightmares.

4. Tolerance stems from the body's attempt to maintain homeostasis. The body will produce compensatory responses as a way of doing this. Withdrawal occurs when compensatory responses continue after drug use is discontinued.

5. According to dissociation theory, hypnosis involves a division of consciousness such that the person experiences two streams of consciousness simultaneously. Social-cognitive theories suggest that hypnotic experiences result from expectations of people who are taking on the "hypnotic" role.

Answer Key for Practice Test Essay Questions

1. Seasonal affective disorder is a cyclic tendency to become depressed during certain times of the year and may be a result of circadian disruptions caused by changes in exposure to daylight. Jet lag is a circadian disruption caused by flying across several time zones in one day. Night shiftwork also causes circadian shifts due to the necessity of different sleeping patterns.

2. Beta waves occur during alert waking states. As sleep begins, theta waves increase. Sleep spindles, which indicate bursts of rapid brain-wave activity, occur in Stage 2. As Stage 3 begins, large delta waves appear, and, in Stage 4, they dominate the EEG pattern. After 20-30 minutes of Stage 4 sleep, the EEG pattern changes as we go back through Stage 3 and Stage 2 sleep and then enter REM sleep.

3. Freud believed that the main purpose of dreams was wish fulfillment, the gratification of our unconscious desires and needs. Activation-synthesis theory suggests that the cortex creates a dream to best fit the pattern of neural activation during sleep. According to problem-solving models, dreams help us to find creative solutions to problems. Cognitive-process dream theories suggest that dreaming and waking thought are produced by the same mental systems in the brain.

4. Genetic factors influence sensitivity and tolerance to drug effects. Both the physical and the social setting in which a drug is taken can influence a user's reaction. Cultural factors can affect how people respond to a drug as well as drug consumption. People's beliefs and expectancies, which are influenced by culture, also affect drug reactions.

5. Most well-controlled studies of hypnosis show that nonhypnotized subjects show the same physiological effects. There is some evidence that hypnosis can increase pain tolerance and cause amnesia beyond placebo effects.

Chapter 7. Learning and Adaptation:
The Role of Experience

Learning Objectives

7.1   Define learning.

7.2   Contrast behavioural and ethological perspectives on learning.

7.3   Define and describe habituation.

7.4   Describe the work of Pavlov in establishing the foundations of classical conditioning.

7.5   Describe the principles of acquisition, extinction, and spontaneous recovery as they apply in classical conditioning.

7.6   Differentiate among unconditioned and conditioned stimuli and responses.

7.7   Describe how stimulus generalization, stimulus discrimination, and higher-order conditioning extend classical conditioning.

7.8   Describe how the principles of classical conditioning can be used to explain the acquisition and treatment of fears and phobias, attraction or aversion to specific stimuli, and physical symptoms with no medical cause.

7.9   Contrast classical and operant conditioning.

7.10   Describe the work of Thorndike and Skinner in establishing the foundations of operant conditioning.

7.11   Describe Skinner's three-term (A-B-C) contingency, differentiating between antecedent stimuli and consequences.

7.12   Differentiate among positive reinforcement, negative reinforcement, positive punishment, negative punishment, and operant extinction.

7.13   Describe the research findings regarding the use of physical punishment in parenting.

7.14   Describe the effect of delayed versus immediate consequences upon learning.

7.15   Contrast shaping and chaining in operant conditioning.

7.16   Describe the role of operant generalization and operant discrimination in operant conditioning.

7.17   Define and recognize the various schedules of reinforcement.

7.18   Describe how escape and avoidance conditioning are combined with classical conditioning in two-factor theory to explain maintenance of classically conditioned associations.

7.19   Describe how operant conditioning can be applied in educational and work settings and in specialized animal training.

7.20   Describe the steps an applied behaviour analyst would use to modify a problem behaviour.

7.21   Define biological preparedness and explain how research on conditioned taste aversions, the variability in phobic stimuli, and instinctive drift support its existence.

7.22   Describe how an understanding of conditioned taste aversions has been applied with humans and with other animals.

7.23   Describe neural pathways in the brain associated with learning.

7.24   Describe the role of cognition in learning, including insight, cognitive maps, expectancy effects, and latent learning.

7.25   Define observational learning and describe the four steps in the process of modeling.

7.26   Describe the purpose, methods, and results of the study examining the use of television to increase prosocial behaviour by Sprafkin and colleagues (1975).

Chapter Overview

This chapter covers the basic processes of learning, which include habituation, classical conditioning, operant conditioning, and modelling. Psychologists have focused both on how we learn and why we learn. Ethologists focused on the functions of behaviour, particularly its adaptive significance; its influence on an organisms' chances of survival and reproduction. Research has suggested that the environment shapes behaviour through both personal and species adaptation. When we enter into environments, the environment shapes our personal behaviour. Similarly, the biology of a species is shaped through the natural selection of behaviours that help members of the species adapt to the environment. The human brain has acquired the capacity to perform psychological functions that historically have helped members of our species to survive and reproduce, according to evolutionary psychologists.

There are several types of learning processes. The simplest type may be habituation, the decrease in response strength to a repeated stimulus. By learning not to respond to familiar stimuli, an organism may conserve resources to pay attention to important stimuli. Classical conditioning, in which an organism learns to associate two stimuli such that one stimulus comes to produce a response that only the other previously did, was made famous through the work of the Russian physiologist Ivan Pavlov with the salivary response of dogs. A stimulus that reflexively produces a response is called an unconditioned stimulus (UCS), and the response is called an unconditioned response (UCR). The stimulus repeatedly paired with the UCS that comes to produce the response is called the conditioned stimulus (CS), and the response is then known as the conditioned response (CR). This entire process is known as acquisition. Forward, short-delay conditioning appears to work best. The CS is presented first and is still present when the UCS appears in this procedure. Extinction occurs when the CS is repeatedly presented without the UCS, such that the response strength diminishes significantly. For example, if a dog has been conditioned to salivate in response to a bell (CS) paired with food (UCS), but the bell is then repeatedly sounded without the food being given to the dog, the dog will stop salivating. Occasionally, a response that has been extinguished will reappear after some time in response to the old CS, a process called spontaneous recovery. Once a CR is acquired, an organism may respond to similar stimuli in the same way, a process called stimulus generalization. The ability to discriminate between stimuli occurs when an organism responds differently to stimuli. When a neutral stimulus comes to produce a response through pairing with an already established CS, higher-order conditioning has occurred. Many examples of this can be seen in everyday life. For example, politicians who appear in front of large Canadian flags are using higher-order conditioning to influence the development of attitudes toward them. Classical conditioning has other applied aspects. The process can be used to both influence the acquisition and elimination of fear. Attraction and aversion to other people and objects are likely also influenced through classical conditioning processes.

Operantly conditioned responses are emitted (voluntarily) rather than elicited like classically conditioned responses are, and they are influenced through their consequences. E.L. Thorndike's Law of Effect says that in a given situation, a response followed by a satisfying consequence will become more likely to occur while a response followed by an unsatisfying consequence will become less likely to occur. The term operant conditioning was coined by B.F. Skinner to describe how an organism operates on its environment to get what it wants and to avoid what it doesn't want. Reinforcement strengthens a response that precedes it, while punishment decreases the strength of a response that precedes it. Skinner's analysis of operant behaviour involved studying the antecedents (A) of the behaviour, the behaviour emitted (B), and the consequences (C) of the behaviour. In operant conditioning, the organism learns an association between the behaviour and its consequences. The antecedent conditions come to signal that a certain consequence will occur if a certain behaviour is emitted. Reinforcement and punishment are the consequences that affect the likelihood of a response under the antecedent conditions. Responses are strengthened by positive reinforcement. Primary reinforcers, such as food and water, are stimuli that satisfy biological needs. Secondary reinforcers, such as money, are conditioned reinforcers because they become associated with primary reinforcers. For example, you can use money to buy food. Negative reinforcement is not the same thing as punishment. Negative reinforcement occurs when a response is strengthened through the removal or avoidance of a stimulus. For example, people use umbrellas because they prevent us from getting wet. Through aversive punishment, a response is weakened by the presentation of a stimulus, such as a slap or a spanking. In response cost, a response is weakened by the removal of a stimulus. For example, taking away TV privileges or car keys is a way that some parents have of punishing their children for undesirable behaviour. Operant conditioning can be used to shape behaviour by rewarding successive approximations of the behaviour. Similarly, chaining is used to condition complex behaviours. The last step of the behaviour chain is trained first, and the prior step is reinforced by the ability to perform the next one until the entire chain of behaviour is performed. Generalization and discrimination work with operant conditioning much like they work with classical conditioning. Operant generalization occurs when an operant response occurs to a new antecedent stimulus similar to an old one. Operant discrimination occurs when an operant response will occur to one antecedent stimulus but not to another. Schedules of reinforcement influence much of operant behaviour. On a continuous schedule, every response is reinforced, while on a partial schedule, only some responses are reinforced. There are both fixed and interval schedules as well as both ratio and interval schedules. On a fixed-ratio schedule, reinforcement is given after a certain number of responses. On a variable-ratio schedule (e.g. VR-6), reinforcement is given after an average number of responses (e.g. sometimes after 3, sometimes after 6, sometimes after 9). On a fixed-interval schedule, the first response that occurs after a certain amount of time is reinforced. Finally, on a variable-interval schedule, the first response after a variable amount of time is reinforced. Ratio schedules tend to produce the highest rate of responding. Following reinforcement, there is typically a pause in responding, which is referred to as a "scallop" on graphs of response rates. Like with classical conditioning, there are many applications of operant conditioning. Skinner's work gave rise to the field of applied behaviour analysis, which combines the behavioural approach with the scientific method in an attempt to solve individual and societal problems through the use of operant conditioning techniques.

Biology asserts certain limits on learning. Martin Seligman's concept of preparedness suggests that animals are biologically "prewired" to easily learn behaviours related to their survival as a species. For example, animals develop conditioned taste aversions to learn to avoid foods and liquids that are bad for them. Similarly, animals may be prepared to fear certain stimuli. This fear then helps them to avoid or escape the stimuli, thus increasing their chances of survival and reproduction. Some responses are difficult to operantly condition because of instinctive drift, the tendency of animals to engage in instinctive behaviour regardless of their training. Biology also affects animals' ability to learn through the action of brain structures like the hypothalamus and through neurotransmitters like dopamine.

Cognition also affects learning. Such models are known as S-O-R models, suggesting that an organism's cognitions influence the relationship between stimulus and response. The expectancy model, for instance, argues that in classical conditioning the CS produces an expectancy (cognition) that the UCS will occur. Cognition is also present in operant conditioning. Cognitive theorists emphasize that organisms develop expectations of the relationships between their behaviour and its consequences.

Much of what we learn is through observation of others. Albert Bandura suggests that observational learning, or modelling, involves four basic steps: attention, retention, reproduction, and motivation. Language frees us from trial-and-error learning and plays a role in teaching us how to perform certain behaviours.

Chapter Outline

Adapting to the Environment
      How Do We Learn? The Search for Mechanisms
      Why Do We Learn? The Search for Functions
      Crossroads of Learning: Biology, Cognition, and Culture
      Habituation

Classical Conditioning: Associating One Stimulus With Another
      Pavlov's Pioneering Research
      Basic Principles
            Acquisition
            Extinction and Spontaneous Recovery
            Generalization and Discrimination
            Higher-Order Conditioning

Problem-Based Learning

General

http://www.wagntrain.com/OC/
An Animal Trainer's Introduction to Operant and Classical Conditioning-This site gives an overview of learning principles from an animal trainer's perspective.

http://www.uwsp.edu/psych/dog/dog.htm
Dr. P's Dog Training-This site contains an extensive amount of information about dog training and learning principles.

Media and Violence

http://www.cln.org/themes/media_violence.html
Part of the Open Learning Agency website-This site contains information on media and violence and is largely Canadian material.

http://www.crtc.gc.ca/eng/social/tv.htm
CRTC website-This site offers news releases, background on the issue of television violence in Canada, resources for parents and a bibliography of some of the available literature.

http://www.media-awareness.ca/english/issues/violence/index.cfm
Media Awareness Network-This site offers information about media and violence from a Canadian perspective.

Key Terms: *Write the letter of the definition next to the term in the space provided.*

Adapting to the Environment, Habituation, and Classical Conditioning

1. ____ adaptive significance

2. ____ anticipatory nausea and vomiting

3. ____ aversion therapy

4. ____ classical conditioning

5. ____ conditioned response

6. ____ conditioned stimulus

7. ____ discrimination (classical conditioning)

8. ____ exposure therapies

9. ____ extinction

10. ____ habituation

11. ____ higher order conditioning

a. a process by which experience produces a relatively enduring change in an organism's behaviour or capabilities

b. how a behaviour influences an organism's chances of survival and reproduction

c. a decrease in the strength of response to a repeated stimulus

d. stimulus that produces a UCR without learning

e. a response that occurs without learning and is elicited by a UCS

f. a stimulus that produces a CR

g. a learned response elicited by a CS

h. stimuli similar to the initial CS elicit a CR

i. a CR occurs to one stimulus but not to others

j. a neutral stimulus becomes a CS after being paired with an already established CS

k. basic goal is to expose a phobic patient to the CS without the UCS

12. ___ learning	l.	when a CS is presented without the UCS, the response gradually weakens
13. ___ spontaneous recovery	m.	the reappearance of a previously extinguished CR after a rest period
14. ___ stimulus generalization	n.	an organism learns to associate two stimuli such that one stimulus comes to produce a response originally produced only by the other stimulus
15. ___ unconditioned response	o.	attempts to condition a repulsion to a stimulus that triggers unwanted behaviour by pairing it with a noxious UCS
16. ___ unconditioned stimulus	p.	people become nauseous and vomit before cancer therapy

Operant Conditioning

1. ___ applied behaviour analysis	a.	a response followed by a satisfying consequence will become more likely to occur and a response followed by an unsatisfying consequence will become less likely to occur
2. ___ aversive punishment	b.	a type of learning in which behaviour is influenced by its consequences
3. ___ avoidance conditioning	c.	a special chamber to study operant conditioning experimentally
4. ___ chaining	d.	a consequence that strengthens an outcome that it follows
5. ___ continuous reinforcement schedule	e.	a signal that a particular response will produce certain consequences
6. ___ delay of gratification	f.	a response is strengthened by the subsequent presentation of a stimulus
7. ___ discrimination (operant conditioning)	g.	stimulus that an organism finds reinforcing because it satisfies biological needs
8. ___ discriminative stimulus	h.	stimulus that through association with primary reinforcers becomes a reinforcer itself
9. ___ escape conditioning	i.	a response is strengthened by the removal or avoidance of a stimulus
10. ___ extinction (operant conditioning)	j.	the weakening and disappearance of a response because it is no longer reinforced
11. ___ fixed interval schedule	k.	a response is weakened by the presentation of a stimulus
12. ___ fixed ratio schedule	l.	a response is weakened by the removal of a stimulus
13. ___ law of effect	m.	the ability to forego an immediate but smaller reward for a delayed but more satisfying outcome
14. ___ negative reinforcement	n.	used to develop a sequence of responses
15. ___ operant conditioning	o.	an operant response occurs to a new antecedent stimulus that is similar to the original one
16. ___ operant generalization	p.	an operant response will occur to one antecedent stimulus but not to another
17. ___ partial reinforcement schedule	q.	every response of a particular type is reinforced
18. ___ positive reinforcement	r.	only some responses are reinforced

19. ___ primary reinforcer	s.	reinforcement is given after a fixed number of responses
20. ___ punishment	t.	reinforcement is given after an average number of responses
21. ___ reinforcement	u.	the first correct response that occurs after a time interval is reinforced
22. ___ response cost	v.	reinforcement occurs after the first response that occurs after a variable time interval
23. ___ secondary reinforcer	w.	organisms learn a response to escape from an aversive stimulus
24. ___ shaping	x.	organisms learn a response to avoid an aversive stimulus
25. ___ Skinner box	y.	both classical and operant conditioning are involved in avoidance learning
26. ___ target behaviour	z.	combines a behavioural approach with the scientific method to solve individual and societal problems
27. ___ token economy	aa.	the specific goal to be changed
28. ___ two-factor theory of avoidance learning	bb.	desirable behaviours are reinforced with tokens that can be exchanged for tangible rewards
29. ___ variable interval schedule	cc.	reinforcing successive approximations toward a desired response
30. ___ variable ratio schedule	dd.	weakens a certain response

Biology and Learning, Cognition and Learning, Observational Learning, and the Role of Language

1. ___ cognitive map	a.	produced by pairing a taste with stomach illness
2. ___ conditioned taste aversion	b.	a conditioned response "drifts back" toward instinctive behaviour
3. ___ insight	c.	the sudden perception of a useful relationship that helps to solve a problem
4. ___ instinctive drift	d.	a mental representation of a spatial layout
5. ___ latent learning	e.	learning that occurs but is not demonstrated until there is an incentive to do so
6. ___ observational learning	f.	learning that occurs by observing the behaviour of a model
7. ___ preparedness	g.	species are biologically prewired to easily learn behaviours related to their survival

Review at a Glance: *Write the term that best fits the blank to review what you learned in this chapter.*

Adapting to the Environment

(1) _____ is a process by which experience produces a relatively enduring change in an organism's behaviour or capabilities. Our capacity for learning increases our likelihood of surviving and reproducing in our environment. Thus, behaviours that help us to so adapt are said to have (2) _____ _____. The environment thus shapes behaviour through (3) . Over time, through the process of evolution, certain behaviours in a species are likely to be selected because of their aid in survival and reproduction, a process called (4) . There are several types of learning. One of the simplest is (5) _____, a decrease in the strength of a response to a repeated stimulus.

Classical Conditioning: Associating One Stimulus With Another

An organism learns to associate two stimuli, with the result that one of the stimuli comes to produce a response previously produced only by the other one in the learning process called (6) _____ _____, a phenomenon studied in dogs by (7) _____. During the period of (8) _____, a response is being learned. Initially a stimulus known as the (9) _____ stimulus produces a response, the (10) _____ response, without learning. A second stimulus is repeatedly paired with the UCS, after several learning trials the second stimulus is presented by itself, and the animal will then respond in a similar way to the second stimulus as it had originally done to the UCS. This second stimulus is then known as the (11) _____ stimulus, and the response is known as the (12) _____ response. Classically conditioned responses can be eliminated through the use of (13) procedures, during which the CS is presented repeatedly without the UCS also being present. Sometimes, extinguished responses will appear weeks, months, or even years later, a phenomenon called (14) _____ _____. Another phenomenon of classical conditioning, called (15) _____ _____, occurs when stimuli similar to the initial CS elicit a CR. Stimulus (16) _____ is the ability to distinguish between stimuli. Finally, a process of pairing a neutral stimulus with an already established CS is known as (17) - _____ conditioning.

Operant Conditioning: Learning Through Consequences

While Pavlov was studying classical conditioning, Edward L. Thorndike was formulating his (18) _____ __ _____, which states that responses that are followed by "satisfying" consequences will become more likely to occur, while those responses followed by "unsatisfying" consequences will become less likely to occur. B. F. Skinner studied (19) _____ conditioning, a type of learning in which behaviour is influenced by its consequences. Skinner studied operant conditioning experimentally by designing a special chamber called a (20) _____ _____. Through his work, Skinner identified several important types of consequences. (21) _____ strengthens a response that precedes it, while (22) _____ weakens a response that precedes it. Skinner identified the ABC's of operant conditioning, or the (23) _____, (24) _____, and (25)_____. An antecedent condition that signifies that a particular response will now produce a consequence is called a (26) _____ stimulus. Consequences determine how we respond to a stimulus. A response is strengthened by the subsequent presentation of a stimulus in the procedure called (27) _____ _____. There are two types of positive reinforcers. (28) _____ reinforcers are stimuli that an organism finds reinforcing because they satisfy biological needs, while (29) _____ reinforcers become reinforcers through their association with primary reinforcers. A response is strengthened by the removal or avoidance of an aversive stimulus through (30) _____ _____. The weakening and eventual disappearance of a response, called operant (31) _____, occurs because the response is no longer being reinforced. In the procedure called (32) _____ _____, a response is weakened by the subsequent presentation of a stimulus. In (33) _____ _____, a response is weakened by the subsequent removal of a stimulus. In general, reinforcement or punishment occurs immediately after a response. Sometimes, people are asked to forego immediate reinforcement to wait for a better, later reinforcement. The ability to do this is called (34) _____ _____ _____. Operant conditioning can be used to create new responses and sequences of behaviours.   (35) _____ is a procedure by which new behaviours or sequences of behaviours are created through reinforcements of successive approximations of the target behaviour. (36) _____ creates a sequence of responses by reinforcing each response with the opportunity to perform the next behaviour in the sequence. Reinforcement typically occurs on schedules of reinforcement. On a (37) _____ schedule, every response is reinforced, while on (38) _____ schedules, only some responses are reinforced. On (39) _____ _____ schedules, reinforcement is given after a fixed number of responses, while on (40) _____ _____ schedules, reinforcement is given for the first response after a certain amount of time. On a (41) _____ _____ schedule, reinforcement is given after a variable number of responses, while on a (42) _____ _____ schedule, reinforcement is given for the first response after an average amount of time. (43) _____ schedules tend to produce the highest rate of response.

Biology and Learning

Pairing a taste with the experience of illness (such as stomach illness, nausea, and vomiting) produces a (44) _____ _____ _____. Martin Seligman has proposed that humans may be biologically prepared to acquire certain fears, a phenomenon also true of other animals and called (45) _____. The Brelands discovered that some animals could not be operantly conditioned because they fell back on behaviours that were part of their evolutionary history instead, a phenomenon called (46) _____ _____.

Cognition and Learning

Cognitive processes seem to play important roles in learning. German psychologist Wolfgang Köhler discovered that chimps were able to learn by (47) _____, the sudden perception of a useful relationship. Psychologist Edward Tolman discovered that rats seem to develop a mental representation or (48) _____ _____ of a maze. Tolman's experiments also supported the concept of (49) _____ learning, learning that occurs but is not demonstrated until there is an incentive to do so. Robert Rescorla found that animals learn to expect that a UCS will occur after the presentation of a CS, and his model of classical conditioning is known as the (50) _____ model.

Observational Learning: When Others Pave The Way

(51) _____ _____ helped pioneer the study of observational learning, which is also known as (52) _____.

Apply What You Know

1. Classical conditioning, operant conditioning, and modelling are used a great deal in advertising. Find one advertisement that uses classical conditioning to persuade us to buy the product, find one advertisement that uses operant conditioning, and find one that uses modelling. Photocopy the ad (or cut it from the newspaper or magazine if it belongs to you), and attach it in the appropriate space on Study Sheet 7.1. Write a brief explanation of how the ad exemplifies the use of that particular model of learning.

2. See Study Sheet 7.2. How might you use operant conditioning to condition this cute little creature to press a lever or stand on its hind legs?

Internet Scavenger Hunt

1. Much recent thought in education has suggested that males and females have different learning styles. Do some library research on this and present the basic arguments and research findings.

Practice Test

<u>Multiple Choice Items</u>: *Please write the letter corresponding to your answer in the space to the left of each item.*

_____ 1. The process that produces a relatively enduring change in an organism's behaviour or capabilities is called ____.

    a. learning
    b. positive reinforcement
    c. negative reinforcement
    d. shaping

_____ 2. Assume that, through a process of natural selection, a particular species of tree squirrels develops a fur colouring that allows it to blend-in more effectively in their natural environment. As a result, they are more difficult to spot in the trees, are less likely to become prey for local predators, and are thus more likely to survive and reproduce. This **best demonstrates** the process of ____.

    a. classical conditioning
    b. personal adaptation
    c. operant conditioning
    d. species adaptation

_____ 3. You have just settled down to begin studying for your exam in this course when your roommate decides to turn on some music. At first, the music distracts you from your studying but after a short time, the music no longer bothers you even though it continues to play. This example **most clearly demonstrates** the process of ____.

    a. extinction
    b. negative reinforcement
    c. classical conditioning
    d. habituation

_____ 4. A stimulus that produces a response without learning is called a(n) ____ stimulus.

    a. conditioned
    b. reflexive
    c. unconditioned
    d. primary

_____ 5. The procedure that seems to work best in producing classically conditioned responses is ____ pairing.

    a. forward short-delay
    b. forward trace
    c. simultaneous
    d. backward

_____ 6. The best explanation for the success of the answer to question #5 is the _____ model.

    a. operant conditioning
    b. expectancy
    c. spontaneous recovery
    d. observational learning

_____ 7. You are conducting an experiment where you are trying to manipulate the immune response of rats by using the principles of classical conditioning. First, for several days of an experiment, you give rats artificially sweetened water with an immune system enhancing drug in it. You later remove the drug and notice that the immune systems of rats are boosted when they consume the sweetened water. In your experiment, the conditioned stimulus is _____.

    a. the sweetened water
    b. the drug
    c. enhanced immune system functioning in response to the drug
    d. enhanced immune system functioning in response to the sweetened water

_____ 8. A woman living in London during WWII learned to associate air-raid sirens with destruction created by bombs dropped from Nazi airplanes. After moving to Canada, sirens no longer predicted such destruction, so her fear responses to sirens subsided over time. In the language of classical conditioned, the fear response has become _____.

    a. discriminated
    b. generalized
    c. extinguished
    d. spontaneously recovered

_____ 9. On a trip back to London forty-four years after the war ended, the same woman hears a recording of an old air-raid siren and becomes very upset. Classical conditioning researchers would suggest that the woman is experiencing _____.

    a. discrimination
    b. generalization
    c. extinction
    d. spontaneous recovery

_____ 10. The sudden perception of a useful relationship that helps to solve a problem is called

    a. trial and error.
    b. cognitive generalization.
    c. operant generalization.
    d. insight.

_____11. Stuart has a rather unusual fear. He is afraid of public speaking but only when he has to make speeches on the weekend. He is a professor and has no trouble speaking in front of large groups of students and he has made effective presentations at conferences, as long as he presents during a weekday. The specificity of Stuart's fear mostly clearly demonstrates the process of _____.

    a. escape conditioning
    b. avoidance conditioning
    c. stimulus generalization
    d. discrimination

_____ 12. The goal of exposure therapies is to expose a phobic person to the feared stimulus without the _____, so that the process of _____ can occur.

    a. CS; habituation
    b. CS; discrimination
    c. UCS; generalization
    d. UCS; extinction

_____ 13. A young child is hungry and wants a cookie but is too short to reach the table where the cookie jar is kept. She tries various things to get the jar, such as jumping or throwing her teddy bear at the jar in hopes of knocking it off the table, but to no avail. Eventually, almost by accident, she realizes that she can pull the tablecloth on which the jar rests and is thus able to reach the jar. In the future, she will be more likely to try this technique again since it was effective. This example **best demonstrates** _____.

    a. Thorndike's law of effect
    b. the principles of classical conditioning
    c. shaping
    d. partial reinforcement

_____ 14. Joey likes to watch wrestling matches on TV but his mother usually does not allow him to do this. However, Joey has noticed that when his mom has a bad day at work and gets very tired, she usually doesn't mind if he watches wrestling. As a result, Joey usually will only ask to watch wrestling if his mother has had a hard day at work. In this instance, the kind of day that Joey's mother has at work would be considered a(n) _____.

    a. conditioned stimulus
    b. discriminative stimulus
    c. negative reinforcer
    d. consequence

_____ 15. In operant conditioning, an organism learns an association between _____.

    a. a CS and a UCS
    b. an antecedent and a CS
    c. an emitted behaviour and an operant behaviour
    d. a behaviour and a consequence

_____ 16. Research by Galef and colleagues has found that rats

    a. only learn through classical conditioning.
    b. have very poor spatial skills.
    c. can learn food preferences by observing other rats.
    d. are not capable of developing cognitive maps.

_____ 17. A mother has been continually nagging her daughter about how messy her room is. Finally, the daughter gets so tired of her mom's complaints that she cleans her room, thus stopping the nagging of her mother. Given the fact that the withdrawal of the mother's nagging served to strengthen the daughter's room-cleaning behaviour, the mother's nagging would be considered a(n) _____.

    a. negative reinforcer
    b. positive reinforcer
    c. aversive punishment
    d. response cost punishment

_____ 18. Parents are interested in getting their son to play piano. In order to do this, they decide to reinforce him by paying him $1.00 for every hour that he practices. Shortly after this, the son decides that he also wants to learn how to play guitar and, since his parents are still paying him, he continues practising both instruments. After a couple of months, the parents decide that the important thing is that their son is involved in music and so they quit paying him to practice the piano, whereupon the son gradually quits playing the piano and continues playing the guitar. The weakening and disappearance of the son's piano playing behaviour would **best** be considered as an example of _____.

    a. operant extinction
    b. negative reinforcement
    c. positive reinforcement
    d. classical extinction

_____ 19. Suzanne was driving down the freeway rather quickly because she was late for a meeting but she noticed a police car parked on the side of the freeway. She quickly applied the breaks and slowed down to the speed limit. In this instance, the police car was a _____.

    a. negative reinforcer
    b. primary stimulus
    c. discriminative stimulus
    d. positive reinforcer

_____ 20. You stay inside on very hot days because you don't want to expose yourself to the heat. By doing so, you don't subject yourself to such problems as sunburns or heatstroke. The learning that has taken place for you is **most similar** to _____.

    a. escape conditioning
    b. a variable ratio schedule of reinforcement
    c. avoidance conditioning
    d. a fixed interval schedule of reinforcement

_____ 21. Chantelle is interested in training her dog "Daisy" to do tricks. She has decided to give Daisy a treat after every fourth time that Daisy performs the trick. The schedule of reinforcement she wants to employ is a _____ schedule.

    a. fixed-ratio
    b. fixed-interval
    c. variable-ratio
    d. variable-interval

_____ 22. Leslie's new teacher is unpopular with the students because she gives "pop" or surprise quizzes. Leslie's teacher believes this method of testing results in more consistent study habits. She is employing a _____ schedule.

    a. variable-interval
    b. fixed-ratio
    c. variable-ratio
    d. fixed-interval

_____ 23. Skinner's work gave rise to a field called _____, which combines a behavioural approach with the scientific method to solve individual and societal problems.

    a. shaping
    b. applied behaviour analysis
    c. chaining
    d. operant conditioning

_____ 24. Through evolution, animals seem to be biologically prewired to more easily learn behaviours that are related to their survival as a species. Seligman has termed this _____.

    a. conditioned taste aversion
    b. preparedness
    c. instinctive drift
    d. biological learning

_____ 25. When a conditioned response "drifts back" to more instinctive behaviour, _____ has occurred.

    a. conditioned taste aversion
    b. preparedness
    c. instinctive drift
    d. evolution

_____ 26. Studies of brain effects on learning have shown that _____.

    a. the hypothalamus is the only part of the brain that controls learning
    b. neurotransmitters are not involved in learning
    c. the cerebellum, but not the cerebral cortex, is involved in learning
    d. no single part of the brain "controls" learning

_____ 27. The _____ model asserts that the key factor in classical conditioning in **not** how often the CS is paired with the UCS but how well the CS predicts the appearance of the UCS.

a. insight
b. expectancy
c. latent learning
d. cognitive

_____ 28. A researcher conducts an experiment where rats in one group (Group 1) receive ten learning trials where they receive a shock after a light is lit. Another group of rats (Group 2) receives the same ten trials where the shock is paired with the light but they also receive ten additional random trials where the light is not followed by a shock. According to the expectancy model of classical conditioning, we would expect that the light to become a CS for fear for the rats _____.

a. only in Group 1
b. only in Group 2
c. in both Group1 and Group 2
d. in neither Group 1 nor Group 2.

_____ 29. Learning that occurs but is not shown until there is an incentive to do so is called _____ learning.

a. backward
b. operant
c. classically conditioned
d. latent

_____ 30. Hannah recently went on a trip to Paris with her mother. They spent their first three days shopping and wandering the streets of Paris. On their fourth day, Hannah accidentally became separated from her mother and had to find her own way back to the hotel. Hannah's mother was surprised that she easily found the hotel. This best demonstrates

a. Thorndike's Law of Effect.
b. latent learning.
c. stimulus discrimination.
d. response cost.

True/False Items: *Write T or F in the space provided to the left of each item.*

_____ 1. Research shows that biology plays no role in learning.

_____ 2. An initially neutral stimulus that through association with an unconditioned stimulus comes to produce a response initially produced only by the unconditioned stimulus is called the conditioned response.

_____ 3. Extinction occurs when a CS is presented repeatedly without the UCS also being present.

_____ 4. When stimuli similar to the initial CS come to produce the same response, the phenomenon is called stimulus discrimination.

_____ 5. Exposure therapies are used to treat phobias.

_____ 6. Operant responses are emitted.

_____ 7. Secondary reinforcers like money become reinforcers through their association with primary reinforcers.

_____ 8. An example of negative reinforcement is spanking a child for bad behaviour.

_____ 9. Interval schedules of reinforcement produce the highest rates of response.

_____ 10. Studies of conditioned taste aversions support the idea that biology constrains learning.

Short Answer Questions

1. What is habituation and why is it important for human behaviour?

2. Describe the process of the acquisition of a classically conditioned response.

3. What does the Law of Effect say?

4. What is the difference between shaping and chaining?

5. How do insight and cognitive maps show that cognition is important in the learning process?

Essay Questions

1. Describe what the function of learning is thought to be.

2. Describe how classical conditioning can be used to both acquire and overcome fear.

3. Describe how the ABC's of operant conditioning interact to produce operant behaviours.

4. Describe the differences between the different types of reinforcement schedules.

5. What are the differences between negative reinforcement, aversive punishment, and response cost?

Study Sheet 7.1 Use of Learning Models in Advertising

Classical Conditioning

Explanation:

Study Sheet 7.1 Use of Learning Models in Advertising

Operant Conditioning

Explanation:

Study Sheet 7.1 Use of Learning Models in Advertising

Modelling

Explanation:

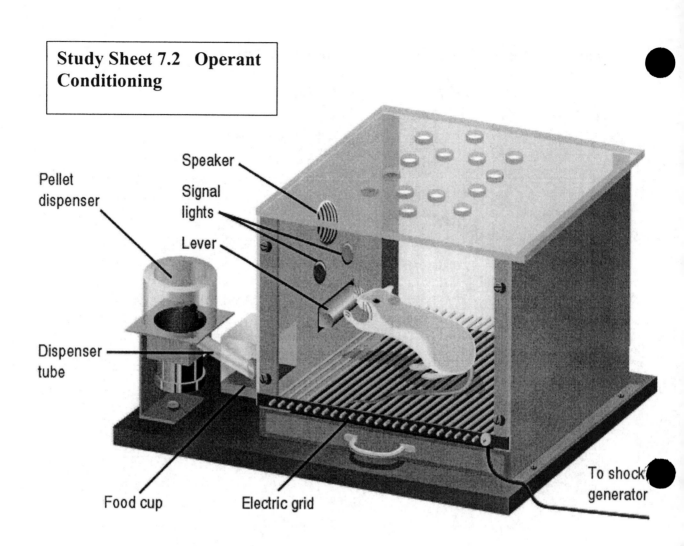

Speaker

Pellet dispenser

Signal lights

Lever

Dispenser tube

Food cup

Electric grid

To shock generator

Answer Keys

Answer Key for Key Terms

Adapting to the Environment, Habituation, and Classical Conditioning

1. b
2. p
3. o
4. n
5. g
6. f
7. i
8. k
9. l
10. c
11. j
12. a
13. m
14. h
15. e
16. d

Operant Conditioning

1. z
2. k
3. x
4. n
5. q
6. m
7. p
8. e
9. w
10. j
11. u
12. s
13. a
14. i
15. b
16. o
17. r
18. f
19. g
20. dd
21. d
22. l
23. h
24. cc
25. c
26. aa
27. bb
28. y
29. v
30. t

Biology and Learning, Cognition and Learning, Observational Learning, and the Role of Language

1. d
2. a
3. c
4. b
5. e
6. f
7. g

Answer Key for Review at a Glance

1. learning
2. adaptive significance
3. personal adaptation
4. species adaptation
5. habituation
6. classical conditioning
7. Pavlov
27. positive reinforcement
28. Primary
29. secondary
30. negative reinforcement
31. extinction
32. aversive punishment
33. response cost

8. acquisition
9. unconditioned
10. unconditioned
11. conditioned
12. conditioned
13. extinction
14. spontaneous recovery
15. stimulus generalization
16. discrimination
17. higher-order
18. Law of Effect
19. operant
20. Skinner box
21. reinforcement
22. punishment
23. antecedents
24. behaviour
25. consequences
26. discriminative

34. delay of gratification
35. Shaping
36. Chaining
37. continuous
38. partial
39. fixed ratio
40. fixed interval
41. variable ratio
42. variable interval
43. Ratio
44. conditioned taste aversion
45. preparedness
46. instinctive drift
47. insight
48. cognitive map
49. latent
50. expectancy
51. Albert Bandura
52. modelling

Answer Key for Practice Test Multiple Choice Questions

1. a
2. d
3. d
4. c
5. a
6. b
7. a
8. c
9. d
10. d
11. d
12. d
13. a
14. b
15. d

16. c
17. a
18. a
19. c
20. c
21. a
22. a
23. b
24. b
25. c
26. d
27. b
28. a
29. d
30. b

Answer Key for Practice Test True/False Questions

1. F
2. F
3. T
4. F
5. T

6. T
7. T
8. F
9. F
10. T

Answer Key for Practice Test Short Answer Questions

1. Habituation refers to a decrease in the strength of a response to a stimulus that is repeated. If we paid attention to every stimulus in our environment, we would quickly become overwhelmed. Thus, through habituation, we learn to pay attention to only those stimuli that are important, and we filter out stimuli that do not provide us with important information.

2. Acquisition refers to the period during which a response is being learned. Initially a stimulus called the unconditioned stimulus will elicit a response, called the unconditioned response, without learning. This is called a natural, unlearned reflex. Learning trials then occur in which a new stimulus, called a conditioned stimulus, is repeatedly paired with the unconditioned stimulus. After a number of such learning trials, the CS is presented alone, and, if the animal or human has been classically conditioned, the response that originally was elicited only by the UCS will now occur in the presence of the CS.

3. Edward L. Thorndike's Law of Effect says that any behaviour that is followed by a satisfying consequence will become more likely to occur in the future and any behaviour that is followed by an unsatisfying consequence will become less likely to occur in the future.

4. Shaping and chaining are used to condition new behaviours and complex sequences of behaviour. When shaping is used, successive approximations toward the final goal are reinforced. For example, to shape a child to study one hour per night, you could reinforce her for studying ten minutes a night. Next, you would only reinforce her for studying twenty minutes a night, and so on. Chaining involves reinforcing the last step of the chain first and working backwards. Each step then is reinforced by the opportunity to perform the next step in the chain.

5. At one time, most psychologists believed in S-R, or stimulus-response learning. That is, the stimulus produced a response without any thought. Today, many psychologists believe in S-O-R models, which argue that cognition is important in behaviour. German psychologist Wolfgang Kohler discovered that chimpanzees could learn to perform tasks through insight, the sudden perception of useful relationships, rather than just through the trial-and-error learning of the conditioning process. Similarly, Edward Tolman discovered that rats being trained through conditioning procedures in a maze were learning a mental representation, or cognitive map, of the maze, and were using it to find food. Such findings challenged the traditional view that cognitive processes were not important in the learning process.

Answer Key for Practice Test Essay Questions

1. Learning has adaptive significance. That is, it helps us to adapt to and survive in our environment. The environment shapes behaviour through both personal and species adaptation. Personal adaptation occurs through the laws of learning. Species adaptation occurs through the process of evolution.

2. Through the process of classical conditioning, some fears may be learned. People become afraid of stimuli paired with noxious stimuli such as pain or electric shock. Systematically exposing a person to the feared stimulus while he or she practices muscular relaxation is a technique (systematic desensitization) used to reduce fear.

3. The antecedent conditions, if present, act as stimuli for emitted behaviours. Such conditions are discriminative stimuli, signals that a particular behaviour will produce a desired consequence. Thus, the voluntary emitted behaviour is performed to produce the desired consequence.

4. On a fixed-ratio schedule, reinforcement occurs after a certain number of responses. On a variable-ratio schedule, reinforcement occurs after an average number of responses. On a fixed-interval schedule, reinforcement occurs after the first response following a fixed time period. On a variable-interval schedule, reinforcement occurs for the first response following a variable time interval.

5. A response is <u>strengthened</u> by the removal or avoidance of a stimulus in negative reinforcement. A response is <u>weakened</u> by the presentation of a stimulus. In response cost, a response is <u>weakened</u> by the <u>removal</u> of a stimulus.

Chapter 8. Memory

Chapter objectives

These questions, with a few additions, are taken from the directed questions found in the margins of the chapter. After reading the chapter, you should be able to answer these questions.

8.1 How is memory likened to an information-processing system?

8.2 What is sensory memory? How did Sperling assess the duration of iconic memory?

8.3 Describe the limitations of short-term memory, and how they can be overcome.

8.4 Why do researchers refer to short-term memory as "working memory?"

8.5 Identify three components of working memory.

8.6 What is the serial position effect? Under what conditions do primacy and recency occur?

8.7 According to the three-component model, why do primacy and recency occur?

8.8 Provide some examples of effortful and automatic processing in your own life.

8.9 Explain the concept of "depth of processing."

8.10 How effectively do maintenance and elaborative rehearsal process information into long-term memory?

8.11 Why do hierarchies, chunking, mnemonic devices, and imagery enhance memory?

8.12 What is a schema? Explain how schemas influence encoding.

8.13 In what sense are schemas and expert knowledge related?

8.14 Explain the concepts of associative networks and priming.

8.15 How do neural network models differ from associative network models?

8.16 Use the concepts of declarative versus procedural memory, and explicit versus implicit memory, to explain the pattern of H. M.'s amnesia.

8.17 Describe some ways to measure explicit and implicit memory.

8.18 Why does having multiple, self-generated retrieval cues enhance recall?

8.19 Do flashbulb memories always provide an accurate picture? Describe some evidence.

8.20 Explain how context-dependent and state-dependent memory illustrate the encoding specificity principle.

8.21 Identify practical principles of encoding and retrieval that can be used to enhance memory.

8.22 Describe Ebbinghaus' "forgetting curve" and factors that contributed to his rapid, substantial forgetting.

8.23   Identify encoding, storage, retrieval, and motivational processes that have been hypothesized to contribute to forgetting.

8.24   Describe the nature and some possible causes of retrograde, anterograde, and infantile amnesia.

8.25   How do Bartlett's research and studies of boundary extension illustrate memory construction?

8.26   Explain how source confusion contributes to misinformation effects.

8.27   Are younger and older children equally susceptible to misinformation effects, and equally accurate in recalling traumatic events? Describe some evidence.

8.28   28.   Do people ever forget traumatic personal events? What are recovered memories and repression controversial topics?

8.29   What major approaches do scientists use to study the brain regions involved in memory?

8.30   What major roles do the hippocampus, cerebral cortex, thalamus, amygdala, and cerebellum play in memory?

8.31   According to some researchers, what basic memory principles account for exceptional memory? Do you agree with this position?

8.32   In what ways is "forgetting" adaptive? How might perfect memory be a burden?

Chapter Overview

Memory as Information Processing

The guiding metaphor used by most cognitive psychologists today to study the mind is that the mind is a processing system that encodes, stores, and retrieves information. Encoding refers to getting information into the system, storage involves retaining information, and retrieval involves getting the information out of memory. Cognitive psychologists also work with a three-component model of memory. Sensory memory holds sensory information, including both visual (or iconic) memory and auditory (or echoic) memory. Information that we pay attention to is passed into short-term, or working memory; other information is lost. The capacity of sensory memory is large, while the capacity of working memory is small, though the latter can be increased via chunking. Both maintenance and elaborative rehearsal techniques can keep information in short-term memory, but information is best transferred to long-term memory via elaborative techniques.

Encoding: Entering Information

The more effectively we encode information, the more likely it is that it can be retrieved. According to the levels of processing concept, the more deeply we process information, the better it will be remembered. Elaborative rehearsal techniques, including techniques like the use of mnemonic devices, increase the depth of processing. Prior knowledge shapes encoding through the use of schemas, which are organized patterns of thought about some aspect of the world.

Storage: Retaining Information

One prominent theory of memory is that it can be represented by an associative network. The idea is memory consists of associated ideas and concepts. Biologically, memory may occur through the firing of synaptically connected neurons. Long-term memory consists of all facts we have learned over time. Cognitive psychologists distinguish between different aspects of long-term memory such as declarative, episodic, semantic, and procedural memories.

Retrieval: Accessing Information

Memory is typically triggered via retrieval cues. The more retrieval cues we have, the more likely we are to remember information. Context, state, and mood can also influence retrieval. We typically remember information better if we are in the same context and state in which the information was originally encoded.

Forgetting

The Ebbinghaus forgetting curve shows that we rapidly lose much information, but the progress of loss levels off after a short period of time. We forget for a number of reasons. Decay theory argues that we forget things because the memory trace decays. Other theories suggest that encoding failures and interference, both proactive and retroactive, contribute to forgetting. We may also be motivated to forget undesirable experiences through repression of them. Amnesia also affects memory loss.

Memory as a Constructive Process

Schemas influence the memory process through providing expectancies about what one perceives or believes is likely to have happened in the past. As a result, sometimes our memories are shaped to fit our schemas. The misinformation effect says that distortion of memory occurs via misleading postevent information. A major controversy has emerged about the validity of children's memories. Some think that children's memories are particularly susceptible to suggestion and bias. The "recovered memory" syndrome is also controversial for the same reasons.

The Biology of Memory

Scientists rely on both naturally- and experimentally-induced lesions, as well as brain imaging to study the biology of memory. The hippocampus and its surrounding tissue have been found to play a major role in encoding long-term declarative memories. The cerebral cortex plays a role in encoding by processing information from the sensory registers and also by storing semantic memories. The frontal lobes of the cortex play a central role in working memory. The amygdala seems to encode emotionally arousing and disturbing aspects of events. The cerebellum plays an important role in the formation of procedural memories.

Chapter Outline

Memory As Information Processing
    A Three-Component Model
        Sensory Memory
        Short-Term/Working Memory
        Long-Term Memory

Encoding: Entering Information
    Effortful and Automatic Processing
    Levels of Processing: When Deeper is Better
    Exposure and Rehearsal
    Organization and Imagery
        Hierarchies and Chunking
        Mnemonic Devices
        Visual Imagery
    How Prior Knowledge Shapes Encoding
        Schemas: Our Mental Organizers
        Schemas and Expert Knowledge

Storage: Retaining Information
    Memory as a Network
        Associative Networks
        Neural Networks
    Types of Long-Term Memory
        Declarative and Procedural Memory
        Explicit and Implicit Memory

Retrieval: Accessing Information
    The Value of Multiple and Self-Generated Cues
    The Value of Distinctiveness
        Flashbulb Memory: Fogging Up the Picture?
    Context, State, and Mood Effects on Memory
        Context-Dependent Memory: Returning to the Scene
        State-Dependent Memory: Arousal, Drugs, and Mood
            Psychological Applications: Improving Memory and Academic Learning

Forgetting
    The Course of Forgetting

Why Do We Forget?
>   Encoding Failure
>   Decay of the Memory Trace
>   Interference, Retrieval Failure, and the Tip-of-the-tongue
>   Motivated Forgetting
Amnesia
Forgetting to Do Things: Prospective Memory

Memory as a Constructive Process
>   Memory Distortion and Schemas: On Ghosts, "Gargoils," and Scenes Beyond the Edge
>   The Misinformation Effect and Eyewitness Testimony
>   Confusing the Source
>   *Research Frontiers: How Accurate Are Young Children's Memories?*
>   Other Factors in Eyewitness Testimony
>   The "Recovered Memory" Controversy: Repression or Reconstruction?

The Biology of Memory
>   Where in the Brain Are Memories Formed?
>   The Hippocampus and Cerebral Cortex
>   The Thalamus and Amygdala
>   The Cerebellum

Exceptional Memory
>   *Research Foundations: Is Exceptional Memory Really Exceptional?*

A Final Thought: The "Curse" of Exceptional Memory

Problem-Based Learning

Recovered Memories

http://web.lemoyne.edu/~hevern/nr-mem.html
Part of the Narrative Psychology Internet and Resource Guide-Offers a large amount of information on both sides of the recovered memory controversy. Includes bibliographical resources, internet resources, and general information.

http://www.fmsfonline.org
Official website of the false memory syndrome foundation.

General
http://human-factors.arc.nasa.gov/cognition/tutorials/index.html
Tutorials from the NASA Cognition Lab website-Contains information and experiments on various aspects of memory including mnemonics, recall and rehearsal.

http://www.exploratorium.edu/memory
Part of the San Francisco Exploratorium website-Contains memory experiments and information about memory.

Key Terms: Write the letter of the definition next to the term in the space provided.

Memory as Information Processing
Encoding: Entering Information
Storage: Retaining Information
Retrieval: Accessing Information

1. ___ associative network

2. ___ chunking

3. ___ context-dependent memory

4. ___ declarative memory

5. ___ dual-coding theory

6. ___ elaborative rehearsal

7. ___ encoding

8. ___ encoding specificity principle

9. ___ episodic memory

10. ___ explicit memory

11. ___ implicit memory

12. ___ levels of processing

13. ___ long-term memory

14. ___ maintenance rehearsal

15. ___ memory

16. ___ mood-congruent recall

17. ___ neural network

18. ___ overlearning

19. ___ priming

20. ___ procedural memory

21. ___ retrieval

22. ___ retrieval cue

23. ___ schema

24. ___ semantic memory

25. ___ sensory memory

a. the processes that allow us to record and later retrieve experiences and information

b. getting information into the system by translating it into a neural code that the brain processes

c. retaining information over time

d. pulling information out of storage

e. part of the memory system that holds sensory information just long enough for it to be recognized

f. holds the information that we are conscious of at any one time

g. another name for short-term memory

h. combining individual items into larger units of meaning

i. simple repetition of information

j. focuses on the meaning of information or relates new information to things we already know

k. our vast library of durable stored memories

l. a U-shaped graphical pattern that shows that recall is influenced by a word's position in a series of items

m. concept that the more deeply we process information the better it will be remembered

n. theory that suggests that if we encode information through both visual and verbal codes we will better remember it

o. an organized pattern of thought about some aspect of the world

p. a massive network of associated ideas and concepts

q. the activation of one concept by another

r. a network in which each concept is represented by a particular pattern or set of nodes that become activated simultaneously

s. our store of factual knowledge concerning personal experiences

t. represents general factual knowledge about the world and language

u. factual knowledge that includes two categories: episodic and semantic memories

v. memory for skills and actions

w. involves conscious or intentional memory retrieval

x. memory that influences our behaviour without conscious awareness

y. any stimulus that activates information in long-term memory

26. ___ serial position effect

z. memory that is easier to recall in the same environment in which it was acquired

27. ___ short-term memory

aa. the principle that memory is enhanced when conditions present during retrieval match those present during encoding

28. ___ state-dependent memory

bb. theory that proposes that our ability to retrieve information is greater when our internal state at the time of retrieval matches that during learning

29. ___ storage

cc. tendency to recall information or events that are congruent with our current mood

30. ___ working memory

dd. continued rehearsal past the point of initial learning

Forgetting
Memory as a Constructive Process
The Biology of Memory
Exceptional Memory
A Final Thought: The "Curse" of Exceptional Memory

1. ___ anterograde amnesia

a. theory that proposes that with time and disuse the physical memory trace in the nervous system fades away

2. ___ decay theory

b. occurs when material learned in the past interferes with recall of newer material

3. ___ infantile amnesia

c. occurs when newly acquired information interferes with the ability to recall information learned at an earlier time

4. ___ source confusion

d. psychodynamic theory that motivational processes may protect us by blocking the recall of anxiety-arousing memories

5. ___ memory consolidation

e. memory loss for events after the initial onset of amnesia

6. ___ misinformation effect

f. memory loss for early experiences

7. ___ proactive interference

g. memory loss for events that occurred prior to the onset of amnesia

8. ___ prospective memory

h. remembering to perform an activity in the future

9. ___ repression

i. the distortion of memory by misleading postevent information

10. ___ retroactive interference

j. our tendency to recall something or recognize it as familiar, but to forget where we encountered it

11. ___ retrograde amnesia

k. hypothetical "binding" of memory process that may occur in the hippocampus

Review at a Glance: *Write the term that best fits the blank to review what you learned in this chapter.*

Memory As Information Processing

(1) _____ refers to the processes that allow us to record and later retrieve experiences and information. Today the mind is visualized as a processing system. It takes in information by translating it into a neural code that your brain processes, a process called (2) _____. The brain retains information over time through (3) _____ and pulls information out of long-term memory through (4) _____ processes. Most cognitive psychologists suggest a three-component model of memory. (5) _____ memory holds incoming sensory information just long enough for it to be recognized. Our visual sensory register is called the (6) _____ store, while the auditory sensory register is called the (7) _____ store. Most information in sensory memory quickly fades away, but information that we pay attention to enters (8) _____ memory, which is also called (9) _____ memory. The capacity of working memory is rather small, but it can be increased through (10) _____, which requires the combination of individual items into larger units of meaning. By rehearsing information, we can keep it in short-term memory longer. (11) _____ rehearsal involves the simple repetition of information, like repeating a phone number in order to remember it, while (12) _____ rehearsal involves focusing on the meaning of information or relating it to things we already know. Our vast library of stored information is called (13) _____ memory.

Encoding: Entering Information

According to the (14) _____ ___ _____ notion, the more deeply we process information, the better it will be remembered. Because of this, (15)_____ rehearsal is the best method of facilitating the transfer of information into long-term memory. Organizational devices such as using hierarchies, chunking, and mnemonic devices help us to remember information. Paivio discovered that we encode information in both verbal and visual codes, which is known as his (16) _____ theory. Prior knowledge also shapes encoding. A (17) _____ is an organized pattern of thought about some aspect of the world.

Storage: Retaining Information

After information is encoded, it is organized and stored in long-term memory. One group of theories suggests that memory is represented as a massive network of associated ideas and concepts, called an (18) _____ network. In such a network, when people think about one concept, it triggers thinking about related concepts throughout the network, through the process called (19) _____ _____. The term (20) _____ refers to the activation of one concept by another. In a (21) _____ network, each concept is represented by a particular pattern or set of nodes that becomes activated simultaneously. There are several types of long-term memory. (22) _____ memory involves factual knowledge and consists of two types. Our store of factual information about the world and language is called (23) _____ memory, while our store of factual memory about our personal experiences is called (24) _____ memory. (25) _____ memory is reflected in skills and actions we perform. Memory retrieval can involve both conscious and unconscious processes. (26) _____ memory involves conscious memory retrieval while (27) _____ memory influences our behaviour without conscious awareness.

Retrieval: Accessing Information

A stimulus that activates of information stored in long-term memory is called a (28) _____ cue. Sometimes memories are so clear that we can picture them like a snapshot in time. Such memories are called (29) _____ memories. Context, state, and mood affect our ability to retrieve information. The principle that states that memory is enhanced when conditions present during retrieval match those that were present during encoding is called the (30) _____ _____ _____.
Sometimes it is easier to remember information if we are in the same environment in which the information was first encoded, a phenomenon called (31) _____ _____ memory. Similarly, our ability to retrieve information is greater when our internal state at the time of retrieval matches our original state during learning, which is called (32) _____ _____ memory. We also tend to recall information or events that are congruent with our current mood, which is known as (33) _____ _____ recall.

Forgetting

Hermann Ebbinghaus pioneered the study of forgetting, discovering that memory declines rapidly and then levels off after initial learning. There are several theories of why we forget things. One theory is that we forget things because we fail to encode them well enough. Another theory, called (34) _____ theory, suggests that with time and disuse the physical memory trace in the nervous system just fades away. Yet another theory, interference theory, suggests that we forget because other items in long-term memory overwrite or impair our ability to retain information. (35) _____ interference occurs when material learned in the past interferes with the learning of new information. (36) _____ interference occurs when newly acquired information interferes with the ability to retrieve information stored at an earlier time. Psychodynamic theorists suggest that we may be motivated to forget particularly disturbing information through (37) _____. Amnesia involves a dramatic forgetting of basic information. (38) _____ amnesia refers to memory loss for events that occur after the initial onset of amnesia while (39) _____ amnesia represents memory loss for events that occurred prior to the amnesia. Most of us can't remember events of our early childhood due to (40) _____ amnesia.

Memory as a Constructive Process

The use of appropriate (41) _____ helps us to organize information as we encode and retrieve it. Sometimes, though, schemas can influence the distortion of information. The distortion of a memory by misleading postevent information is called the (42) _____ effect. Misinformation effects also occur because of (43) _____ _____, our tendency to recall something or recognize it without being able to remember where we encountered it.

The Biology of Memory

The (44) _____ and its adjacent tissues seem to play a key role in encoding long-term declarative memories. The cerebral cortex also seems to play an important role in encoding. One hypothetical process called (45) _____ _____ suggests that the diverse aspects of an experience are first processed by different parts of the cortex and are then consolidated or "bound" together in the hippocampus.

Apply What You Know

1. Construct two lists of 20 words. Learn one list using maintenance rehearsal techniques. Learn the other list using elaborative rehearsal techniques, such as making up a story using the words or creating mental images of the concepts the words represent in your mind. Measure your immediate recall of the words right after you've learned them by recording the number of words you can recall from each list. Then measure your recall of both lists a day later. Do you find that you better remember words from one list as measured by immediate recall? If so, why? How about after one day? If so, why?

2. Suppose that you are an attorney and are interested in using the misinformation effect to sway the testimony of an eyewitness. Describe how you could do so.

Internet Scavenger Hunt

1. Research in education suggests that males and females may have different learning styles, suggesting that males and females should be taught in somewhat different ways. Using what you learned from your research in the "Internet Scavenger Hunt" exercise in Chapter 7, describe some differences in the ways that males and females might be taught.

Practice Test

Multiple Choice Items: *Please write the letter corresponding to your answer in the space to the left of each item.*

_____ 1. In the three stage memory model, iconic memory is part of _____ memory.

    a. sensory
    b. short-term
    c. long-term
    d. echoic

_____ 2. Both elaborative and maintenance rehearsal keep information active in ____ memory but ____ rehearsal is more effective in transferring information to long-term memory.

    a. short-term; elaborative
    b. sensory; maintenance
    c. short-term; maintenance
    d. sensory; elaborative

_____ 3. According to psychologist Alan Baddeley, working memory is divided into _____ components.

    a. sensory, short-term, and long-term memory
    b. episodic, procedural, and semantic memory
    c. auditory, visual-spatial, and central executive
    d. encoding, storage, and retrieval

_____ 4. New professor Cyko L. Gist is faced with the unenviable task of trying to memorize all of his new students' names, so he decides to employ elaborative rehearsal techniques to do this. To help his long-term recall of student Melody Balobalo, Gist should _____.

    a. repeat her name over and over again
    b. associate a mental image of her with a ball bouncing up and down over a song melody
    c. divide her name into chunks like Mel - O - Dy Bal - O - Bal – O
    d. use only short-term memory

_____ 5. Of the following, the one which is not one of the three basic memory processes is _____.

    a. encoding
    b. attention
    c. storage
    d. retrieval

_____ 6. Which of the following concepts does not fit with the other three?

   a. Digit Span Test
   b. working memory
   c. episodic memory
   d. magical number 7 plus or minus 2

_____ 7. Words at the end of a list are typically remembered better than words presented in the middle, when recalled immediately. This is known as the _____ effect and it presumably happens because the last few words on the list remain in _____ memory.

   a. serial position; sensory
   b. recency; long-term
   c. primacy; short-term
   d. recency; short-term

_____ 8. Making a grocery list and taking notes for a class are both examples of _____, which is encoding that is initiated intentionally and requires conscious attention.

   a. effortful processing
   b. automatic processing
   c. maintenance rehearsal
   d. state-dependent memory

_____ 9. The method of loci is a memory enhancing technique based on _____ and is consistent with the predictions of _____ theory.

   a. imagery; dual-coding
   b. chunking; dual-coding theory
   c. hierarchies; encoding specificity
   d. acronyms; encoding specificity

_____ 10. If you go to a movie, you know that the movie isn't going to start as long as the lights are on. Once the movie starts, you also know that it is considered polite not to talk during the movie and that if you need to leave, it is best to try not to disturb others. This collection of thoughts is best considered to be an example of _____.

   a. overlearning
   b. a schema
   c. chunking
   d. implicit memory

_____ 11. If you think for a moment about the concept SCHOOL, it is likely that other concepts such as TEXTBOOKS, TEACHERS, and EXAMS may also come to mind. The fact these other words can be triggered by the word SCHOOL is best considered as an example of _____.

   a. elaborative rehearsal
   b. proactive interference
   c. dual encoding
   d. priming

_____ 12. According to Craik and Lockhart's (1972) levels of processing theory which instructions would most likely lead to the best memory?.

    a. POTATO "Is the word in capital letters?"
    b. HORSE "Does the word rhyme with course?"
    c. ANIMAL "Is the word printed in black ink?"
    d. TABLE "Does the word fit in the sentence, (The man peeled the _____)?"

_____ 13. Deryk, a first year student, participated in a memory experiment as part of his introductory psychology class. He was shown pictures of four different loonies and asked to say which coin was the correct one. Deryk's inability to choose the correct coin was most likely due to

    a. retroactive interference
    b. encoding failure
    c. dual specificity
    d. elaborative forgetting

_____ 14. According to the _____, memory is better when the conditions present during encoding match those that are present during retrieval.

    a. dual processing theory
    b. decay theory
    c. encoding specificity principle
    d. the principles of implicit memory

_____ 15. Imagine that you have studied for an exam in a quiet environment and your physiological arousal has been low while you were studying. If on the day of the exam, you were given the test in a quiet environment and your physiological arousal remained low, the concept of state-dependent memory would predict that your recall would _____ and the concept of context-dependent memory would predict that your recall would _____.

    a. be worse; also be worse
    b. be better; be worse
    c. be worse; be better
    d. be better; also be better

_____ 16. Jim has a hard time remembering to do things that he plans to do in the future, such as mailing letters or remembering to call someone. These memories are examples of what are called _____ memories and the _____ is thought to be play an important role in their recreation.

    a. retroactive; parietal lobe
    b. prospective; frontal lobe
    c. anterograde; amygdale
    d. retrograde; hippocampus.

_____ 17. An eyewitness from a crime is asked to look through some mug shots to see if he can identify the person who committed a crime. After doing this, he sees a police line up of suspects and identifies one of the men as the person who committed the crime because he looks very familiar. Unfortunately, the man in the line up looks familiar not because the eyewitness saw him commit the crime but because he saw his face in the mug shot books a few hours ago and the eyewitness has forgotten this. This example best demonstrates the phenomenon of _____.

a. proactive interference
b. retrograde amnesia
c. source confusion
d. memory consolidation

_____ 18. The _____ appears to be an "encoding station" for long-term declarative memory.

a. cerebral cortex
b. thalamus
c. hippocampus
d. cerebellum

_____ 19. Which of the following statements best describes eyewitness testimony?

a. Men and women are equally inaccurate at eyewitness identification.
b. Identification based on voice is more accurate than identification based on vision.
c. Marijuana is more damaging to eyewitness memory than alcohol.
d. Women are more confident than men about the accuracy of their identifications.

_____ 20. At dinner, Suzanne noticed that her son Ryan seemed more hungry than usual and she asked him what he had eaten for breakfast. In this instance she was testing Ryan's _____ memory.

a. echoic
b. episodic
c. working
d. semantic

_____ 21. The process of getting information into the brain by translating it into a neural code that the brain processes is called _____.

a. retrieval
b. recall
c. storage
d. encoding

_____ 22. Recognizing someone's voice when you hear it on the phone shows that you have a _____ for that person.

a. chunk
b. icon
c. mental representation
d. elaboration

_____ 23. According to the _____ concept, the more deeply we encode information, the better we will remember it.

a. dual-coding
b. levels of processing
c. maintenance rehearsal
d. chunking

_____ 24. An organized pattern of thought about some aspect of the world is called a _____.

a. chunk
b. code
c. proposition
d. schema

_____ 25. A massive network of associated ideas and concepts is called a(n) _____ network.

a. associative
b. schema
c. neural
d. priming

_____ 26. Studies of _____ show that it is generally easier to remember information in the same environment in which it was originally learned.

a. state-dependent learning
b. schemas
c. context-dependent learning
d. decay

_____ 27. Krysta's boyfriend Paul is angry with her because she accidentally called him Tom, her ex-boyfriend's name. In her defence, she explained to him that the mistake was an example of _____.

a. retroactive interference
b. motivated forgetting
c. elaborative forgetting
d. proactive interference
e.

_____ 28. Memory loss for early life experiences is called _____.

a. infantile amnesia
b. anterograde amnesia
c. retroactive interference
d. Korsakoff's syndrome

_____ 29. The distortion of memory by misleading postevent information is called _____.

    a. anterograde amnesia
    b. Korsakoff's syndrome
    c. the misinformation effect
    d. priming

_____ 30. The _____ and its surrounding tissue seem to play key roles in encoding long-term declarative memories.

    a. hypothalamus
    b. hippocampus
    c. cerebellum
    d. amygdala

True/False Items: _Write T or F in the space provided to the left of each item._

_____ 1. Combining individual items into larger units of meaning is called chunking.

_____ 2. The best technique for transferring information from short-term memory to long-term memory is maintenance rehearsal.

_____ 3. A U-shaped pattern that shows that recall is influenced by a word's position in a series of items is called the primacy effect.

_____ 4. According to Paivio's dual coding theory, memory is improved by encoding information using both verbal and visual cues.

_____ 5. An organized pattern of thought about some aspect of the world is called a schema.

_____ 6. Our store of factual knowledge concerning our own personal experiences is called declarative memory.

_____ 7. Studies of context dependent memory show that it is easier to remember something in a different environment from which it was first encoded.

_____ 8. Proactive interference occurs when newly acquired information interferes with the ability to recall information learned at an earlier time.

_____ 9. Studies of the biology of memory have shown that the hippocampus plays a major role in encoding long-term declarative memories.

_____ 10. Synaptic connections seem to become stronger as a result of stimulation.

Short Answer Questions

1. Describe the three-component model of memory.

2. Describe the two different types of rehearsal.

3. What are associative and neural networks?

4. What are the major types of amnesia?

5. What is the misinformation effect?

Essay Questions

1. Describe the process of encoding information.

2. Describe the various types of long-term memory.

3. Why do we forget?

4. What is meant when psychologists say that memory involves a "constructive process?"

5. Where in the brain are memories formed?

Answer Keys

Answer Key for Key Terms

Memory as Information Processing
Encoding: Entering Information
Storage: Retaining Information
Retrieval: Accessing Information

1. p		16. cc	
2. h		17. r	
3. z		18. dd	
4. u		19. q	
5. n		20. v	
6. j		21. d	
7. b		22. y	
8. aa		23. o	
9. s		24. t	
10. w		25. e	
11. x		26. l	
12. m		27. f	
13. k		28. bb	
14. i		29. c	
15. a		30. g	

Forgetting
Memory as a Constructive Process
The Biology of Memory
Exceptional Memory
A Final Thought: The "Curse" of Exceptional Memory

1. e		7. b	
2. a		8. h	
3. f		9. d	
4. j		10. c	
5. k		11. g	
6. i			

Answer Key for Review at a Glance

1. memory
2. encoding
3. storage
4. retrieval
5. Sensory
6. iconic
7. echoic
8. short-term
9. working
10. chunking

24. episodic
25. Procedural
26. Explicit
27. implicit
28. retrieval
29. flashbulb
30. encoding specificity principle
31. context dependent
32. state dependent
33. mood congruent

11. Maintenance
12. elaborative
13. long-term
14. levels of processing
15. elaborative
16. dual-code
17. schema
18. associative
19. spreading activation
20. priming
21. neural
22. Declarative
23. semantic

34. decay
35. Proactive
36. Retroactive
37. repression
38. Anterograde
39. retrograde
40. infantile
41. schemas
42. misinformation
43. source confusion
44. hippocampus
45. memory consolidation

Answer Key for Practice Test Multiple Choice Questions

1. a
2. a
3. c
4. b
5. b
6. c
7. d
8. a
9. a
10. b
11. d
12. d
13. b
14. c
15. d

16. b
17. c
18. c
19. a
20. b
21. d
22. c
23. b
24. d
25. a
26. c
27. d
28. a
29. c
30. b

Answer Key for Practice Test True/False Questions

1. T
2. F
3. F
4. T
5. T

6. F
7. F
8. F
9. T
10. T

Answer Key for Practice Test Short Answer Questions

1. The three component model of memory consists of sensory memory, short-term, or working memory, and long-term memory. Sensory memory holds incoming sensory information just long enough for it to be recognized. Short-term memory holds the information that we are conscious of at any given time. Long-term memory is our vast store of more durable stored memories.

2. Maintenance rehearsal involves the simple repetition of information and is useful for retaining information in short-term memory. Elaborative rehearsal involves focusing on the meaning of information or relating it to other things we already know. Elaborative rehearsal is a better technique than maintenance rehearsal for transferring information from short-term to long-term memory.

3. An associative network is a massive network of associated ideas and concepts. In a neural network, each concept is represented by a pattern or set of nodes that becomes activated simultaneously. There is no single node for a concept in a neural network, while there is in an associative network.

4. Retrograde amnesia represents memory loss for events that occurred prior to the onset of amnesia. Anterograde amnesia involves memory loss for events that occur after the initial onset of amnesia. Infantile amnesia refers to an inability to remember information from the first few years of life.

5. The misinformation effect is the distortion of memory by misleading postevent information.

Answer Key for Practice Test Essay Questions

1. Encoding refers to the process of getting information into the system by translating it into a neural code that your brain processes. Encoding may involve effortful processing, which is encoding that is initiated intentionally and requires conscious attention. This may involve maintenance and elaborative rehearsal, making lists, and taking notes. Much encoding is also done by automatic processing, which occurs without intention and requires minimal attention. The deeper that information is encoded the more likely it will be able to be retrieved.

2. Declarative memory involves factual knowledge and includes episodic memory, which is our store of factual knowledge about our life experiences, and semantic memory, which represents general factual knowledge about the world. Procedural memory is our memory for skills and actions.

3. There are several theories of forgetting. Failure to encode information in a useful fashion at the time of learning often leads to later forgetting. Decay theory says that with time and disuse the physical memory trace in the nervous system fades away. According to interference theory, we forget information because other items in long-term memory overwrite it or impair our ability to retain it. Proactive interference occurs when material learned in the past interferes with recall of newer information. Retroactive interference occurs when newly acquired information interferes with the ability to recall information learned at an earlier time. Psychodynamic theorists believe that some information is lost due to motivated forgetting. Such a process may keep us from remembering traumatic or other upsetting memories.

4. We may reconstruct a memory in a way that intuitively "makes sense" and therefore feels real and accurate. Schemas often help us to distort information because we try to shape information to fit our schemas, rather than the other way around. Postevent information can distort memory in this way, a process called the misinformation effect.

5. Studies show that the hippocampus and its adjacent tissue play a major role in encoding long-term declarative memories. The cerebral cortex plays a vital role in encoding by processing information from the sensory registers. Semantic memory also seems to be stored in the cerebral cortex. The frontal lobes seem to play a central role in carrying out the functions of working memory. The amygdala seems to encode emotionally arousing and disturbing aspects of events. The cerebellum may play an important role in the formation of procedural memories.

Chapter 9. Thought, Language, and Intelligence

Learning Objectives

9.1   Define language and describe the three critical properties of language.

9.2   Contrast surface and deep structures of language.

9.3   Describe the basic elements of language.

9.4   Contrast biological and social learning perspectives of language acquisition.

9.5   Describe the cognitive effects of learning a second language.

9.6   Outline the development of language among children.

9.7   Using the linguistic relativity hypothesis, explain how language influences thinking.

9.8   Define concepts and propositions and explain their interrelation.

9.9   Contrast and recognize examples of deductive and inductive reasoning.

9.10   Describe and recognize examples of the four stages of problem solving.

9.11   Recognize examples of obstacles to problem solving: mental sets, confirmation bias, and functional fixedness.

9.12   Define and provide examples of algorithms and heuristics.

9.13   Define creativity and explain how it facilitates problem solving.

9.14   Define intelligence.

9.15   Outline the history of intelligence testing, including the work of Galton, Binet, Terman, and Wechsler.

9.16   Contrast the strategies for calculating intelligence quotients by Stern and Wechsler.

9.17   Differentiate between aptitude and achievement testing.

9.18   Describe standards for developing a psychological test, including standardization and various types of reliability and validity.

9.19   Differentiate the psychometric and cognitive processes approach to the study of intelligence.

9.20   Describe the major theories of intelligence developed by Spearman, Cattell and Horn, Gardner, and Sternberg.

9.21   Define emotional intelligence and distinguish it from intelligence.

9.22   Describe biological and environmental factors related to intelligence, including brain size and genetics.

9.23   Describe the cultural and ethnic variation in scores on intelligence tests.

9.24   Describe gender differences in cognitive and behavioural skills and the potential reasons for them.

9.25   Describe the purpose, methods, and results of the research on stereotypes and intelligence conducted by Steele (1997).

9.26   Define cognitive disability and intellectual giftedness and describe how individuals scoring at the extremes of intelligence differ from individuals scoring within the normal range of intelligence.

Chapter Overview

Language

Language consists of a system of symbols and rules for combining these symbols in such a way that can produce an infinite number of possible messages or meanings. Language is symbolic and uses sounds, written signs, or gestures to refer to objects, events, ideas, and feelings. With language we can talk about not only the present but the past, future, and imaginary events, a feature of language called displacement. Language has both a surface and a deep structure. The surface structure is the way symbols are combined (through rules of grammar called syntax) while the deep structure refers to the underlying meaning. Phonemes are the smallest units of sound in a language while morphemes are the smallest units of meaning. The development of language seems to be both biological and psychological. All infants, regardless of culture or society, vocalize the entire range of phonemes found in the world's languages. Some linguists believe that there is a critical period during which language is most easily learned. Learning through imitation, rewards, and punishments, also seems to be important in the development of language, though it cannot completely explain the development of language skills. A second language is best learned and spoken most fluently when learned during the sensitive period of childhood. Language seems to affect thinking processes. Benjamin Lee Whorf, in fact, argued that language determines what we are capable of thinking, though most modern linguists disagree with that assertion. We do seem to think in propositions, statements that express fact. Propositions consist of concepts, basic units of semantic memory. Many concepts in turn are defined by prototypes, the most typical and familiar members of a category.

Reasoning and Problem Solving

We reason through both deductive (top-down) and inductive (bottom-up) reasoning. Sometimes, though, we run into stumbling blocks in reasoning. These stumbling blocks include being distracted by irrelevant information, failing to apply deductive rules, and belief bias, the tendency to abandon logical rules in favour of one's own personal beliefs. To solve a problem, we must first frame it. Following that, we generate potential solutions, test the solutions, and evaluate the results. Problem-solving schemas help us to select information and solve problems. Algorithms are formulas for solving problems, while heuristics are general problem-solving strategies that we employ to solve problems. Means-ends analysis, which can involve the generation of subgoals, is used to move us from an initial state to a desired goal state. The representativeness heuristic is used to determine whether a new stimulus is a member of a particular class or category, while the availability heuristic can bias our perceptions by focusing on what is available in our memories. Similar to belief bias is the confirmation bias, by which we search only for information that supports our beliefs. Yet another problem with problem solving is functional fixedness, which involves being unable to think about alternative uses for an object. On the other hand, divergent thinking and incubation can aid problem solving.

Intelligence

Intelligence is a concept that refers to individual differences in the ability to acquire knowledge, to think and reason effectively, and to deal adaptively with the environment. The measurement of mental abilities was begun by French psychologist Alfred Binet. He assumed that mental abilities developed with age and that the rate at which people gain mental competence is a characteristic of the person and is stable over time. German psychologist William Stern developed the idea of the intelligence quotient (IQ), which was originally expressed as the ratio mental age/chronological age x 100. In the United States, Lewis Terman and David Wechsler developed the most prominent IQ tests. Other tests that measure mental abilities are achievement tests, which measure learning, and aptitude tests, which measure potential for future learning and performance.

There are standards for psychological tests to be considered good tests. Reliability refers to the consistency of measurement while validity refers to whether a test is measuring what it is supposed to measure. Test-retest reliability, internal consistency, and interjudge reliability are ways of measuring reliability, while construct validity, content validity, and predictive validity are all measures of validity. A third requirement for good tests is standardization.

The nature of intelligence is a widely debated topic in psychology. Charles Spearman argued for one general factor that he called "g" which he argued underlies all mental abilities. Thurstone argued for seven distinct primary mental abilities. Cattell and Horn argued that intelligence is of two types, crystallized and fluid. Crystallized intelligence consists of the ability to apply existing knowledge while fluid intelligence consists of the ability to deal with novel situations. In that tradition, Robert Sternberg has developed a triarchic theory of intelligence. Sternberg suggests that intelligence consists of planning and regulating task behaviour, executing behavioural strategies, and encoding and storing information. Finally, emotional intelligence refers to the abilities to read and respond to others' emotions appropriately, to motivate oneself, and to be aware of and to control one's own emotions.

Heredity and environment both influence intelligence. The reaction range for intelligence, or any trait for that matter, refers to the range of possibilities that the genetic code allows. Studies of ethnic group differences show that African-Americans score, on average, 12-15 IQ points below the White-American average, while Asian-Americans score, on average, above the White-American mean. Hispanic-Americans score, on average, roughly the same as White-Americans. Studies of African-Americans have shown that the mean differences with White-Americans have declined over the past 25 years as greater educational and vocational opportunities for African-Americans have emerged, suggesting an environmental component to group differences in intelligence. Sex differences in cognitive abilities have also been discovered. Males perform better on spatial tasks and tasks involving mathematical reasoning. Females perform better on tests of perceptual speed, verbal fluency, mathematical calculation, and precise manual tasks. Finally, about 3-5 percent of the North American population is disabled, requiring special help, while the intellectually gifted also need special educational opportunities.

Chapter Outline

Language
    The Nature and Structure of Language
        Surface and Deep Structure
        Language From the Bottom Up
    Acquiring a Language
        Biological Foundations
        Social Learning Processes
        Bilingualism: Learning a Second Language
    Linguistic Influences on Thinking
    Concepts and Propositions
        Research Frontiers: Can Animals Acquire Human Language?

Reasoning and Problem Solving
    Reasoning
        Stumbling Blocks in Reasoning
    Problem Solving
        Understanding, or Framing, the Problem
        Generating Potential Solutions
        Testing the Solutions
        Evaluating Results
        Problem-Solving Schemas
        Algorithms and Heuristics
        Uncertainty, Heuristics, and Decision Making
        Confirmation Bias
        Psychological Applications: Guidelines for Creative Problem Solving

Intelligence
    Intelligence in Historical Perspective
        Sir Francis Galton: Quantifying Mental Ability
        Alfred Binet's Mental Tests
        The Stanford-Binet and Wechsler Scales
        Group Tests of Aptitude and Achievement
    Scientific Standards for Psychological Tests
        Reliability
        Validity
        Standardization and Norms
    The Nature of Intelligence
        The Psychometric Approach: The Structure of Intellect
        Cognitive Process Approaches: Processes Underlying Intelligent Thinking
        Brain Size and Intelligence: Is Bigger Better?
    Influences on Intelligence
        Cultural and Group Differences in Intelligence
        Beliefs, Expectations, and Cognitive Performance
        Research Foundations: Gender and Racial Stereotypes, Self-Concept, and Cognitive Performance
    Extremes of Intelligence
        The Cognitively Disabled
        The Intellectually Gifted

Problem-Based Learning

Autism and Savants
http://www.naar.org
National Alliance for Autism Research-This site contains journal information and links to other sites.

http://groups.msn.com/TheAutismHomePage
The Autism Home Page-This website contains general information about autism as well as links to a large bibliography of journal articles. This site also includes information about Savant Syndrome.

Disabilities and Giftedness
http://ericec.org
ERIC Clearinghouse on Disabilities and Gifted Education-This site contains general information about disabilities and gifted education, a database and many links to other sites.

Multiple Intelligence
http://surfaquarium.com/MI/
Walter McKenzie's Multiple Intelligence Page-This site contains simple and general information on multiple intelligence. It's strength is its links to a number of entertaining and interesting demonstrations and tests.

Key Terms: *Write the letter of the definition next to the term in the space provided.*

Language

1. ___ concepts
2. _e_ deep structure
3. _q_ displacement
4. ___ imaginal thought
5. _a_ language
6. ___ linguistic relativity hypothesis
7. _l_ mental representations
8. _h_ morphemes
9. _m_ motoric thought
10. _g_ phonemes
11. ___ propositional thought
12. ___ propositions
13. ___ prototypes
14. ___ semantics
15. ___ surface structure
16. ___ syntax
17. _i_ telegraphic speech

a. includes images, ideas, concepts, and principles
b. consists of a system of symbols and rules for combining symbols
c. consists of the way symbols are combined within a given language
d. rules of grammar
e. the underlying meaning of combined symbols
f. rules for connecting symbols to what they represent
g. the smallest units of sound that are recognized as separate in a given language
h. the smallest units of meaning in a language
i. two-word sentences uttered by two-year-old children
j. belief that language determines what we are capable of thinking
k. thought that expresses a statement
l. thought that consists of images
m. thought that relates to mental representations of movement
n. statements that express facts
o. basic units of semantic memory
p. the most typical and familiar member of a category
q. the feature of language that indicates that past, future, and imaginary events and objects that are not physically present can be symbolically represented

Reasoning and Problem Solving

1. ___ algorithms
2. ___ availability heuristic
3. ___ belief bias
4. ___ confirmation bias
5. ___ deductive reasoning
6. ___ divergent thinking
7. ___ functional fixedness
8. ___ heuristics
9. ___ incubation
10. ___ inductive reasoning
11. ___ means-ends analysis
12. ___ mental set
13. ___ problem-solving schemas
14. ___ representativeness heuristic
15. ___ subgoal analysis

a. reasoning from general principles to a conclusion about a specific case

b. reasoning involving developing a general principle from specific facts

c. the tendency to abandon logical rules in favour of our own personal beliefs

d. the tendency to stick to solutions that have worked in the past

e. mental blueprints for selecting information and solving specialized classes of problems

f. formulas or procedures that automatically generate correct solutions

g. general problem-solving strategies that we apply to certain classes of situations

h. a strategy by which we identify differences between the present situation and one's desired state and then make changes to reduce the difference

i. attacking a large problem by forming subgoals

j. used to infer how closely something or someone is to a prototype

k. leads us to pass judgements and decisions based on the availability of information in memory

l. tendency to look only for information that will confirm our beliefs

m. the generation of novel ideas that depart from the norm

n. the tendency to be blind of new ways to use an object

o. not working on a problem for a while, after which a flash of insight occurs

Intelligence

1. ___ achievement test
2. ___ aptitude test
3. ___ cognitive process theories
4. ___ construct validity
5. ___ content validity
6. ___ crystallized intelligence
7. ___ emotional intelligence
8. ___ factor analysis
9. ___ fluid intelligence

a. individual differences in the ability to acquire knowledge, think, reason effectively. and respond adaptively

b. mental age/chronological age x 100

c. a test designed to find out how much someone has learned

d. a method for measuring potential for future learning and performance

e. a method for measuring individual differences related to a psychological concept based on a sample of relevant behaviour in a scientifically designed and controlled condition

f. consistency of measurement

g. consistency measured by giving a test twice to the same group of participants and correlating the scores

h. consistency of measurement within a test itself

i. how well a test measures what it is designed to measure

10. ___ intelligence

11. ___ intelligence quotient

12. ___ interjudge reliability

13. ___ internal consistency

14. ___ knowledge acquisition components

15. ___ mental age

16. ___ metacomponents

17. ___ normal distribution

18. ___ norms

19. ___ performance components

20. ___ predictive validity

21. ___ primary mental abilities

22. ___ psychological test

23. ___ psychometrics

24. ___ reaction range

25. ___ reliability

26. ___ savants

27. ___ standardization

28. ___ test-retest reliability

29. ___ triarchic theory of intelligence

30. ___ validity

j. the degree to which a test is measuring discriminant validity

k. whether the items on a test measure all the knowledge and skills that are assumed to comprise the construct of interest

l. determined by how highly test scores correlate with a criterion

m. creating a well-controlled environment for administering a test and determining norms

n. provide a basis for comparing an individual's score with others' scores

o. a bell-shaped curve of scores

p. the statistical study of psychological tests

q. a statistical tool that analyzes patterns of correlations between test scores to discover clusters of measures

r. Thurstone's seven distinct abilities

s. the ability to apply previously acquired knowledge to current problems

t. the ability to deal with novel problem-solving situations

u. involves abilities to read and respond to other's emotions appropriately, to motivate oneself, and to be aware of and to control one's emotions

v. people disabled in a general sense who have exceptional skills in some areas

w. theory addressing both the cognitive processes involved in intelligence and the forms that intelligence can take

x. higher-order processes used to plan and regulate task performance

y. mental processes used to perform a task

z. processes that help us encode and store information

aa. the range of possibilities that the genetic code allows for a trait

bb. theories that explain why people differ in cognitive skills

cc. consistency of measurement when different people score the same test

dd. the level of mental performance that is characteristic at a particular chronological age

Review at a Glance: *Write the term that best fits the blank to review what you learned in this chapter.*

Language

Humans have a remarkable ability to represent the world through symbols. (1) _____ _____ take a variety of forms, including images, ideas, concepts, and principles. (2) _____ consists of a system of symbols and rules for combining those symbols in ways that can produce an infinite number of possible messages or meanings. Language is symbolic and can represent the present as well as past, future, and imaginary events and objects, the latter of which is a feature of language called (3) _____. Language has both structure and rules. The (4) _____ structure of a language consists of the way symbols are combined within a given language. The rules for such combination are called the (5) _____ of a language. The underlying meaning of the combined symbols is called (6) _____ structure. Human languages have a hierarchical structure. The smallest units of sound that are recognized as separate in a given language are called (7) _____, while the smallest units of meaning in a language are called (8) _____. Language can influence how we think. Benjamin Lee Whorf, in his (9) _____ _____ hypotheses, argues that language actually <u>determines</u> what we are capable of thinking. Thinking may be considered to be the "internal language of the mind." Verbal sentences that we hear are called (10) _____ thought. Images that we can "see" in our minds are called (11) _____ thought, while (12) _____ thought relates to mental representations of motor movements. Much of our thinking, in fact, occurs in terms of statements that express facts, which are called (13) _____. We seem to understand the world, in part, by understanding concepts. According to Rosch (1977), concepts are defined by (14) _____, the most familiar and typical members of a category.

Reasoning and Problem Solving

Two types of reasoning affect our abilities to make decisions and solve problems. (15) _____ reasoning involves reasoning from general principles to a conclusion about a specific case, while (16) _____ reasoning involves starting with specific facts and developing a general principle from them. To solve problems, we often employ (17) _____ _____ _____, which are step-by-step scripts for selecting information and solving specialized classes of problems. Formulas that automatically generate correct solutions are called (18) _____. Shortcut problem-solving strategies that we often employ rather than algorithms to solve problems are called (19) _____. One type of heuristic is (20) _____ _____ _____, during which we identify differences between the desired state and our present state and make changes to reduce the differences. Often this strategy involves (21) _____ analysis, by which people form intermediate steps toward a problem solution. Another heuristic allows us to infer how closely something or someone fits our prototype for a particular class, or concept. This type of heuristic is called the (22) _____ heuristic. A heuristic that leads us to base judgements and decisions on the availability of information in memory is called the (23) _____ heuristic.

Intelligence

In the early days of mental testing, examiners like Alfred Binet tried to determine whether a child was performing at the correct mental level for children of that age. The result of the testing was a score called the (24) _____ age. German psychologist William Stern developed the (25) _____ _____, based on the ratio of mental age to chronological age. Psychologists today distinguish between tests that measure how much someone has learned, or (26) _____ tests, and tests that measure potential for future learning and performance, or (27) _____ tests. Good tests have both reliability and validity. The consistency of measurement of a test is called (28) _____. One way to measure reliability, known as (29) _____ _____ reliability, is to administer the same measure to the same group of participants on two different occasions and to correlate the scores. Determining the consistency of measurement within the test itself is known as (30) _____ _____. (31) _____ refers to how well a test actually measures what it is supposed to measure. (32) _____ validity refers to how well a measure can predict some other criterion, like a future behaviour. Creating a standardized environment and (33) _____, helps to meet the third measurement requirement for a good test, (34) _____. There is great debate about the nature of intelligence. British psychologist Charles Spearman believed that there is a general factor known as (35) _____, in mental abilities. American psychologist L. L. Thurstone argued that there are seven distinct, or (36) _____ _____ abilities that underly human mental performance. Cattell and Horn suggest two types of intelligence. (37) _____ intelligence involves the ability to apply previously acquired knowledge to solve new problems while (38) _____ intelligence is used to deal with novel problem-solving situations. (39) _____ _____ has argued for multiple intelligences. One of the newer theories of intelligence is that it is not purely cognitive. An intelligence that involves the abilities to read and respond to others' emotions appropriately, to motivate oneself, and to be aware of and to control one's own emotions is called (40) _____ intelligence. Robert Sternberg has developed a (41) _____ theory of intelligence. He suggests that people use higher-order processes, or (42) _____, to plan and regulate task performance, (43) _____ components to actually do the task, and (44) _____ _____ components to encode and store information.

Apply What You Know

1. Examining the female-male differences in problem-solving you see on p. 421, use both evolutionary psychological theory and theories of socialization to explain why those differences exist. Use Study Sheets 9.1 and 9.2.

2. Examining ethnic differences in intelligence, use theories of socialization to explain why those differences exist, and discuss the findings that support this theoretical explanation.

Internet Scavenger Hunt

1. Find several intelligence tests on the WWW. Evaluate whether they meet the criteria for a sound psychological test. Use Study Sheet 9.3.

2. Thinking about Sternberg's triarchic theory of intelligence, describe how the items on the tests you located measure up to the criteria of being free of cultural, ethnic, and sex bias.

Practice Test

Multiple Choice Items: *Please write the letter corresponding to your answer in the space to the left of each item.*

___a___ 1. The three essential properties that define ___ are that it is symbolic, it has structure, and it is generative.

    a. language
    b. a prototype
    c. fluid intelligence
    d. a heuristic

___a___ 2. Consider the statement, "Last night, I shot an elephant in my pajamas." Since this sentence has two different interpretations (the pajamas could be worn by the man OR they could be worn by the elephant), this means that this sentence has _____ and _____.

    a. two different deep structures; one surface structure
    b. two different surface structures; one deep structure
    c. two different surface structures; two different deep structures
    d. one surface structure; one deep structure

___d___ 3. Prior to 6 months of age, infants around the world are able to vocalize _____ but at about 6 months of age they begin vocalizing _____.

    a. only 5-10 phonemes; only the phonemes associated with their native language
    b. only the phonemes associated with their native language; the phonemes of all languages
    c. only 5-10 phonemes; the phonemes of all languages
    d. the phonemes of all languages; only the phonemes associated with their native language

___b___ 4. While at the park, 19-month-old Suzy points to the swing set and says, "Push swing!" After she has had enough and wants to leave, she turns to her father and says, "Go car." Utterances such as these are called _____.

    a. baby talk
    b. telegraphic speech
    c. motherese
    d. child-speak

___c___ 5. Many _____ are difficult to describe in words but we often can define them using _____, which are typical and familiar members of a particular class.

    a. prototypes; concepts
    b. concepts; propositions
    c. concepts; prototypes
    d. phonemes; morphemes

_____ 6. One morning, John decides to have oatmeal for breakfast and he performs very well on a math test that he takes later that day. He doesn't think too much about this until a few weeks later when he does very well on an English test and recalls that he had oatmeal for breakfast before this test too. He concludes that eating oatmeal in the morning helps him to perform better on exams. This example **best demonstrates** the _____.

a. use of the representativeness heuristic
b. process of inductive reasoning
c. use of problem-solving schemas
d. process of deducting reason

_____ 7. You are hungry and would like something to eat. You decide to look through the pantry and see a box of macaroni and cheese that looks good. Without really thinking about it, you know how to do all the various steps involved in making this meal such as filling a pot with water, boiling the water, cooking the pasta, mixing in the cheese sauce, and finding a plate on which to put the finished meal. Based on the discussion in the text, this type of specialized knowledge is **best considered** as an example of _____.

a. a problem solving schema
b. a mental set
c. deductive reasoning
d. a norm

_____ 8. According to Tversky and Kanheman, the errors in logic that occur in response to the "Linda the feminist bank teller" problem (where participants think it is more likely that Linda is a feminist bank teller than simply a bank teller) are due to the fact that they confuse _____.

a. representativeness with availability
b. representativeness with probability
c. availability with confirmation bias
d. availability with probability

_____ 9. Shelley is attempting to solve a problem and at this point in time, she is trying to generate as many solutions as possible and trying to incorporate new and unusual ideas into her potential solutions. Shelley is engaged in _____ thinking.

a. convergent
b. propositional
c. divergent
d. confirmatory

_____ 10. Suppose you take a psychological test and receive a score of 82 (out of a possible 100) on it. Imagine that you take the same test again 2 days later and this time you receive a score of 46. Other people who have taken the test twice have also had similar positive and negative changes in scores. These results mean that this test has _____.

a. high internal consistency
b. low internal consistency
c. low test-retest reliability
d. high test-retest reliability

_____a_____ 11. The ability to apply previously learned knowledge to current problems that heavily involves verbal reasoning and factual knowledge is called _____ intelligence.

a. crystallized
b. fluid
c. psychometric
d. deductive

_____a_____ 12. Compared to other existing theories of intelligence, Gardner's theory of multiple intelligences is **most unique** in that he _____.

a. argues that additional abilities such as musical talents and interpersonal skills should also be considered part of intelligence
b. believes that intelligence consists of several distinct abilities
c. asserts that there are only 3 different types of intelligence: linguistic, mathematical, and visual-spatial
d. believes that a general "g" factor was largely responsible for intelligence

_____a_____ 13. According to Sternberg's triarchic theory, the types of intelligence that can be demanded by the environment are _____.

a. mathematical, linguistic, and visual-spatial
b. musical, bodily-kinesthetic, and personal
c. crystallized and fluid
d. analytical, practical, and creative

_____a_____ 14. Highly debated research by Philippe Rushton examined racial differences on over 60 measures including intelligence and a host of physical and social variables. He suggested that there was a consistent pattern with individuals of _____ decent scoring the highest, those of _____ decent the lowest and _____ fell in the middle.

a. East Asian; African; Caucasian
b. Caucasian; East Asian; African
c. African; Caucasian; East Asian
d. Caucasian; African; East Asian

_____A_____ 15. The fact that IQ differences between black and white students has _____ in recent years is generally taken as evidence that this difference may largely be due to _____ factors.

a. decreased; unchangeable genetic
b. increased; unchangeable genetic
c. remained the same; changeable environmental
d. decreased; changeable environmental

__d__ ✓ 16. Approximately _____ percent of the Canadian population can speak both English and French.

    a. 2
    b. 44
    c. 34
    d. 16

X __b__ 17. Snoopy, dreaming once more of being a World War I flying ace, sits on top of his doghouse and flies once more into battle against the evil Red Baron. Snoopy's unique use of his doghouse suggests that he is **not** suffering from _____.

    a. problem-solving set
    b. functional fixedness
    c. heuristics
  ✓ d. deep structure

__d__ ✓ 18. If Captain Picard leaves Deep Space Nine at 0900 hours and travels at Warp 4 in his shuttlecraft, he can rendezvous with the Starship Enterprise in 4.2 hours. However, in order to reach the ship so quickly, he would have to travel through the Neutral Zone, and his presence would undoubtedly be noticed by Romulan warships, which would attack and destroy his craft. Thus, Picard realizes that he will have to take another route to the ship and thus devises what comes to be known as the "Picard loop" to get around the neutral zone. The Captain has applied _____.

    a. crystallized intelligence ability
    b. an algorithm
    c. deductive reasoning skill
  ✓ d. means-ends analysis

__a__ 19. A step-by-step problem strategy for solving a problem or achieving a goal is called a(n) _____.

    a. algorithm
    b. heuristic
    c. exemplar
    d. prototype

X __b__ 20. Having given up his bumbling ways to become a high school teacher at alma mater Riverdale High, the formerly bungling Jughead looks to former teacher Miss Grundy as his role model, believing that she is the ideal representative of the category "teacher." Jughead would be said to be employing the _____ model of categorization.

X C
    a. classical
    b. prototype
    c. exemplar
    d. functional

_a_ 21. Salovey & Mayer (1990) argue that "emotional intelligence" includes _____.

    a. being able to recognize the emotions of others
    b. a lack of self-control
    c. not examining your feelings when making decisions
    d. a need for power

_____ 22. The education act in all provinces in Canada states that

    a. disadvantaged students must be integrated into the regular classroom.
    b. gifted students must be integrated into the regular classroom.
    c. both disadvantaged and gifted students must be integrated into the regular classroom.
    d. disadvantaged students must be segregated from the regular classroom.

_b_ 23. The smallest units of meaning in a language are called ____.

    a. phonemes
    b. morphemes
    c. surface structures
    d. deep structures

_d_ 24. The fact that all adult languages throughout the world have a common underlying deep structure suggests that _____.

    a. deep structure is more important than surface structure
    b. phonemes are more important than morphemes
    c. morphemes are more important than phonemes
    d. language has a biological basis

_a_ 25. Reasoning from the "top down" is called _____ reasoning.

    a. deductive
    b. inductive
    c. schematic
    d. propositional

_a_ 26. Based on the fact that he has seen 10,776 murders on TV in the last week, LaWanda believes that she is far more likely to be murdered than to die of old age. LaWanda seems to be ____.

    a. using the representativeness heuristic
    b. applying an algorithm
    c. using the availability heuristic
    d. subject to the confirmation bias

√ _c_ 27. According to Stern's work in Germany, ____ was originally defined as mental age/chronological age x 100.

    a. aptitude
    b. achievement
√ c. IQ
    d. problem-solving ability

_b_ 28. A(n) ____ test is thought to measure an applicant's potential for future learning and performance.

    a. achievement
    b. aptitude
√ c. intelligence
    d. psychological

_a_ 29. The statistical study of psychological tests is called ____.

    a. psychometrics
    b. standardization
    c. the establishment of norms
√ d. the "g" factor

_b_ 30. What percentage of the North American population are classified as cognitively disabled?

24/30

    a. .5
    b. 3-5
    c. 10-12
    d. 20-25

True/False Items: *Write T or F in the space provided to the left of each item.*

_____ 1. The surface structure of a language consists of the way symbols are combined within a given language.

_____ 2. Phonemes are the smallest units of sound that are recognized as separate in a given language.

_____ 3. The linguistic relativity hypothesis suggests that language determines how we think.

_____ 4. The most typical and familiar members of a concept are called prototypes.

_____ 5. Reasoning from general principles to a conclusion about a specific case is called inductive reasoning.

_____ 6. Using problem-solving schemas to solve problems is called a mental set.

_____ 7. The availability heuristic is involved in exaggerating the likelihood that something will occur because it easily comes to mind.

_____ 8. Content validity refers to how highly test scores correlate with criterion measures.

_____ 9. Fluid intelligence refers to the ability to deal with novel problem-solving situations for which personal experience does not provide a solution.

_____ 10. According to Sternberg's triarchic theory of intelligence, metacomponents are used to encode and store information.

Short Answer Questions

1. What is the difference between the surface and deep structure of a language?

2. What is a proposition?

3. What are algorithms and heuristics?

4. Describe the three scientific standards for sound psychological tests.

5. What abilities comprise emotional intelligence?

Essay Questions

1. What processes, both biological and environmental, are involved in learning a language?

2. Describe three major stumbling blocks in the reasoning process.

3. Describe the general process involved in problem-solving.

4. Describe Sternberg's triarchic theory of intelligence.

5. How do both heredity and environment seem to affect intelligence?

Study Sheet 9.1 Male-Female Differences in Problem-Solving

List of Problem-Solving Tasks Favouring Women	Evolutionary Explanation	Sociocultural Explanation

Study Sheet 9.2 Male-Female Differences in Problem-Solving

List of Problem-Solving Tasks Favouring Men	Evolutionary Explanation	Sociocultural Explanation

Study Sheet 9.3
WWW Intelligence Tests

URL (Web Address) of Test:

http://

Reliability:

Validity:

Standardization:

Answer Keys

Answer Key for Key Terms

Language

1. o	6. j	11. k	16. d
2. e	7. a	12. n	17. i
3. q	8. h	13. p	
4. l	9. m	14. f	
5. b	10. g	15. c	

Reasoning and Problem Solving

1. f	2. k	3. c	4. l
5. a	6. m	7. n	8. g
9. o	10. b	11. h	12. d
13. e	14. j	15. i	

Intelligence

1. c	2. d	3. bb	4. j
5. k	6. s	7. u	8. q
9. t	10. a	11. b	12. cc
13. h	14. z	15. dd	16. x
17. o	18. n	19. y	20. l
21. r	22. e	23. p	24. aa
25. f	26. v	27. m	28. g
29. w	30. i		

Answer Key for Review at a Glance

1. Mental representations
2. Language
3. displacement
4. surface
5. syntax
6. deep
7. phonemes
8. morphemes
9. linguistic relativity
10. propositional
11. imaginal
12. motoric
13. propositions
14. prototypes
15. deductive
16. inductive
17. problem solving schemas
18. algorithms
19. heuristics
20. means ends analysis
21. subgoal
22. representativeness
23. availability
24. mental
25. intelligence quotient
26. achievement
27. aptitude
28. reliability
29. test retest
30. internal consistency
31. Validity
32. Predictive
33. norms
34. standardization
35. g
36. primary mental
37. Crystallized
38. fluid
39. Howard Gardner
40. emotional
41. triarchic
42. metacomponents
43. performance
44. knowledge acquisition

Answer Key for Practice Test Multiple Choice Questions

1. a	11. a	21. a
2. a	12. a	22. c
3. d	13. d	23. b
4. b	14. a	24. d
5. c	15. d	25. a
6. b	16. d	26. c
7. a	17. b	27. c
8. b	18. d	28. b
9. c	19. a	29. a
10. c	20. c	30. b

Answer Key for Practice Test True/False Questions

1.	T	6.	F
2.	T	7.	T
3.	T	8.	F
4.	T	9.	T
5.	F	10.	F

Answer Key for Practice Test Short Answer Questions

1. Surface structure consists of the way symbols are combined within a given language. Deep structure refers to the underlying meaning of the combined symbols.

2. A proposition is a statement that expresses a fact. All propositions consist of concepts that contain a subject and a predicate.

3. Algorithms are formulas or procedures that automatically generate correct solutions. Heuristics are general problem-solving strategies that we apply to certain classes of situations. They are mental shortcuts that may or may not provide correct solutions.

4. There are three major standards for sound psychological tests. Reliability refers to the consistency of measurement. Validity measures the extent to which a test measures what it is designed to measure. Standardization has two facets: creating a standardized environment for testing and the establishment of norms for comparison.

5. Emotional intelligence involves the abilities to read others' emotions accurately, to respond to them appropriately, to motivate oneself, to be aware of one's emotions, and to regulate and to control one's own emotional responses.

Answer Key for Practice Test Essay Questions

1. Some linguists believe that there is a sensitive period during which language is most easily learned, suggesting a biological foundation for the acquisition of language. This period typically extends from infancy to puberty or early adolescence. In terms of social learning, parents influence their children's acquisition of language in a variety of ways. Parents use *motherese* to maintain their children's interest and attract their attention. Rewarding of appropriate vocalizations and nonrewarding of inappropriate ones have been hypothesized to influence acquisition. Such rewards may focus more on deep structure than on grammar.

2. Sometimes we can be distracted by irrelevant information. The ability to pay attention only to relevant information is a key to effective problem-solving. A second problem in the reasoning process involves failure to apply deductive rules. The use of formal logic and algorithms such as mathematical formulas can help us solve problems more accurately. A third problem is called belief bias. Belief bias is the tendency to abandon logical rules in favour of our own personal beliefs.

3. The first step in problem-solving is understanding, or framing, the problem. If we frame a problem poorly at the beginning, incorrect problem-solving strategies are likely to be followed. The second step involves generating potential solutions. To do that, we might first determine what procedures will be considered and then use those procedures to test whether they are helpful in moving us toward solution. If a procedure is not useful, we move to another procedure and test it. The final stage of problem-solving involves evaluating the results.

4. Robert Sternberg's triarchic theory of intelligence addresses the psychological processes involved in intelligence and the different forms that intelligence takes. It is a three-component model. Metacomponents are higher-order cognitive processes used to plan and regulate performance on a task. Performance components are used to perform a task. Knowledge-acquisition components allow us to learn from experience, store information, and combine new insights with previously acquired knowledge. Sternberg has stressed that we should look at analytical intelligence, which involves academically-oriented knowledge, practical intelligence, which refers to the skills needed to cope with everyday demands, and creative intelligence, which helps us to deal with novel problems. The three components of the triarchic model are likely involved in all three kinds of intelligence Sternberg proposes.

5. There is evidence that genetic factors play an important role in intelligence. For example, monozygotic twins seem to be more alike in intelligence than are dizygotic twins. The reaction range for intelligence, as well as that for other traits, provides upper and lower limits for the development of intelligence, meaning that intelligence is not fixed at birth and is influenced as well by environmental factors. Heredity and environmental factors such as culture, ethnicity, and parental influences interact in complex ways to influence intelligence.

Chapter 10. Motivation and Emotion

Learning Objectives

10.1   Define and differentiate motivation and emotion.

10.2   Compare and contrast the various perspectives on motivation, including instinct theories, drive theory, incentive and expectancy theories, psychodynamic theories, and humanistic theories.

10.3   Describe what is meant by the concept of homeostasis, and how the concept of homeostasis was developed into drive reduction theory of motivation.

10.4   Describe set point theory and how it regulates the physiological signals involved in the initiation and cessation of eating.

10.5   Describe the brain mechanisms involved in hunger and satiety, including the role of leptin.

10.6   Identify several environmental and cultural factors that influence eating, including factors that pressure women feel to be thin.

10.7   Describe the roles of genetics and environmental factors in obesity.

10.8   Describe the relation between dieting and weight loss.

10.9   Describe the symptoms and causes of anorexia and bulimia.

10.10 Outline how sexual behaviours and attitudes changed in the last half-century.

10.11 Explain the stages of the sexual response cycle.

10.12 Describe the organizational and activational effects of sex hormones.

10.13 Outline the psychological factors that stimulate or inhibit sexual functioning, including cultural norms and environmental stimuli.

10.14 According to social learning and catharsis principles, explain how viewing pornography affects sexual aggression.

10.15 Describe the determinants of sexual orientation, including both biological and environmental theories.

10.16 Explain what is meant by sensation seeking and why it conflicts with drive theory, and describe the biological basis of sensation seeking.

10.17 Describe the types of achievement goals associated with motives for success and fear of failure.

10.18 Explain why people with high versus low achievement needs select tasks that differ in difficulty.

10.19 Describe the effect of job enrichment and incentive programs in the workplace.

10.20 Differentiate the three main types of motivational conflict.

10.21   Name and describe the four major components of emotions, including the two classes of behavioural responses.

10.22   Describe what is known about the brain areas involved in emotion, concentrating on the role of the amygdala.

10.23   Describe the role of cognitive appraisals in emotion.

10.24   Describe the relation between fundamental emotional patterns of expression and both facial expressions of emotion and cultural display rules.

10.25   Describe the relations between emotional arousal, task complexity, and task performance.

10.26   Compare and contrast theories and research pertaining to emotion, including the James-Lange (somatic), Cannon-Bard, and Schachter-Singer (two-factor) explanations for emotional perception and labeling.

Chapter Overview

Perspectives on Motivation

Motivation is a process that influences the direction, persistence, and vigour of goal-directed behaviour. Instinct theories of motivation, prominent a century ago, soon gave way to other models. The body's biological systems are balanced to ensure survival. Homeostasis, a state of internal equilibrium, is important to maintain, and many behaviours may be motivated by the need to return to homeostasis. Drive theory assumed that physiological disruptions to homeostasis produce drives to reduce the tension caused by the disruptions. Incentive theories, on the other hand, focus attention on external stimuli as motivators of behaviour. According to expectancy x value theory, goal-directed behaviour is jointly determined by the person's expectation that a behaviour will lead to a goal and the value that the person places on the goal. Many cognitive theorists also distinguish between extrinsic motivation, which is motivation produced by the desire to obtain rewards and to avoid punishments, and intrinsic motivation, which is performing an activity for its own sake. Psychodynamic theorists suggest that unconscious motives, thoughts, and inner tensions are an important motivator of behaviour. Humanistic theorists such as Maslow stress need hierarchies, particularly the need to fulfill our potential, or self-actualization.

Hunger and Weight Regulation

The body monitors its energy supplies, and this information interacts with other signals to regulate food intake. Homeostatic mechanisms are designed to prevent us from running low on energy. Some researchers believe that there is a set point around which body weight is regulated. Studies of humans and rats show a temporary drop-rise in glucose patterns prior to experiencing hunger. As we eat, stomach and intestinal distention act as satiety signals, and peptides such as cholecystokinin stimulate brain receptors to decrease eating. Fat cells regulate food intake and weight by secreting leptin. Many parts of the brain also influence eating. Early studies indicated that the lateral hypothalamus seemed to be a "hunger-on" centre. The ventromedial hypothalamus seemed to be a "hunger-off" centre. However, modern research indicates that it is not that simple. Various neural circuits within the hypothalamus regulate food intake. Many of these pathways involve the paraventricular nucleus. Eating is also affected by psychological factors. Eating is positively reinforced by good taste and is negatively reinforced by hunger reduction. Beliefs, attitudes, habits, and psychological needs also affect food intake. Studies of obesity have indicated a strong genetic component. Eating disorders such as anorexia nervosa, where people severely restrict their food intake because of a fear of being fat, and bulimia nervosa, where the fear of being fat causes binging and purging, pose serious health problems.

Sensation-Seeking

The motivation to seek out stimulation and novelty is called sensation-seeking. Those higher in sensation-seeking tend to enjoy activities involving higher risks, are less likely to become depressed, and engage in a wider variety of sexual activities with more partners. High sensation-seekers may have a less "reactive" nervous system.

Sexual Motivation

People engage in sex for a variety of reasons. Secretions of gonadotropins from the pituitary glands affect the rate at which the sex organs secrete androgens and estrogens. These sex hormones have both organizational effects that direct the development of sex organs and activational effects that stimulate sexual desire and behaviour. Psychological factors like sexual fantasy can also trigger sexual arousal. The psychological meaning of sex depends strongly on cultural contexts and learning. Cultural norms influence what stimuli are sexually arousing and what sexual behaviours occur. Studies of pornography are controversial. Violent pornographic films seem to increase, at least temporarily, men's aggression toward women and may promote rape myths. Sexual orientation may have three dimensions: self-identity, sexual attraction, and actual sexual behaviour. Many researchers believe in a genetic basis for sexual orientation. Altering prenatal sex hormones can also influence sexual orientation. These findings, for human, though, are correlational and controversial.

Achievement Motivation

Need for achievement is influenced by both motive for success and fear of failure. Individual perceptions, family influences, and cultural influences all influence achievement motivation.

Motivation in the Workplace

People work for a number of different reasons, including money, personal accomplishment, opportunities for mastery, growth, and satisfying interpersonal relationships. Job enrichment programs attempt to increase people's intrinsic motivation to work. Employee participation in programs like management by objectives (MBO) is increasingly being stressed by industrial-organizational psychologists as an important way to increase worker motivation.

Motivational Conflict

Approach-approach, avoidance-avoidance, and approach-avoidance conflicts influence motivation through having to choose between two attractive alternatives, two unattractive alternatives, and attractive and unattractive aspects of the same goal respectively.

The Nature and Functions of Emotions

Emotions are positive or negative affect states consisting of a pattern of cognitive, physiological, and behavioural reactions to events that have relevance to important goals or motives. Emotions have important adaptive functions. Negative emotions may help us to narrow attention and actions to deal with a threatening situation. Positive emotions may help us to broaden our thinking and behaviour so that we explore, consider new ideas, try out new ways to achieve goals, play, and savour what we have. The emotions we have share four common features: they are responses to stimuli, they involve cognitive appraisal, they involve physiological responses, and they include behavioural tendencies. Innate biological factors and learning may both influence which eliciting stimuli elicit which emotions. Appraisal processes relate to what we think is desirable and undesirable. Culture can also affect appraisal.

Biological factors also play an important role in emotions. Subcortical structures such as the hypothalamus, amygdala, and other limbic system structures are particularly involved. The ability to regulate emotion depends heavily on the prefrontal cortex. Joseph LeDoux has discovered that the thalamus sends messages along two independent neural pathways: to the cortex and to the amygdala. This dual system means that emotional responses can occur both through cortex interpretation and through a more primitive system through the amygdala, which is likely important for survival. Left-hemisphere activation may underlie certain positive emotions, and right-hemisphere activation might influence negative ones. Such activation may also underlie subjective well-being.

Autonomic and hormonal processes may also influence emotions. Some basic emotions, such as anger and fear, show distinctive autonomic processes. The behavioural component of emotions involves expressive behaviours, or emotional displays. Modern evolutionary theorists stress the adaptive value of such displays and suggest that some fundamental emotional patterns may be innate. Paul Ekman's studies of emotional expressions have shown a wide degree of cross-cultural agreement in evaluations of expressions. The studies also show that different parts of the face provide the best clues for certain emotions and that women are generally more accurate judges of emotional expression. Different cultures have different display rules for emotions.

Interactions Among the Components of Emotion

According to the James-Lange theory of emotion, which today lives on as the somatic theory of emotion, bodily reactions produce perceptions of emotional states. An offshoot, the facial-feedback hypothesis, suggests that feedback to the brain from facial muscles produces emotions. The Cannon-Bard theory stresses the simultaneous messages sent by the thalamus to the cortex and the body's internal organs. Schachter's two-factor theory stresses cognitive appraisal of physiological arousal and situational cues leading to perception of an emotion.

Chapter Outline

Perspectives on Motivation
    Instinct Theory and Modern Evolutionary Psychology
    Homeostasis and Drive Theory
    Incentive and Expectancy Theories
    Psychodynamic and Humanistic Theories

Hunger and Weight Regulation
    The Physiology of Hunger
        Signals That Start and Terminate a Meal
        Signals That Regulate General Appetite and Weight Brain Mechanisms
    Psychological Aspects of Hunger
    Environmental and Cultural Factors
    Obesity
        Genes and Environment
        Dieting and Weight Loss
    Eating Disorders
        Causes of Anorexia and Bulimia
            Psychological Applications: The Battle to Control Eating and Weight

Sexual Motivation

    Sexual Behaviour: Patterns and Changes
    The Physiology of Sex
        The Sexual Response Cycle
        Hormonal Influences
    The Psychology of Sex
        Sexual Fantasy
        Desire, Arousal, and Sexual Dysfunction
    Cultural and Environmental Influences
        Cultural Norms
        Arousing Environmental Stimuli
        Pornography, Sexual Violence, and Sexual Attitudes
    Sexual Orientation
        Prevalence of Different Sexual Orientations
        Determinants of Sexual Orientation
            Research Frontiers: Sensation-Seeking

Achievement Motivation
    Motivation for Success: The Thrill of Victory
    Fear of Failure: The Agony of Defeat
    Achievement Needs and Situational Factors
    Family and Cultural Influences

Motivation in the Workplace
    Why Do People Work?
        Job Satisfaction and Performance
    Enhancing Work Motivation
        Enriching and Redesigning Jobs
        Modifying External Incentives

Goal-Setting and Management by Objectives

Motivational Conflict

The Nature and Functions of Emotions
      The Adaptive Value of Emotions
      The Nature of Emotions
            Eliciting Stimuli
            The Cognitive Component
            The Physiological Component
            The Behavioural Component

Interactions Among the Components of Emotion
      The James-Lange Somatic Theory
      The Cannon-Bard Theory
            The Role of Autonomic Feedback
            The Facial Feedback Hypothesis
      Cognitive-Affective Theories
            Research Foundations: Cognition-Arousal Relations

Problem-Based Learning

Lie Detection

http://www.polygraph.org
American Polygraph Association-This site is the home page for the American Polygraph Association.

http://dmoz.org/Science/Social_Sciences/Psychology/Forensics_and_Law/Brain_Fingerprinting
This site contains numerous letters and articles for and against brain fingerprinting. Unfortunately, there are no journal articles.

Sexuality

http://www.ssc.wisc.edu/ssss
The Society for the Scientific Study of Sexuality-This site contains information about numerous areas of sexuality, journal abstracts, employment opportunities, etc.

Key Terms: *Write the letter of the definition next to the term in the space provided.*

Perspectives on Motivation
Hunger and Weight Regulation
Sensation-Seeking

1. ___ anorexia nervosa

2. ___ bulimia nervosa

3. ___ CCK (cholecystokinin)
4. ___ drive theory

5. ___ expectancy x value
   theory

6. ___ extrinsic motivation

7. ___ glucose
8. ___ homeostasis

9. ___ incentives
10. ___ instinct
11. ___ intrinsic motivation
12. ___ leptin

13. ___ metabolism
14. ___ motivation

15. ___ need hierarchy

16. ___ paraventricular nucleus
    (PVN)
17. ___ self-actualization
18. ___ sensation-seeking

a. a process that influences the direction, persistence, and vigour of goal-directed behaviour

b. an inherited characteristic that automatically produces a particular response when the organism is exposed to a particular stimulus

c. a state of internal physiological equilibrium

d. theory that physiological disruptions to homeostasis produce states of internal tensions that motivate organisms

e. proposes that goal-directed behaviour is produced by a person's strength of expectation that behaviour will lead to a goal and the value the person places on the goal

f. performing an activity to obtain an external reward or to avoid a punishment

g. performing an activity for its own sake

h. a progression of needs, with deficiency needs at the bottom and growth needs at the top

i. the need to fulfill our potential

j. the body's rate of energy utilization

k. a simple sugar that is the body's major source of fuel

l. a peptide that stimulates brain receptors to terminate eating

m. a hormone that decreases appetite

n. a cluster of neurons packed with receptor sites for transmitters that stimulate or reduce appetite

o. disorder in which victims have an intense fear of being fat and thus severely restrict their food intake

p. disorder in which victims binge eat and then purge the food

q. the motivation to seek out stimulation and novelty

r. environmental stimuli that "pull" an organism toward a goal

Sexual Motivation
Achievement Motivation
Motivation in the Workplace
Motivational Conflict
The Nature and Functions of Emotions
Interactions Among the Components of Emotion

1.	___ androgens	a.	"masculine" sex hormones
2.	___ approach-approach conflict	b.	"feminine" sex hormones
3.	___ approach-avoidance conflict	c.	one's emotional and erotic preference for partners of a particular sex
4.	___ avoidance-avoidance conflict	d.	a four-stage pattern of sexual response
5.	___cognitive appraisal	e.	positive or negative affective states
6.	___display rules	f.	idea that facial muscular feedback to the brain plays a key role in the nature and intensity of emotion
7.	___emotions	g.	emotional displays
8.	___empathy	h.	behaviours directed at achieving a goal
9.	___estrogens	i.	innate patterns of emotion
10.	___expressive behaviours	j.	theory that emotions are caused by arousal and cognitive labelling
11.	___ facial feedback hypothesis	k.	an instrument that measures physiological responses
12.	___fundamental emotional patterns	l.	occurs when others' emotional displays can evoke similar emotional reactions in us
13.	___instrumental behaviours	m.	norms for emotional expression within a given culture
14.	___job enrichment	n.	theory that tensing facial muscles alters the temperature of blood entering the brain, thus influencing emotion
15.	___ management by objectives	o.	interpretation of eliciting stimuli
16.	___need for achievement	p.	represents the desire to accomplish tasks and to attain standards of excellence
17.	___polygraph	q.	programs that attempt to increase intrinsic motivation
18.	___sexual motivation	r.	combines goal setting with employee participation and feedback
19.	___sexual response cycle	s.	involves choosing between two attractive alternatives
20.	___somatic theory of emotions	t.	a person must choose between two undesirable alternatives
21.	___two-factor theory of emotion	u.	involves being attracted to and repulsed by the same goal
22.	___vascular theory of emotional feedback	v.	theory that bodily reactions cause our emotions

Review at a Glance: *Write the term that best fits the blank to review what you learned in this chapter.*

Perspectives on Motivation

(1) _____ is a process that influences the direction, persistence, and vigour of goal-directed behaviour. An inherited characteristic, common to all members of a species, that automatically produces a particular response is called an (2) _____. According to Hull's (3) _____ theory, states of internal tension motivate people to behave in ways that return them to (4) _____. (5) _____ motivation involves external rewards to motivate behaviour, while (6) _____ motivation involves performing an activity for its own sake. Abraham Maslow proposed the concept of a (7) _____ _____, a progression of needs from deficiency needs at the bottom to (8) _____ _____, the need to fulfill our potential, at the top.

Hunger and Weight Reduction

The body's rate of energy (or caloric) utilization is called (9) _____. When we eat, digestive enzymes break food down into various nutrients, including (10) _____, a simple sugar that is the body's major source of fuel. Several hormones called peptides help to terminate a meal. For example, (11) _____ is released into the bloodstream by the small intestine as food arrives in the stomach, travels to the brain, and stimulates brain receptors. A hormone that decreases appetite is called (12) _____. Early studies of the brain indicated "hunger-on" and "hunger-off" centres. A proposed "hunger-on" centre of the brain is called the (13) _____ _____. A proposed "hunger-off" centre is called the (14) _____ hypothalamus. However, later research did not support the early ideas. A cluster of neurons that are packed with receptor sites for various transmitters that stimulate or reduce appetite is called the (15) _____ nucleus. Victims of (16) _____ _____ have an intense fear of being fat and severely restrict their food intake to the point of self-starvation. People who suffer from (17) _____ _____ are also overconcerned about being fat but binge eat and then purge the food.

Sexual Motivation

A four-stage pattern of sexual response is called the (18) _____ _____ _____. The "masculine" sex hormones, or (19) _____, and the "feminine" sex hormones, or (20) _____, affect sexual behaviour. (21) _____ _____ refers to one's emotional and erotic preference for partners of a particular sex.

Sensation-Seeking

The motivation to seek out stimulation and novelty is called (22) _____ _____.

Achievement Motivation

(23) _____ _____ _____ represents the desire to accomplish tasks and attain standards of excellence. A negatively oriented motivation to avoid failure is called (24) _____ of failure.

Motivation in the Workplace

Reflecting Maslow's humanistic theory, (25) _____ _____ programs attempt to increase (26) _____ motivation by making jobs more fulfilling and providing workers with opportunities for growth. Another important development in the workplace is called (27) _____ _____ _____, which combines goal setting by management with employee participation and feedback.

Motivational Conflict

Motivational goals sometimes conflict with each other. An (28) _____ - _____ conflict involves opposition between two attractive alternatives, an (29) _____ - _____ conflict involves a choice between two undesirable alternatives, and an (30) _____ - _____ conflict involves being attracted to and repulsed by the same goal.

The Nature and Functions of Emotions

(31) _____ are positive or negative affect states consisting of a pattern of cognitive, physiological, and behavioural reactions to events that have relevance to important goals or motives. Emotional responses result from our interpretation or (32) _____ _____ of stimuli. We often infer an internal state in another person by examining his or her emotional displays, or (33) _____ behaviours. Others' emotional displays can evoke similar emotional responses in us, a process known as (34) _____. Modern evolutionary theorists stress the adaptive value of emotional expression. Humans have innate emotional patterns, which are also known as (35) _____ _____ patterns. Culture also affects emotional displays. The norms for emotional expression within a given culture are called (36) _____ _____. Emotional reactions may give rise to (37) _____ behaviours, which are directed at achieving a goal.

Interactions Among the Components of Emotion

According to the (38) _____ or (39) _____ theory of emotion, bodily reactions determine emotions, rather than the other way around. According to the (40) _____ hypothesis, facial muscles involved in emotional expression send messages to the brain, which then interprets the pattern as an emotion. The (41) _____ theory of emotional feedback suggests that this occurs because tensing facial muscles alters the temperature of blood entering the brain. The (42) _____ theory of emotion proposed that when we encounter an emotion-arousing situation, the thalamus simultaneously sends sensory messages to the cerebral cortex and to the body's internal organs. Schachter's (43) _____ theory of emotion states that physiological arousal and cognitive labelling of the arousal produces an emotion.

Apply What You Know

1. Describe your own behaviours that support both drive theories and sensation-seeking theories.

2. Give examples of all three motivational conflicts from your own life.

3. Using Study Sheet 10.1, keep a journal of your emotions throughout one day. Describe what behaviours and thoughts you are engaged in as you are experiencing your emotions at that particular time. What patterns of behaviours and thoughts seem to emerge for both positive and negative emotions as you examine your own data? Does your data support any of the theories of emotions described in your textbook? If so, which ones, and why?

Internet Scavenger Hunt

1. Search the WWW for sites which provide recommendations to travellers on etiquette in other countries. Analyze differences in appropriate behaviours across cultures, and attempt to determine how display rules for emotions are different in different cultures. Describe your findings.

Practice Test

Multiple Choice Items: *Please write the letter corresponding to your answer in the space to the left of each item.*

_____ 1. Sara and Frank are competing for the same new job. They both very much want the job and believe that it would substantially help their careers. Frank isn't sure that he has the job or interview skills needed to get the job and as a result, he puts a little less effort into his resume and job interview. Sara on the other hand believes that she has good interview skills and thinks that she has the talent to get the job. As a result, she prepares at bit harder for this position. The expectancy x value theory of motivation would **most likely** explain this difference in motivation as being due to _____.

    a. their different expectations regarding their goal-related behaviours
    b. their different growth needs
    c. the different values they placed on the job
    d. their different internal drives

_____ 2. Tim is just learning to play the piano and somewhat surprisingly, he already enjoys playing it even though he isn't very good. Tim's parents would like to see him develop his skills so they decide to pay Tim $10.00 at the end of each week if he has satisfactorily practiced all his lessons. Motivation theorists familiar with the overjustification hypothesis would argue that the rewards being offered by Tim's parents may _____ Tim's interest in piano by _____ motivation.

    a. increase; enhancing his extrinsic
    b. decrease; undermining his extrinsic
    c. increase; enhancing his intrinsic
    d. decrease; undermining his intrinsic

_____ 3. According to a brain-imaging study at McGill University, sensation-seeking is linked to:

    a. a limbic system sensitive to amphetamine stimulation
    b. a dopamine system insensitive to amphetamine stimulation
    c. a limbic system insensitive to amphetamine stimulation
    d. a dopamine system especially sensitive to amphetamine stimulation

_____ 4. For people who are overweight, their bodies tend to respond to the food deprivation often involved in dieting by _____ the rate of basal metabolism. As fat mass decreases, leptin levels _____, which stimulates appetite and makes it harder to keep dieting.

    a. decreasing; decrease
    b. decreasing; increase
    c. increasing; decrease
    d. increasing; increase

_a_ 5. Research on the prevalence of anorexia and bulimia has determined that these disorders are ____.

   a. most common in industrialized cultures where beauty is equated with thinness
   b. equally common in almost all cultures of the world
   c. most common in cultures that have to deal with food scarcity and famine
   d. most common in cultures where people lack personal control and freedom

_a_ 6. During the ____ phase of the sexual response cycle, physiological arousal builds rapidly and blood flow increases to the organs in and around the genitals in a process called vasocongestion.

   a. plateau
   b. excitement
   c. arousal
   d. resolution

_d_ 7. According to Masters and Johnson, in proper order, the four stages of the human sexual response cycle are ____, ____, ____, and ____.

   a. plateau; excitement; orgasm; resolution
   b. plateau; excitement; resolution; orgasm
   c. excitement; orgasm; resolution; plateau
   d. excitement; plateau; orgasm; resolution

_c_ 8. The fact that children in the Marquesas Islands of French Polynesia have ample opportunity to observe sexual behaviour and boys in this society are sometimes masturbated by their parents when the boys are distressed **best demonstrates** how ____ factors can impact sexual behaviour.

   a. genetic
   b. personal psychological
   c. cultural
   d. biological

_d_ 9. Real world correlational evidence gathered on the effect of pornography on behaviour ____.

   a. provides clear support for the social learning theory position
   b. provides clear support for the psychoanalytic position
   c. does not clearly support either the social learning theory or psychoanalytic position
   d. provides clear support for both the social learning theory and psychoanalytic positions

_c_ ✓ 10. All of the following findings have been observed in research on sexual orientation **except** the finding that homosexual ____.

    a.   children seem to know early in life that they are somehow different from their same-sex peers.
    b.   children are more likely to engage in gender nonconforming behaviours.
    c.   and heterosexual males have different adult levels of sex hormones.
    d.   women are more likely to be considered "tomboys" and to be interested in boy's toys.

_d_ 11. The fact that children who are blind from birth express the basic emotions in roughly the same way as sighted children was presented to demonstrate that ____.

    a.   even the emotions of children are based largely on cognitive appraisals
    b.   basic human emotions are determined by sensory information sent directly to the amygdala
    c.   the emotional responses of children appear to largely be learned
    d.   humans may have innate fundamental emotion patterns

_b_ 12. In the United States, someone who sticks her thumb up is likely trying to hitchhike or is telling someone that everything is OK. However, in Greece, this same gesture is considered obscene. This difference **best demonstrates** how culturally based norms called ____ can influence emotional expressions.

    a.   eliciting stimuli
    b.   display rules
    c.   primary appraisals
    d.   instrumental behaviours

_d_ 13. The ____ theory of emotion asserts that the thalamus sends messages directly to the cortex and these messages determine the experience of emotion. The physiological arousal that accompanies the emotion is determined by separate messages sent from the thalamus to the body's internal organs.

    a.   James-Lange
    b.   Cannon-Bard
    c.   facial feedback
    d.   somatic

_d_ 14. Fran really would like to do well in this course. She isn't so much motivated by wanting to get better grades and test scores than her classmates nor is she afraid of doing poorly but she is very much interested in learning and gaining some expertise for the material, even though some of the content is quite challenging for her. Fran appears to have a ____ and her particular way of manifesting this suggests that she is motivated by ____ goals.

    a.   strong fear of failure; mastery
    b.   high need for achievement; competitive
    c.   strong motive for success; competitive
    d.   high need for achievement; mastery

_C_ ✓ 15. In cultures that encourage _____, such as China and Japan, measures of achievement motivation more strongly represent the desire to fit into the family and social group and to meet the expectations and work goals of these groups.

a. intrinsic motivation
b. mastery goals
c. collectivism
d. individualism

_d_ 16. Lazarus' theory of emotion and Schachter's two-factor theory of emotion are similar in that they both ____.

a. minimize the importance of cognitive appraisals
b. view emotion as primarily a physiological process
c. contradict the Cannon-Bard theory of emotion
d. acknowledge the importance of situational cues in determining emotions

_d_ 17. Polygraphs measure all of the following except _____.

a. respiration
b. heart rate
c. skin conductance
d. brain waves

_d_ ✓ 18. Others' emotional displays can evoke similar emotional responses in us, a process known as ____.

a. emotional intelligence
b. a fundamental emotional pattern
c. an instinct
d. empathy

_b_ 19. Behaviours directed at achieving some goal are called _____ behaviours.

a. emotional
b. instrumental
c. empathic
d. instinctual

_b_ ✓ 20. Tilly Seaker likes to bungee jump off of skyscrapers in the nude every few days. Tilly's behaviour is probably best explained by _____.

a. drive theory
b. sensation-seeking theory
c. the desire to maintain homeostasis
d. avoidance-avoidance conflicts

_a_ 21. _____ represent environmental stimuli that "pull" an organism toward a goal.

    a. Drives
    b. Incentives
    c. Homeostatic states
    d. Intrinsic motivators

_a_ 22. At the top of Maslow's pyramid, the need to fulfill our potential is called ____.

    a. self-actualization
    b. a cognitive need
    c. an aesthetic need
    d. an esteem need

_b_ 23. When _____ levels decline, hunger is likely to be felt when ____ levels increase, eating diminishes.

    a. CCK; blood glucose
    b. leptin; blood glucose
    c. blood glucose; CCK
    d. blood glucose; LH

_a_ 24. Of the following, the one which is not a <u>psychological</u> factor that regulates food intake is ____.

    a. CCK
    b. attitudes
    c. habits
    d. psychological needs

_d_ 25. A disorder in which a person has an intense fear of being fat and thus severely restricts their food intake to the point of self-starvation is called ____.

    a. bulimia nervosa
    b. CCK
    c. leptin
    d. anorexia nervosa

_c_ 26. The hormones that appear to have the primary influence on sexual desire are the ____.

    a. estrogens
    b. leptins
    c. androgens
    d. initiators

_C_ 27. Results of studies examining the facial feedback hypothesis are best explained by
_____.

    a. the two-factor theory
    b. cognitive-affective theories
    c. the vascular theory of emotional feedback
    d. Lazarus' theory of coping

_a_ 28. An incentive theory of drug use would argue that heroin addicts seek heroin because

    a. the drug makes them feel good.
    b. of a biological heroin drive.
    c. of a need to escape withdrawal.
    d. the drug has altered their brain chemistry.

_a_ 29. A goal setting technique used by managers that involves combining goal setting with
employee participation and feedback is called _____.

    a. task significance
    b. job feedback
    c. task identity
    d. management by objectives

_b_ 30. At this point in your review of this chapter, you have to decide to answer the rest of the
practice test questions (a very undesirable alternative) or study for your biology test
(another undesirable alternative) You are experiencing a(n) _____ conflict.

    a. approach-approach
    b. approach-avoidance
    c. avoidance-avoidance
    d. hopeless

21/30

True/False Items: *Write T or F in the space provided to the left of each item.*

_____ 1. According to Hull's drive theory, drives are produced by physiological disruptions to
homeostasis.

_____ 2. Performing an activity to obtain an external reward or to avoid punishment is called
intrinsic motivation.

_____ 3. Studies of the lateral hypothalamus and the ventromedial hypothalamus have
definitely shown that they are "hunger-on" and "hunger-off" centres respectively.

_____ 4. According to Fredrickson and Roberts' (1997) objectification theory, American culture
teaches women to view their bodies as objects.

_____ 5. Sensation-seeking refers to the motivation to seek out stimulation and novelty.

_____ 6. The four stage pattern of sexual response described by Masters and Johnson (1966)
includes excitement, plateau, orgasm, and resolution.

_____ 7. Psychophysiological findings suggest that left hemisphere activation might underlie certain positive emotions.

_____ 8. According to the James-Lange theory, subcortical activity in the thalamus leads to autonomic arousal and emotion.

_____ 9. Results of studies examining the facial feedback hypothesis support the James-Lange theory.

_____ 10. An approach-approach conflict involves making a choice between two attractive alternatives.

Short Answer Questions

1.   What role may homeostasis play in motivation?

2.   What are the psychological aspects of hunger?

3.   How are hormones involved in sexual motivation?

4.   What are cultural display rules?

5.   What does the two-factor theory of emotion say?

Essay Questions

1. Describe the physiological processes involved in hunger.

2. How are both genetics and environmental factors involved in obesity?

3. How can employers enhance work motivation?

4. How does physiology affect the experience of emotions?

5. How are appraisal processes involved in emotion?

Study Sheet 10.1   Emotions Throughout The Day

Time	Emotions Experiencing	Thoughts	Behaviours
8:00 a.m.			
10:00 a.m.			
12:00 noon			
2:00 p.m.			
4:00 p.m.			
6:00 p.m.			
8:00 p.m.			
10:00 p.m.			

Answer Keys

Answer Key for Key Terms

Perspectives on Motivation
Hunger and Weight Regulation
Sensation-Seeking

1. o
2. p
3. l
4. d
5. e
6. f
7. k
8. c
9. r

10. b
11. g
12. m
13. j
14. a
15. h
16. n
17. i
18. q

Sexual Motivation
The Nature and Functions of Emotions
Interactions Among the Components of Emotion
Achievement Motivation
Motivation in the Workplace
Motivational Conflict

1. a
2. s
3. u
4. t
5. o
6. m
7. e
8. l
9. b
10. g
11. f

12. i
13. h
14. q
15. r
16. p
17. k
18. c
19. d
20. v
21. j
22. n

Answer Key for Review at a Glance

1. Motivation
2. instinct
3. drive
4. homeostasis
5. Extrinsic
6. intrinsic
7. need hierarchy
8. self actualization
9. metabolism
10. glucose
11. CCK (cholecystokinin)

23. need for achievement
24. fear
25. job enrichment
26. intrinsic
27. management by objectives
28. approach-approach
29. avoidance-avoidance
30. approach-avoidance
31. emotions
32. cognitive appraisal
33. expressive

12. leptin
13. lateral hypothalamus
14. ventromedial
15. paraventricular

16. anorexia nervosa
17. bulimia nervosa
18. sensation seeking
19. sexual response cycle
20. androgens
21. estrogens
22. sexual orientation

34. empathy
35. fundamental emotional
36. display rules
37. instrumental
38. James-Lange
39. somatic
40. facial feedback
41. vascular
42. Cannon-Bard
43. two-factor

Answer Key for Practice Test Multiple Choice Questions

1. a	16. d
2. d	17. d
3. d	18. d
4. b	19. b
5. a	20. b
6. b	21. b
7. d	22. a
8. c	23. c
9. c	24. a
10. c	25. d
11. d	26. c
12. b	27. c
13. b	28. a
14. d	29. d
15. c	30. c

Answer Key for Practice Test True/False Questions

1. T	6. T
2. F	7. T
3. F	8. F
4. T	9. T
5. T	10. T

Answer Key for Practice Test Short Answer Questions

1. Homeostasis is a state of internal physiological equilibrium that the body strives to maintain. Homeostatic regulation involves both unlearned and learned behaviours. According to drive theory, physiological disruptions to homeostasis produce drives, which motivate organisms to behave in ways that reduce drive.

2. From a behavioural perspective, eating is positively reinforced by good taste and negatively reinforced by hunger reduction. We have expectations that eating will be pleasurable, so cognitions about eating are important in motivation. Our beliefs, attitudes, and cultural standards about caloric intake as well as body image are important factors affecting eating.

3. The pituitary gland secretes hormones called gonadotropins into the bloodstream. These hormones affect the rate at which the gonads (testes in the male and ovaries in the female) secrete androgens and estrogens. These sex hormones have both organizational effects on the body by directing the development of the sex organs and activational effects by stimulating sexual desire and behaviour.

4. Cultural display rules are the norms for emotional expression within a given culture. Display rules dictate when and how particular emotions are to be expressed

5. The two-factor theory of emotion states that both physiological arousal and cognitive labelling create an emotional experience. Situational cues provide us with the necessary information we need to understand and label the nature of the physiological response that we are feeling.

Answer Key for Practice Test Essay Questions

1. One key ingredient affecting hunger is glucose. Studies have determined that a temporary drop-rise pattern in blood glucose levels occurs prior to experiencing hunger and may be a signal to the brain that helps initiate feeding. As we eat, stomach and intestinal distention provide satiety signals to the brain, suggesting that we are getting full. The intestines respond to food by releasing peptides that help terminate a meal. For example, CCK (cholecystokinin) is released into the bloodstream, travels to the brain, and stimulates receptors in several brain regions, resulting in the cessation of eating. Leptin signals influence neural pathways to decrease appetite and increase energy expenditure. Many pathways involving the paraventricular nucleus (PVN) may also regulate food intake.

2. Over 200 genes have been identified as possible contributors to human obesity. The combined effects of some of those genes rather than a single gene itself may produce an increased risk of obesity. Societal and cultural factors such as an abundance of inexpensive, tasty, high-fat foods; a cultural emphasis on things like "supersizing," and technological advances that decrease the need for daily physical activity interact with genetic propensities to influence the development of obesity.

3. There are a number of ways that employers can enhance job motivation. Job enrichment programs attempt to increase intrinsic motivation by making jobs more fulfilling and providing workers with opportunities for personal growth. Increasing skill variety such that a worker can use many talents and skills seems to be a successful way of increasing job motivation. Similarly, increasing a worker's sense of task identity, his or her sense of completing a job from start to finish, can help. Other ways of increasing motivation involve increasing a worker's sense of task significance, increasing worker autonomy, and providing clear feedback about job performance. Management by objectives programs attempt to increase motivation by combining goal setting with employee participation and feedback. Finally, improving external incentives such as pay and bonuses can increase motivation.

4. Subcortical structures such as the hypothalamus, amygdala, hippocampus, and other structures in the limbic system play major roles in emotions. The prefrontal cortex likely plays an important role in our ability to regulate emotion. The thalamus sends messages via two independent neural pathways, one to the cortex and one to the amygdala. This dual system for processing means that some emotions likely do not involve conscious thought while others do. Other theorists argue that neurotransmitters such as dopamine, serotonin, norepinephrine, and endorphins play major roles in the experience of emotion. Some research findings suggest that left hemisphere activation might underlie certain positive emotions while right hemisphere activation might underlie some negative ones. Finally, the release of hormones into the bloodstream likely also influence emotions by triggering physiological responses.

5. Appraisals relate to what we think is desirable or undesirable for us or for the people we care about. Some appraisals are more automatic, particularly for emotions such as fear. This may be because of the instinctual nature of some emotions. Other appraisals are more cognitively based and include evaluative and personal dimensions. This is why different people may have entirely different emotional reactions to the same stimuli.

Chapter 11. Development Over the Lifespan

Learning Objectives

11.1 Describe the four broad issues that guide developmental research.

11.2 Describe 5 different developmental functions.

11.3 Differentiate among cross-sectional, longitudinal, and sequential designs.

11.4 Describe prenatal development and how it can be influenced by STDs, alcohol, and other drugs.

11.5 Discuss fetal behaviour.

11.6 Describe the *newborn's* sensory capabilities, perceptual preferences, reflexes, and learning capabilities.

11.7 Discuss the developmental functions for sensory-perceptual development.

11.8 Explain how nature and nurture jointly influence physical growth and motor development during infancy.

11.9 Describe the cognitive processes identified by Piaget and his four stages of cognitive development, including research that supports and contradicts his basic ideas.

11.10 Outline some of the more recent challenges to Piaget's theory, including those by Vygotsky, and researchers using information-processing and theory of mind approaches.

11.11 Differentiate between preconventional, conventional, and postconventional moral reasoning as outlined by Kohlberg, and explain how moral reasoning is affected by culture and gender.

11.12 Discuss individual differences in temperament.

11.13 Describe social development of the child, including Erikson's stages of psychosocial development, and research on imprinting and attachment.

11.14 Describe how infant attachment is measured, and how disruptions in attachment can affect psychological development.

11.15 Describe the data relating day care, and divorce and remarriage (in the Psychological Applications section), to psychosocial development.

11.16 Outline parenting styles associated with positive and negative child outcomes.

11.17 Describe how socialization shapes children's beliefs about gender.

11.18 Describe factors that influence adolescents' psychological reactions to puberty.

11.19 Describe how adolescents' reasoning abilities change, and the ways in which their thinking is egocentric.

11.20 Identify different ways adolescents approach the challenge of establishing an identity.

11.21 Describe the extent to which, in different ethnic groups, parent-teen relationships are characterized by "storm and stress".

11.22 Describe how peer relationships change during adolescence.

11.23 Describe the major physical and cognitive changes that occur in the stages of early through late adulthood, and discuss research that tests whether elderly adults are "older but wiser."

11.24 Describe the three major social developmental challenges of adulthood outlined by Erikson.

11.25 Describe how marital satisfaction typically changes over time, including a description of the major events associated with these changes.

11.26 Outline the stages of establishing a career.

11.27 Discuss the evidence for the myths of the "midlife crisis" and the stress associated with retirement.

11.28 Describe the 5 stages of death and dying outlined by Kübler-Ross.

Chapter Overview

Major Issues and Methods

Developmental psychology examines biological, physical, social, and behavioural changes that occur with age. Four broad issues: nature and nurture, critical and sensitive periods, continuity versus discontinuity, and stability versus change guide developmental research. Developmental psychologists employ both cross-sectional research to study cohorts at the same point in time and longitudinal research to study the same cohort at different points in time.

Prenatal Development

Prenatal development consists of three stages: zygote, embryo, and fetus. The 23rd pair of chromosomes in the zygote determines the child's sex. The pairing of two X chromosomes creates a female, and the pairing of an X and Y chromosome creates a male. Teratogens like nicotine, alcohol, other drugs, mercury, lead, and radiation can cause abnormal prenatal development.

Infancy and Childhood

The sensory-perceptual abilities of newborns are poor, but develop quickly. The physical and motor development of newborns follow both the cephalocaudal and proximodistal principles.

Environmental and cultural influences affect physical and motor development as well and interact with biological factors. Swiss psychologist Jean Piaget suggested that children learn about the world through their schemas. Assimilation is the process by which new experiences are incorporated into existing schemas, while accomodation is the process by which schemas are changed by new experiences. Piaget's stage model of cognitive development proposes that infants in the sensorimotor stage learn about the world through their sensory experiences, and interactions with objects. During this stage, children also attain a sense of object permanence. Symbolic thought develops in the preoperational stage, while during the concrete operational stage children begin to be able to perform basic mental operations, such as reversibility and serial ordering. Abstract reasoning which includes the ability to form and systematically test hypotheses first occur during the formal operational stage. Research on Piaget's theory has found that the general cognitive abilities he suggested occur in the same order across cultures, but children acquire many cognitive skills much earlier than he suggested. Furthermore, children may perform skills that indicate they may be at one stage in some ways and in another in other ways.Lev Vygotsky proposed a zone of proximal development in which children, with assistance, may do more than they might be capable of independently. Information processing approaches to cognitive development stress developmental changes in information-search strategies, information-processing speed, memory capabilities, and metacognition. Kohlberg's stage model of moral development suggests that children develop morally from reasoning based on anticipated rewards and punishments to reasoning based on social expectations and laws to the highest level of moral reasoning based on general principles. Kohlberg's critics claim that the theory is culturally and gender biased. Erikson argued that social development occurs throughout the lifespan in eight major psychosocial stages, each of which involves a particular "crisis" in how we relate to others. Much recent research in developmental psychology has focused on attachment, the strong emotional bond between children and their caregivers. British theorist John Bowlby hypothesized that attachment develops through indiscriminate attachment to discriminate attachment behaviour to specific attachment to specific caregivers. Mary Ainsworth's research using the Strange Situation Test to measure attachment and anxiety has revealed different patterns of attachment, including securely attached, insecurely attached, anxious-resistant, and anxious-avoidant infants. There is much research showing the relation of early attachment styles to later behaviours. Studies of isolates and children raised in orphanages suggest that infancy is a sensitive, but not critical, period during which attachment forms most easily and can facilitate subsequent development. Studies have found that day-care children do not show less attachment to their parents than children raised exclusively in the home. High-quality day-care can also aid children from disadvantaged backgrounds, but the quality of family experiences is often more important in predicting social adjustment and academic performance. Styles of parenting including authoritative, authoritarian, indulgent, and neglectful can also influence children's development. Through socialization, children develop gender identity and gender constancy, which influence their sense of what it means to be a girl or a boy.

Adolescence

Adolescence begins at puberty, at which time hormonal secretions stimulate the development of both primary and secondary sex characteristics. Such physical changes have important psychological ramifications for adolescents. Adolescent thinking can become highly self-focused, resulting in adolescent egocentrism. The search for one's identity can be a major goal of adolescence. During this time, relationships with parents and peers can change.

Adulthood

Physical status typically peaks during one's twenties and then declines at midlife. Perceptual speed, memory for new factual information, and recall often decline as one ages. Fluid intelligence seems to decline steadily beginning in young adulthood, while crystallized intelligence declines later. Regular exercise and perceptual-motor activities help people to retain cognitive functioning at later ages. Social clocks influence whether we are satisified with our lives by setting expectations for when we should marry and have children, amongst other life goals. Research on the "mid-life crisis" suggest that it is largely a myth. People at all ages experience conflict, disappointments, and frustrations. Retirement can be a "golden" time for those who desire it. Eventually, everyone will die. Elisabeth Kübler-Ross' pioneering work emphasized several distinct stages people work through as they approach death, although the sequence and the existence of all stages for all people is questionable. Nevertheless, death has many psychological ramifications for people.

Chapter Outline

Major Issues and Methods

Prenatal Development
     Genetics and Sex Determination
     Environmental Influences

Infancy and Childhood
     The Amazing Newborn
          Newborn Sensation and Perception
          Newborn Learning
     Sensory-Perceptual Development
     Physical, Motor, and Brain Development
          Environmental and Cultural Influences
               Research Frontiers: Effects of Early Experience on Human Perceptual-Motor Abilities
     Cognitive Development
          Piaget's Stage Model
          Assessment of Piaget's Theory: Stages, Ages, and Culture
          Vygotsky: The Social Context of Cognitive Development
          Information-Processing Approaches
          Theory of Mind: Children's Understanding of Mental States
     Moral Development
          Kohlberg's Stage Model
          Culture, Gender, and Moral Reasoning
     Personality and Social Development
          Erikson's Psychosocial Theory
               Research Foundations: Were you a shy Baby or a Fussy Baby? Does Early Temperament Predict Adult Functioning?
          Attachment
          Attachment Deprivation
          The Day-Care Controversy
          Styles of Parenting
          Gender Identity and Socialization

Adolescence
    Physical Development
    Cognitive Development
        Abstract Reasoning Abilities
        Social Thinking
    Social and Personality Development
        The Search for Identity
        Relationships With Parents
            Psychological Applications: Understanding How Divorce and
            Remarriage Affect Children and Adolescents
        Peer and Friendship Relationships

Adulthood
    Physical Development
    Cognitive Development
        Information Processing and Memory
        Intellectual Changes
        Use it or Lose it? Maintaining Cognitive Functioning
        Older But Wiser?
    Social and Personality Development
        Stages and Critical Events
        Marriage and Family
        Establishing a Career
        Midlife Crisis: Fact or Fiction?
        Retirement and the Golden Years
        Death and Dying

Problem-Based Learning

Adolescence
http://www.personal.psu.edu/faculty/n/x/nxd10/adolesce.htm
Adolescence: Change and Continuity-This site was developed by students at Pennsylvania State University. It contains information on many aspects of adolescent development and links to articles and other resources.

Aging
http://www.aoa.gov/index.asp
Administration on Aging-This multidisciplinary site contains numerous links covering all aspects of aging.

http://www.apa.org
American Psychological Association-This is the APA's website and it contains information about careers, student concerns, some full text articles, news and events, and information about many areas such as clinical disorders, aids, violence, anger and aging.

Midlife
http://midmac.med.harvard.edu
MIDMAC-This site contains information about midlife, research projects, and a bibliography of research in this area.

Key Terms: Write the letter of the definition next to the term in the space provided.

Major Issues and Methods
Prenatal Development

1. ___ critical period
2. ___ cross-sectional design
3. ___ embryo
4. ___ fetal alcohol syndrome
5. ___ fetus
6. ___ longitudinal design
7. ___ sensitive period
8. ___ teratogen
9. ___ zygote

a. an age range during which certain experiences must occur for development to proceed normally
b. an optimal age range for certain experiences
c. used to compare people of different ages at the same point in time
d. used to repeatedly assess the same cohort as it grows older
e. a fertilized egg
f. name for the cell mass from the second through the eighth week after conception
g. name for the developing organism from the ninth week after conception until birth
h. environmental agents that can cause abnormal prenatal development
i. a severe group of abnormalities that result from prenatal exposure to alcohol

Infancy and Childhood

1. ___ accommodation
2. ___ assimilation
3. ___ attachment
4. ___ authoritarian parenting
5. ___ authoritative parenting
6. ___ cephalocaudal principle
7. ___ concrete operational stage
8. ___ conservation
9. ___ conventional moral reasoning
10. ___ egocentrism
11. ___ formal operational stage
12. ___ gender constancy

a. automatic, inborn behaviours that occur in response to specific stimuli
b. the genetically programmed biological process that governs our growth
c. reflects the tendency for development to proceed in a head-to-foot direction
d. states that development begins along the innermost parts of the body and continues outward
e. organized patterns of thought and action
f. the process by which new experiences are incorporated into existing schemas
g. the process by which new experiences cause existing schemas to change
h. stage in which infants understand their world through sensory experiences and physical interactions with objects
i. an infant's understanding that an object continues to exist even when it can't be seen
j. stage in which children begin to symbolically represent the world through words and mental images
k. the principle that basic properties of objects stay the same even thought their outward appearance may change
l. difficulty in viewing the world from someone else's perspective

13. ___ gender identity

m. stage at which children can perform basic mental operations involving tangible objects and situations

14. ___ imprinting

n. stage at which individuals can think both concretely and abstractly and can form and test hypotheses

15. ___ indulgent parenting

o. the difference between what a child can do independently and with assistance

16. ___ maturation

p. a person's beliefs about the mind and ability to understand others' mental states

17. ___ neglectful parenting

q. moral reasoning based on anticipated punishment or rewards

18. ___ object permanence

r. moral reasoning based on conformity to social expectations, laws, and duties

19. ___ postconventional moral reasoning

s. moral reasoning based on general moral principles

20. ___ preconventional moral reasoning

t. a series of stages that involve "crises" of how we view ourselves in relation to others

21. ___ preoperational stage

u. a biologically based general style of reacting emotionally and behaviourally to the environment

22. ___ proximodistal principle

v. a biologically primed form of attachment

23. ___ psychosocial stages

w. the strong emotional bond between children and their primary caregivers

24. ___ reflexes

x. when approached by an unfamiliar person, becoming afraid, crying, and reaching for the caregiver; occurs from 6-7 months to about 1 ½ years old

25. ___ schemas

y. becoming anxious and crying when separated from a primary caregiver

26. ___ sensorimotor stage

z. a standard procedure for examining infant attachment

27. ___ separation anxiety

aa. parenting that is controlling but warm

28. ___ sex-role stereotypes

bb. parenting that is controlling and cold

29. ___ socialization

cc. parenting that is warm, caring, and permissive

30. ___ Strange Situation Test

dd. parenting that is rejecting and permissive

31. ___ stranger anxiety

ee. a sense of "maleness" and "femaleness"

32. ___ temperament

ff. the understanding that being male or female is a permanent part of a person

33. ___ theory of mind

gg. beliefs about characteristics and behaviours that are sex appropriate

34. ___ zone of proximal development

hh. the process by which we acquire the beliefs, values, and behaviours of a group

Adolescence
Adulthood

1. ___ adolescent egocentrism

a. an overestimation of the uniqueness of feelings and experiences and a feeling of being "on stage"

2. ___ postformal thought

b. a period of rapid maturation in which a person becomes capable of sexual reproduction

3. ___ puberty

c. a set of cultural norms concerning the optimal age range for work, marriage, parenthood, and other major life experiences

4. ___ social clock

d. a fifth stage of cognitive development in which people can reason logically about opposing points of view and accept contradictions and irreconcilable differences

Review at a Glance: *Write the term that best fits the blank to review what you learned in this chapter.*

Major Issues and Methods

Developmental psychologists examine changes that occur as we age. A (1) _____ _____ is an age range during which certain experiences must occur for development to proceed normally. A (2) _____ period is an optimal age range for certain experiences. Developmental psychologists use both (3) _____ - _____ designs, which compare people of different cohorts at the same time and (4) _____ designs, which repeatedly test the same people as they grow older.

Prenatal Development

A fertilized egg is known as a (5) _____. From the second through the eighth week after conception, the cell mass is called an (6) _____, and after that the developing organism is called a (7) _____. Environmental influences can affect prenatal development. (8) _____ are environmental agents that can cause abnormal development, such as (9) _____ _____ _____, which results from prenatal exposure to alcohol.

Infancy and Childhood

Newborn children are equipped with automatic, inborn behaviours, or (10) _____ that are elicited by specific stimuli. The genetically programmed biological process that governs our growth is called (11) _____. Physical and motor development follow both the (12) _____ principle, which reflects the tendency for development to proceed in a head-to-foot direction and the (13) _____ principle, which states that development begins on the innermost parts of the body and proceeds toward the outermost parts. Cognitive development was studied most famously by (14) _____. He argued that children organize the world in terms of (15) _____. (16) _____ is the process by which new information causes existing schemas to change, while (17) _____ is the process by which new experiences are incorporated into existing schemas. Piaget suggested that children go through four distinct cognitive stages. In the (18) _____ stage, infants understand their world through their sensory experiences and physical interactions with objects. During this stage, an infant comes to understand that an object continues to exist even when it cannot be directly experienced, a concept Piaget called (19) _____ _____. Children enter the (20) _____ stage around the age of two and begin to represent the world symbolically through words and mental images. Preoperational children also show (21) _____, which reflects their difficulty in viewing the world from any perspective other than their own. In the (22) _____ _____ stage, children can now perform basic mental functions involving tangible objects and situations. Finally, in the (23) _____ operational stage, individuals can think abstractly and form hypotheses. Another theorist, (24) _____, argued that there is a zone of (25) _____ _____, the difference between what a children can do independently and what they can do with assistance. Kohlberg's theory of moral development suggests that children proceed from a stage of morality based on anticipated punishments or rewards, called (26) _____ moral reasoning, to conformity based on social expectations, laws, and duties, called (27) _____ moral reasoning, to the highest level of moral reasoning, (28) _____ moral reasoning, which is based on general moral principles. Theorist Erik Erikson proposed that people develop through eight major (29) _____ stages. (30) _____ refers to the strong emotional bond that develops between children and their primary caregivers. As an infant's attachment develops, two types of anxiety occur. (31) _____ anxiety occurs first, followed by (32) _____ anxiety. A standard procedure used to measure attachment developed by Mary Ainsworth and colleagues is called the (33) _____ _____ _____. Four parenting styles have been associated with different patterns of child-rearing. Controlling but warm parents are called (34) _____, while controlling but cold parents are called (35) _____. Parents who have warm, caring relationships with their children but who provide little or no rules or guidance are called (36) _____ parents, and parents who are cold toward their children and who provide little or no rules of guidance are called (37) _____ parents. Parents also help their children develop a sense of "femaleness" or "maleness" called (38) _____ _____. As gender identity develops, children acquire beliefs about characteristics and behaviours that are appropriate for girls and for boys. These beliefs are known as (39) _____ _____.

Adolescence

Adolescents tend to think that their experiences and feelings are unique, which is known as the (40) _____ _____. They also tend to believe that everyone else is watching what they are doing. The two phenomena together are what Elkind calls (41) _____ _____.

Adulthood

Several theorists have proposed a fifth stage of cognitive development called (42) _____ thought, in which people can reason logically about opposing points of view. Neugarten has suggested that people match what is going on in their lives with a (43) _____ _____, which is a set of cultural norms concerning the optimal age for marriage, parenthood, and other life goals.

Apply What You Know

1. Find four children who should be in different Piagetian cognitive stages. Observe their behaviour and interview them to determine what behaviours and thoughts correspond to those suggested by Piaget as appropriate for that particular stage. Determine some behaviours and thoughts that don't correspond to what Piaget believed. Use Study Sheet 11.1.

2. Study Sheet 11.2 provides Neugarten's findings about social clocks in the 1970's. Devise a survey for measuring student's social clocks for the same events today, and compare and contrast your findings to what Neugarten observed.

Internet Scavenger Hunt

1. Conduct an internet search on some of the key figures in Developmental Psychology: Jean Piaget, Lev Vygotsky, Erik Erikson, Sigmund Freud. In particular, you might look for discussions of how their life experiences influenced their theories.

2. There are several sites on the internet which provide information to parents and grandparents on child and adolescent development. If you look at the most frequently asked questions, you may obtain some idea of the 'issues' currently relevant to parents of children of different ages. If you search well enough, you will also be able to conduct a cross-cultural comparison of information currently of interest to parents in a variety of cultures/countries, because many have English versions available.

Practice Test

Multiple Choice Items: *Please write the letter corresponding to your answer in the space to the left of each item.*

____ 1. In developmental research, a _____ period is an age range during which specific experiences must take place if normal development is to occur. This is in contrast to a ____ period, where it is optimal although not necessarily essential for these experiences to occur.

    a. sensitive; critical
    b. critical; receptive
    c. critical; sensitive
    d. explicit; sensitive

____ 2. A self-esteem researcher is interested in how self-esteem varies across the life span and decides to conduct a survey comparing people of different ages to address this issue. He recruits participants to be in one of four different age groups (20-29, 30-39, 40-49, 50-59), has them complete a self-esteem survey, and then analyses the data to see if any patterns emerge. This study would be considered an example of a ____ design.

    a. longitudinal
    b. double-blind
    c. cross-sectional
    d. sequential

_____ 3. If a zygote receives a Y chromosome from its father, this means that the egg _____.

    a. will be a female
    b. will be a male
    c. could be either a male or a female, depending on the contribution of the mother
    d. will have the characteristics of both a male and a female

_____ 4. Consistent with the concept of _____ , a study found that children over age three who grew up with older brothers or sisters performed _____ on a cognitive task than children with no siblings or younger siblings.

    a. a zone of proximal development; better
    b. egocentrism; worse
    c. animism; better
    d. irreversibility; worse

_____ 5. Results from studies examining the information-processing abilities of young children are often used to argue that cognitive development is _____, but there are some theorists who assert that children still learn new ways of processing information as they age.

    a. determined by sensitive periods
    b. schema-driven
    c. discontinuous
    d. continuous

_____ 6. In response to the moral dilemma where a man must decide if he should steal a medication to save his dying wife, a child says that he shouldn't steal the medication because if he does, he'll be punished. This child would be classified as being in Kohlberg's _____ level of moral reasoning.

    a. preconventional
    b. preoperational
    c. conventional
    d. concrete operational

_____ 7. _____ refers to the strong emotional bond that develops between human children and their primary caregivers and its creation appears to be governed by a _____ period since it is most easily established during the first 1- to 2-years of a child's life.

    a. Attachment; sensitive
    b. Attachment; critical
    c. Imprinting; sensitive
    d. Imprinting; critical

_____ 8. _____ anxiety refers to how young toddlers become upset when they are apart from their primary caregivers and it appears to follow _____ patterns in different cultures.

    a. Stranger; similar
    b. Separation; similar
    c. Stranger; different
    d. Separation; different

_d_ 9. Nguyen is participating in an attachment experiment involving the strange situation. When his mother is present with the stranger, Nguyen explores the room and is friendly with the stranger. However, when the mother leaves, he becomes upset and starts to cry. When she returns, Nguyen happily greets her and then returns to his previous explorations. Nguyen would most likely be classified as a(n) _____ child.

    a. resistant-avoidant
    b. anxious-resistant
    c. anxious-avoidant
    d. securely attached

_a_ 10. A couple with three kids is considering divorce but is wondering if they should remain together for the sake of their children. Research suggests that the **most important** factor that they should take into consideration is _____.

    a. how old the children are.
    b. how long they have been married.
    c. the amount of conflict in the relationship.
    d. whether or not adultery is involved.

_d_ 11. Ned is growing up in a family where his parents provide him with a great deal of warmth and he feels that he has very close relationships with both of his parents. In terms of discipline, his parents are relatively lax and allow him to do as he pleases. As result, Ned is somewhat immature and self-centred. Diana Baumrind would **most likely** classify Ned's parent's as using a(n) _____ parenting style.

    a. tolerant
    b. indulgent
    c. lenient
    d. liberal

_d_ 12. A father believes that there are certain behaviours that are more appropriate for boys than for girls. His wife has heard him share these beliefs and she wonders if they are partly responsible for the fact that he actually relates differently to his son, with whom he tends to use more verbal and physical prohibition, than he does with his daughter. In this example the father's beliefs would be examples of _____ while the fact that he treats his children differently depending on their gender demonstrates the concept of _____.

    a. gender identities; gender constancies
    b. sex-role stereotypes; gender preferences
    c. sex-role stereotypes; sex typing
    d. gender identities; sex typing

_a_ ✓ 13. ____ who reach puberty ____ their peers tend to be more popular and have more positive body images.

    a. Boys; earlier than
    b. Boys; at the same time as
    c. Boys; later than
    d. Girls; earlier than

_b_ x c 14. Your Grandmother is just about to have her 77th birthday. According to results from studies examining information processing changes that occur with age, of the following areas the one which you would expect to be **least impaired** by the process of aging would be ____.

    a. memory for new factual information
    b. recall memory
    c. memory for personal events
    d. speed of processing

_d_ x a 15. Studies indicate that most people who retire ____ more likely to become anxious, depressed, or lonely. The risks that are associated with retirement become more likely when the retirement is ____.

    a. are not; forced
    b. are not; voluntary
    c. are; forced
    d. are; voluntary ✓

_a_ 16. Piaget was one of the first to suggest that children actively interpret information about their environments. They likely do this through the processes of ____ and ____.

    a. accommodation; assimilation
    b. moral development; accommodation
    c. object permanence; assimilation
    d. developing an anxious style of attachment; developing a zone of proximal development

_d_ 17. McKim at the University of Saskatchewan and co-workers in Ontario examined the effects of home care versus out-of-home care on the security of attachment of 24 to 30 month old infants. They found that

    a. out-of-home care infants had very low security of attachment.
    b. home care infants had very low security of attachment.
    c. quality of out-of-home care was more important than the number of caregivers in the infant's life.
    d. infants with less sensitive mothers who also employed extensive out-of-home care were the least secure.

_a_ 18. In some parts of the Northwest Territories, where drinking is common, fetal alcohol syndrome is estimated to occur in _____ births.

    a. one of every three
    b. one of every twenty
    c. one of every forty four
    d. one of every one hundred

_b_ 19. Vygotsky believed that _____.

    a. development occurs in discrete stages for everyone
    b. cognitive development depends on the people in a child's world and the tools that the culture provides to support thinking
    c. the learning of language does not influence cognitive development
    d. children should learn on their own and should not be assisted

_b_ 20. Research by University of Toronto and McMaster University research has demonstrated that young infants .

    a. become increasingly adept at localizing sounds.
    b. appear to perceive music as adults do.
    c. become increasingly adept at detecting phonemic changes.
    d. are capable of detecting higher auditory frequencies than adults.

_c_ 21. The prenatal period that begins approximately 2 months after conception and continues until birth is known as the _____.

    a. zygote stage
    b. embryonic period
    c. fetal period
    d. germinal phase

_d_ 22. A study of over 300 Canadian World War 2 veterans by Arbuckle, et al. (1992) found that greater intellectual decline with age was associated with.

    a. higher education.
    b. more stressful occupations.
    c. greater amounts of game playing (cards, video games, etc.)
    d. lower intellectual activity.

_d_ 23. Apparently having a few too many rocks in their heads, Fred and Wilma Flintstone let daughter Pebbles hang out to all hours with boyfriend Bamm-Bamm. They allow her to let her bedroom become a filthy, rotting mess of empty pizza boxes, and, when she comes home after winning the title of Miss Bedrock, ignore her pleas for praise in order to concentrate on planning their latest trip to Rock Vegas. Fred and Wilma's parenting style would best be described as _____.

    a. authoritarian
    b. authoritative
    c. indulgent
    d. neglectful

24. Having eaten only a small amount of porridge, young Baby Bear is distracted for a moment by the morning antics of the Teletubbies and moves into the Bear living room to watch TV. During this time, devious parents Papa and Mama Bear remove Baby Bear's porridge and put it in the freezer. Returning to the table after boring soap operas come on, Baby Bear sees that his porridge is no longer there and believes that it has vanished forever. Baby Bear has not yet developed _____, which develops during the _____ period.

    a.   object permanence; sensorimotor
    b.   centration; preoperational
    c.   object permanence; preoperational
    d.   centration; sensorimotor

25. Looking back over a long life of violence before he says his final "Hasta la vista, baby," an old, wrinkled, stooped-over Terminator wonders if his life would have been better if he had been a florist. Term is experiencing Erikson's _____.

    a.   generativity vs. stagnation
    b.   integrity vs. despair
    c.   identity vs. role confusion
    d.   industry vs. inferiority

26. Benoit and Parker (1994) compared the attachment styles of infants, their mothers and their grandmothers. They found _____ percent agreement in the attachment classification of infants and their mothers.

    a.   17
    b.   88
    c.   20
    d.   33

27. I recently observed a 4-year-old girl at the local fast food establishment "Taco Bell." At the conclusion of their meal, she asked her mother if they should "leave money on the table." Her mother responded that they didn't do that at this place even though they did do so at other restaurants. The girl nodded her head. In this case, Piaget would argue that the little girl was using _____ in her development of knowledge of what to do at "restaurants."

    a.   accommodation
    b.   object permanence
    c.   sensorimotor thought
    d.   gender identity

28. By definition, adolescence begins at _____.

    a.   the time a child gets his or her first job
    b.   hormonal sensitization of brain structures
    c.   the initial development of primary sex characteristics
    d.   puberty

_C_ 29. Adolescents' overestimation of their uniqueness and their feeling of being "on stage" are part of Elkind's (1978) notion of ____.

    a. puberty
    b. intimacy vs. isolation
    c. adolescent egocentrism
    d. identity diffusion

_a_ 30. Studies of men's and women's careers show that ____.

    a. women are more likely to have "career gaps" to take care of elderly relatives
    b. men are more likely to have "career gaps"
    c. the first stage of most careers is a "maintenance" stage
    d. men experience more "interrole conflict" than women do

True/False Items: *Write T or F in the space provided to the left of each item.*

_____ 1. A critical period is an age range during which certain experiences must occur for development to proceed normally.

_____ 2. A longitudinal design is used to compare people of different ages at the same point in time.

_____ 3. Smoking during pregnancy is an example of a teratogen.

_____ 4. The proximodistal principle stresses that development proceeds in a head-to-foot direction.

_____ 5. According to Piaget, assimilation is the process by which new experiences cause existing schemas to change.

_____ 6. In the preoperational stage, children learn how to use abstract reasoning.

_____ 7. Studies of children's information processing show that metacognition declines with age.

_____ 8. Studies of Kohlberg's model of moral development find that the stages he proposed are equally common in all cultures, supporting a biological basis for moral development.

_____ 9. Cross-cultural studies support the hypothesis that most infants are insecurely attached.

_____ 10. Research into the relationships between adolescents and their parents has found that "storm and stress" is the rule rather than the exception.

Short Answer Questions

1. What is object permanence?

2. What is the zone of proximal development?

3. What is attachment?

4. What changes in cognitive development are hypothesized to take place in adolescence?

5. What intellectual changes occur in adulthood?

Essay Questions

1. How do both genetics and environmental influences affect prenatal development?

2. What major changes take place in each of Piaget's stages of cognitive development?

3. Describe Kohlberg's stage model of moral development.

4. Describe Erikson's stages of psychosocial development.

5. What does the research on the developmental effects of day-care indicate?

Study Sheet 11.1 Using Piaget's Theory

<u>Supporting</u>   <u>Not Supporting</u>

Sensorimotor

Preoperational

Concrete Operational

Formal Operational

Study Sheet 11.2   **Social Clocks**

	Late 70's*		Today	
	Men	Women	Men	Women
Best Age for a Man to Marry (20-25)	42%	42%		
Best Age for a Woman to Marry (19-24)	44%	36%		
When Should Most People Become Grandparents (45-50)	64%	57%		
Best Age for Most People to Finish School and Go To Work (20-22)	36%	38%		
When Most Men Should Be Settled On a Career (24-26)	24%	36%		
When Most Men Hold Their Top Jobs (45-50)	38%	31%		
When Most People Should Be Ready To Retire (60-65)	66%	41%		
When a Man Has the Most Responsibilities (35-50)	49%	50%		
When a Man Accomplishes the Most (40-50)	46%	41%		
The Prime of Life for a Man (35-50)	59%	66%		
When a Woman Has the Most Responsibilities (25-40)	59%	53%		
When a Woman Accomplishes the Most (30-45)	57%	48%		

*Data are taken from a study by Passuth, Mines, & Neugarten, 1984). Percentages refer to the percentages of the sample who agreed with the statement that the age range in parentheses is the appropriate age range for the event.

Answer Keys

Answer Key for Key Terms

Major Issues and Methods
Prenatal Development

1. a
2. c
3. f
4. i
5. g

6. d
7. b
8. h
9. e

Infancy and Childhood

1. g
2. f
3. w
4. bb
5. aa
6. c
7. m
8. k
9. r
10. l
11. n
12. ff

13. ee
14. v
15. cc
16. b
17. dd
18. i
19. s
20. q
21. j
22. d
23. t
24. a

25. e
26. h
27. y
28. gg
29. hh
30. z
31. x
32. u
33. p
34. o

Adolescence
Adulthood

1. a
2. d

3. b
4. c

Answer Key for Review at a Glance

1. critical period
2. sensitive
3. cross-sectional
4. longitudinal
5. zygote
6. embryo
7. fetus
8. Teratogens
9. fetal alcohol syndrome
10. reflexes
11. maturation
12. cephalocaudal
13. proximodistal
14. Piaget

23. formal
24. Vygotsky
25. proximal development
26. preconventional
27. conventional
28. postconventional
29. psychosocial
30. Attachment
31. Stranger
32. separation
33. Strange Situation Test
34. authoritative
35. authoritarian
36. indulgent

15. schemas
16. Accommodation
17. assimilation
18. sensorimotor
19. object permanence
20. preoperational
21. egoentrism
22. concrete operational

37. neglectful
38. gender identity
39. sex-role stereotypes
40. personal fable
41. adolescent egocentrism
42. postformal
43. social clock

Answer Key for Practice Test Multiple Choice Questions

1. c
2. c
3. b
4. a
5. d
6. a
7. a
8. b
9. d
10. c
11. b
12. c
13. a
14. c
15. a

16. a
17. d
18. a
19. b
20. b
21. a
22. d
23. d
24. a
25. b
26. b
27. a
28. d
29. c
30. a

Answer Key for Practice Test True/False Questions

1. T
2. F
3. T
4. F
5. F

6. F
7. F
8. F
9. F
10. F

Answer Key for Practice Test Short Answer Questions

1. Object permanence is the belief that children develop during the sensorimotor stage of cognitive development that an object continues to exist even when it no longer can be seen.

2. Vygotsky's idea of the zone of proximal development is the difference between what a child can do independently and what he or she can do with some assistance. Thus, a child may be able to do more than someone thinks he or she can, if some help is given.

3. Attachment refers to the strong emotional bond that develops between children and their primary caregivers.

4. There are several cognitive changes that occur in adolescence. Piaget proposed that adolescents acquire formal operational thinking, which is characterized by more abstract thinking and the ability to form hypotheses. Elkind (1978) proposed that adolescents engage in adolescent egocentrism, which involves an overestimation of the uniqueness of one's feelings and experiences and a feeling of being "on stage."

5. Fluid intelligence begins to decline steadily in young adulthood, whereas crystallized intelligence peaks during middle adulthood and declines after that. Poorer perceptual speed, memory, vision, and hearing may contribute to these intellectual declines. People who have above-average education, cognitively stimulating jobs, are involved in cognitively-stimulating activities on a regular basis, marry spouses with greater intellectual abilities than their own, and maintain a higher level of perceptual processing speed tend to have less steep declines in cognitive functioning. Regular physical exercise and perceptual-motor activities also help to preserve cognitive abilities.

Answer Key for Practice Test Essay Questions

1. At conception an egg and sperm unite to form the zygote. The 23rd pair of chromosomes determine the baby's sex. If the union produces an XY combination in the 23rd pair, the resulting child will be a boy. If the combination is XX, the resulting child will be a girl. The TDF gene on the Y chromosome initiates the development of testes in the male at 6-8 weeks after conception. If there is no Y chromosome (and thus no TDF gene), testes do not form, and if there is an absence of sufficient androgen activity in this critical period, a female pattern of organ development occurs. Environmental agents called teratogens can cause abnormal prenatal development. Teratogens include things like nicotine, alcohol consumption, mercury, lead, and radiation.

2. During the sensorimotor period, children come to understand their world through their sensory experiences and interactions with objects. During this stage they develop object permanence and start to develop the basic skills of language. During the preoperational stage beginning about the age of 2, children start to be able to represent the world through symbols such as words and mental images. During this stage children can also start to think about past and future events and engage in pretend play. They have difficulty understanding the principle of conservation. Children's thinking at this time also reflects their egocentrism. Children in the concrete operational stage understand the concept of reversibility, the serial ordering of objects (e.g. smallest to largest) and can form mental representations of a series of steps needed to accomplish a goal, an important step in problem-solving. Finally, children in the formal operational stage can use abstract and hypothetico-deductive thought.

3. Kohlberg believed that people pass through three main levels of moral development. The first stage is called preconventional moral reasoning and is based on anticipated punishments and rewards. Individuals in this stage are simply interested in getting rewards and avoiding punishments and see morality in those terms. The second level is called conventional moral reasoning and is the stage that Kohlberg felt most people reach as adults. Conventional moral reasoning is based on conformity to social expectations. Thus, a person in this level behaves morally because he or she seeks to gain approval from others and feels that it is one's duty to show respect for authority and to maintain order. The third level is called postconventional moral reasoning. This level is based on well-thought-out moral principles. These are principles that can be above laws and rules and are often based on principles of justice and equality.

4. Erikson argued for eight psychosocial stages of development. The first is called trust vs. mistrust and is characterized by the development of a sense of trust toward others based on experiences in the first year of life. Autonomy versus shame and doubt follows as children start to exercise their individuality. Parents who don't allow that may have children who develop shame and doubt. From ages three to six, children's curiosity about the world shows up in initiative versus guilt. Given freedom to explore, children will develop a sense of initiative. From six to puberty, a child who experiences pride will develop "industry," a striving to achieve. Without this, a child will develop a sense of inferiority. In adolescence, the major issue is "identity versus role confusion" as adolescents try to develop a sense of identity, "who they are." In young adulthood (20-40), the major issue is "intimacy versus isolation" and involves making connections with others, particularly in terms of finding a life partner and developing a family. In middle adulthood (40-65), the major issue is "generativity versus stagnation" as people feel they are moving forward with family and career or are not. Finally, the last stage is called "integrity versus despair," as people look back over their lives and experience a sense of satisfaction or regret.

5. Research into the day-care controversy has revealed some interesting results. Day care does not seem to disrupt infants' attachments to their parents unless the day care is poor, the child spends many hours there, parents are not sensitive to their child at home, and the child has multiple day-care arrangements. Infants and toddlers are slightly less engaged with their mothers and less sociable toward them if they attend day-care. Infants and pre-schoolers from low income families seem to benefit socially and cognitively from high-quality day-care. For infants from middle- and upper-income homes, day-care, regardless of quality, seems to have little subsequent effect (positively or negatively) on children once they enter elementary school. The quality of home and family experiences seem to be more important predictors of development for these children.

Chapter 12. Personality

Learning Objectives

12.1 Describe three characteristics of behaviour that are seen as reflecting an individual's personality.

12.2 Outline the primary elements of Freud's psychodynamic theory, including levels of consciousness, roles of the pleasure and reality principle, and the three personality structures.

12.3 Describe the various forms of defence mechanisms and explain their function.

12.4 Describe each of Freud's psychosexual stages and explain how they contribute to adult personality.

12.5 Explain how the neoanalytic theorists Adler and Jung and object relations' theorists departed from Freudian theory.

12.6 Describe the major difficulties in evaluating psychodynamic theories.

12.7 Describe the roles of self-consistency and congruence in Rogers' self-theory.

12.8 Explain how positive regard prevents conditions of worth from developing.

12.9 Describe current research on self-esteem, self-verification, and self-enhancement and how it assists in evaluating the humanistic-phenomenological perspective.

12.10 Describe the gender and cultural differences that have been found in self-concept research.

12.11 Describe the trait perspective of personality, including factor analysis approaches and the five-factor model.

12.12 Describe Eysenck's theory of personality that focuses upon extraversion and neuroticism.

12.13 Describe the Five Factor Model of personality.

12.14 Describe what is known about the biological bases of personality traits

12.15 Describe research evidence regarding stability of personality over time and across situations, including factors that influence consistency.

12.16 Describe how personality factors, such as Type A and C personalities, optimism-pessimism, and conscientiousness relate to health.

12.17 Explain what is meant by reciprocal determinism.

12.18 Describe Rotter's theory of expectation and the role of locus of control.

12.19 Describe Bandura's social learning theory and the four sources of information that influence self-efficacy.

12.20 Summarize the six principles of effective goal setting.

12.21 Describe the various methods used to measure personality variables.

12.22 Describe how personality can be assessed through structured interviews, behavioural assessment, and remote behavioural sampling strategies.

12.23 Compare and contrast rational and empirical approaches to personality scale development, providing examples of each.

12.24 Describe the assumptions and give examples of projective tests.

Chapter Overview

What is Personality?

Personality refers to the relatively enduring and distinctive ways of thinking, feeling, and acting that characterize a person's responses to life situations.

The Psychodynamic Perspective

Freud believed strongly in the ideas of unconscious processes and psychic energy as motivators of behaviour. Freud's structural theory of personality suggests that three interacting structures (id, ego, and superego) form the core of personality. The id operates according to the pleasure principle, seeking immediate gratification for its sexual and aggressive impulses. The ego, operating primarily at a conscious level, operates according to the reality principle, finding ways that the id can safely discharge its impulses. The superego is the moral arm of personality and strives to check the desires of the id. Freud believed that the interaction between all three structures of personality, along with the release of psychic energy not only motivated behaviour but also could result in anxiety if the three structures of personality don't work together in harmony. Defence mechanisms such as repression are used by the ego to deal with anxiety. Freud also proposed a series of psychosexual stages through which children develop. Sexual pleasure is focused on different parts of the body during these stages (oral, anal, phallic, latency, and genital). Needless to say, Freud's theory has been controversial in the field of psychology. Much research does not support the basic suppositions of the theory, but some research does support the importance of the unconscious in motivating behaviour. Former Freudian disciples who grew disenchanted with Freudian theory developed their own theories, and, as a group, they became known as the neoanalysts. These theorists suggested that social and cultural factors play a far more important role in the development of personality than Freud had believed and argued that Freud had placed too much importance on childhood events in his theory. Important neoanalysts include Jung and the object-relations theorists, including Melanie Klein.

The Humanistic Perspective

Humanistic psychologists stress people's striving for self-actualization, the realization of one's potential. One of the most important theorists, Carl Rogers, believed that we have needs for self-consistency (in self-perceptions) and congruence (between self-perceptions and experience). Inconsistency creates threat and anxiety. Rogers believed that we are born with a need for positive regard from others and that conditional positive regard, which means that others give us approval only if we behave or think in ways that they approve of, can hurt us in a number of ways. Research on the self has pointed to the importance of self-esteem for healthy functioning. People try to self-verify their perceptions and engage in self-enhancement behaviours to develop their self-esteem.

Trait and Biological Perspectives

Two of the more prominent theories of traits are Cattell's sixteen personality factors theory and the five factor model, which, not surprisingly, argue that there are sixteen different personality factors and five different personality factors, respectively. Biological explanations for traits focus on three different causes: activity of the nervous system, genes, and evolution. Studies of brain activity have indicated some differences between introverts and extraverts. Twin studies, covered in Chapter 4, have indicated that monozygotic twins are far more alike in personality than are dizygotic twins, suggesting a genetic basis of personality traits. Evolutionary personality theory suggests that traits developed throughout human history because they helped us to physically survive and because they aid in reproduction (see Chapter 4 for a discussion).

Social Cognitive Theories

Social cognitive theories, as the name would indicate, combine behavioural and cognitive theories in an attempt to understand behaviour. According to Bandura's principle of reciprocal determinism, person factors (including personality and cognitive processes), the environment, and behaviour all affect each other. Julian Rotter argued that the likelihood that we will engage in a certain behaviour is governed by expectancy and how much we desire or dread the expected outcome of our behaviour. Locus of control is a term that Rotter devised to refer to the degree to which we believe that internal or external factors control our behaviour. Bandura has suggested that self-efficacy strongly affects how people regulate their lives. Performance experiences, observational learning, emotional arousal, and verbal persuasion all affect one's sense of self-efficacy.

Personality Assessment

Personality assessment is accomplished through a number of means, including interviews, behavioural assessment, personality scales, and projective tests. In behavioural assessment, elaborate coding systems are used by psychologists in observing behaviours of interest. Objective personality scales, such as the Minnesota Multiphasic Personality Inventory follow the empirical approach to the study of personality. Projective tests, such as the Rorschach inkblot test and the Thematic Apperception Test are tests of interpretations of ambiguous stimuli. People's responses to the stimuli are thought by some psychologists to be "projections" of inner needs, feelings, and ways of viewing the world.

Chapter Outline

What is Personality?

The Psychodynamic Perspective
    Freud's Psychoanalytic Theory
        Psychic Energy and Mental Events
        The Structure of Personality
        Conflict, Anxiety, and Defence
        Psychosexual Development

Problem-Based Learning

General

http://fas.psych.nwu.edu/personality.html
The Personality Project from the department of psychology at Northwestern University. This site contains information for students, links to research literature on many aspects of personality, online projects, and psychological organizations.

http://www.ship.edu/~cgboeree/perscontents.html
Personality Theories-This site which is maintained by Dr. C. George Boeree at Shippensburg University is an electronic text containing many theories and biographical information about the theorists.

http://www.personalityresearch.org
Great Ideas in Personality-This site contains research programs, a large number of links to other sites, a bibliography of journals and books, student information, and course outlines. It covers many aspects of personality including behaviour genetics, personality disorders, and psychoanalysis. It also contains a large list of researchers in personality, the university they are affiliated with, and links to their websites.

Psychoanalysis

http://www.cyberpsych.org/apf/index.html
American Psychoanalytic Association-This site contains information about programs, news and events, links to other sites and a bibliography of books and journal literature on psychoanalysis.

Key Terms: *Write the letter of the definition next to the term in the space provided.*

What is Personality?
The Psychodynamic Perspective

1. ___ analytic psychology	a.	the distinctive and relatively enduring ways of thinking, feeling, and acting that characterize a person's responses to life situations
2. ___ archetypes	b.	powers the mind and constantly presses for direct or indirect release
3. ___ defence mechanisms	c.	the innermost core of the personality that is the source of all psychic energy
4. ___ ego	d.	the seeking of immediate gratification or release, regardless of reality
5. ___ Electra complex	e.	the part of personality that tests reality to decide how best to allow the id to satisfy its desires
6. ___ id	f.	the realization that id impulses should only be satisfied in societally appropriate ways
7. ___ object relations theories	g.	the moral part of the personality
8. ___ Oedipal complex	h.	strategies used by the ego to deny or to distort reality

9. ___ personality

    i. a defence mechanism by which the ego uses some of its energy to prevent anxiety-arousing memories, feelings, and impulses from entering consciousness

10. ___ pleasure principle

    j. a defence mechanism by which a repressed impulse is released in the form of a socially acceptable behaviour

11. ___ psychic energy

    k. stages during which psychic energy is focused on particular erogenous zones of the body

12. ___ psychosexual stages

    l. consists of a boy's erotic feelings toward his mother, guilt, and castration anxiety

13. ___ reality principle

    m. consists of a girl's erotic feelings toward her father, guilt, and anxiety

14. ___ repression
15. ___ sublimation
16. ___ superego

    n. Jung's theory of personality
    o. inherited tendencies to interpret experiences in certain ways
    p. theories that focus on the images or mental representations that people form of themselves and other people as a result of early experience with caregivers

The Humanistic Perspective

1. ___ conditions of worth
2. ___ congruence

3. ___ fully functioning person
4. ___ gender schema
5. ___ need for positive regard

6. ___ need for positive self-regard
7. ___ self

8. ___ self-actualization
9. ___ self-consistency
10. ___ self-enhancement

11. ___ self-esteem
12. ___ self-verification

13. ___ threat
14. ___ unconditional positive regard

    a. the total realization of one's human potential
    b. an organized, consistent set of perceptions and beliefs about oneself
    c. an absence of conflict among self-perceptions
    d. consistency between self-perception and experience
    e. evoked by any experience that is inconsistent with our self-concept
    f. need for acceptance, sympathy, and love from others

    g. communicates that love is independent of how the child behaves
    h. wanting to feel good about ourselves
    i. dictate when we approve or disapprove of ourselves
    j. people who do not hide behind masks or adopt artificial roles

    k. how positively or negatively we feel about ourselves
    l. need to preserve self-concept by maintaining self-consistency and congruence
    m. a tendency to gain and preserve a positive self-image
    n. organized mental structures that contain our understanding of the attributes and behaviours that are appropriate and expected for males and females

Traits and Biological Perspectives
Social Cognitive Theories
Personality Assessment

1. ___ behavioural assessment

2. ___ empirical approach

3. ___ factor analysis

4. ___ internal-external locus of control

5. ___ Minnesota Multiphasic Personality Inventory

6. ___ projective tests

7. ___ rational approach

8. ___ reciprocal determinism

9. ___ remote behaviour sampling

10. ___ self-efficacy

11. ___ self-monitoring

12. ___ social cognitive theory

13. ___ Type A personality

14. ___ Type C personality

a. a statistical tool that identifies clusters of correlated behaviours

b. paying attention to situational cues and adapting behaviour appropriately

c. a personality type of people who live under great pressure and are very demanding of themselves

d. a personality type that may be a risk factor for cancer

e. a cognitive-behavioural approach to personality, developed by Albert Bandura and Walter Mischel, that emphasizes the role of social learning, cognitive processes, and self-regulation

f. principle that the person's behaviour and the environment influence each other

g. an expectancy concerning the degree of personal control we have in our lives

h. beliefs concerning ability to perform behaviours needed to achieve desired outcomes

i. tests, such as the Rorschach and the TAT, that present ambiguous stimuli to the subject; the responses are assumed to be based on a projection of internal characteristics of the person onto the stimuli

j. assessment based on an explicit coding system that contains the behavioural categories of interest

k. self-reports of behaviour from respondents' natural environments using "beeper" or computer prompts

l. creating items for a personality test based on a theorist's conception of a personality trait

m. an approach to test construction in which items (regardless of their content) are chosen that differentiate between two groups that are known to differ on a particular personality variable

n. a widely used personality test whose items were developed using the empirical approach and by comparing various kinds of psychiatric patients with normal patients

Review at a Glance: *Write the term that best fits the blank to review what you learned in this chapter.*

The Psychodynamic Perspective

According to Freud, instinctual drives generate (1) _____ _____, which powers the mind and presses for release. Freud divided the personality into three separate but interacting structures. The (2) _____ exists totally within the unconscious mind and operates according to the (3) _____ principle. The (4) _____ operates primarily at a conscious level, testing reality and trying to satisfy the id's desires in appropriate ways, according to the (5) _____ _____. The moral arm of personality is called the (6) _____. As the personality involves a dynamic interaction between all three personality structures, anxiety may occur if they do not work in harmony. The ego may resort to (7) _____ _____, which may distort reality when a person feels anxiety. For example, in (8) _____, the ego uses some of its energy to prevent anxiety-provoking memories, feelings, and impulses from entering consciousness. Another technique the ego uses is (9) _____, by which the sinister underlying impulses are completely masked. Freud believed that much of adult personality structure is set during childhood. He proposed that children pass through five (10) _____ stages of development: oral, anal, phallic, latency, and genital. During the phallic stage, boys sexually desire their mothers but fear castration by their father, resulting in the (11) _____ _____, while girls similarly sexually desire their fathers but fear their mother's response, resulting in the (12) _____ _____. Successful resolution of these complexes leads to identification with the same-sex parent, according to Freud. Neo-Freudians, who broke away from Freudian theory, developed their own ideas about personality. Carl Jung developed his theory of (13) _____ psychology. Jung believed that all humans have a collective unconscious that consists of memories accumulated throughout the entire history of the human race. These memories are represented as (14) _____, inherited tendencies to interpret experiences in certain ways. (15) _____ _____ theorists believe that early experiences with caregivers influence the images that people form of themselves and of others.

The Humanistic Perspective

Humanistic psychologists believe that humans are motivated to realize their full potential, a process called (16) _____ _____. They believe that we have a tendency to maintain our self-concept after it is established and thus have a need for an absence of conflict among self-perceptions, or (17) _____ _____, and a need for consistency between self-perceptions and experience, or (18) _____. A prominent humanistic theorist, Carl Rogers, believed that we are born with an innate need for (19) _____ _____, that is, for acceptance, sympathy, and love from others. (20) _____ _____ _____ from parents communicates to the child that he or she is inherently worthy of love. However, when other people withhold approval unless an individual thinks or acts in a certain way, they have placed (21) _____ _____ _____ on that individual. People who had achieved self-actualization were called (22) _____ - _____ persons by Rogers. Research on the self has shown that how positively or negatively we feel about ourselves, or our sense of (23) _____ - _____ has important implications for our lives. The proposition that people are motivated to preserve their self-concept and maintain their self-consistency and congruence is called (24) _____ - _____. Processes used to gain and maintain a positive self-image are called (25) _____ - _____ activities.

Trait and Biological Perspectives

A statistical approach often used by trait theorists that identifies clusters of specific behaviours that are associated with one another so that they are seen as reflecting a basic trait on which people can vary is called (26) _____ _____. One of the most popular trait theories is called Big Five theory, which suggests that there are five major personality traits. The acronym (27) _____ can be used to remember the traits: Openness, Conscientiousness, Extraversion, Agreeableness, and Neuroticism. Eysenck believed that the factors of introversion-extraversion and stability-instability (neuroticism) underlie normal personality. Biological approaches have suggested that activity of the nervous system, genetics, and evolution all play a role in the development of personality traits. According to (28) _____ _____ theory, human personality traits have come to exist because of the role they play in both survival and reproduction.

Social Cognitive Theories

According to Bandura's principle of (29), _____ _____, the person, the person's behaviour, and the environment all influence one another in a pattern of two-way causal links. Julian Rotter believed that a sense of personal control plays an important influence on our behaviours. People with an (30) _____ locus of control believe that they control their own behaviour, while people with an (31) _____ locus of control believe that external factors control their behaviour. Bandura also believed that people who believe that they have abilities to perform the behaviours needed to achieve desired outcomes have a good sense of (32) _____ - _____.

Personality Assessment

There are many techniques used to assess personality. (33) _____ are particularly valuable for the direct personal contact established between researcher and respondent. In (34) _____ _____, psychologists use an explicit coding system to code the behaviours of interest. Through (35) _____ _____ _____, researchers and clinicians collect samples of behaviour from respondents as they live their daily lives. Personality scales, such as the most widely used personality inventory, the (36) _____, are developed in two major ways. In the (37) _____ approach, items are based on the theorist's conception of the personality trait to be measured, while in the (38) _____ approach, items are chosen because previous research has shown that the items were answered differently by groups of people known to differ in the personality characteristic of interest. Tests that assume that when a person is presented with an ambiguous stimulus, his or her interpretation of it will indicate inner feelings, anxieties, or desires are called (39) _____ tests.

Apply What You Know

1. Using Study Sheet 12.1, rate both your actual and ideal characteristics. Using the principles of humanistic psychology, describe how you could move your "actual self" toward your "ideal self."

2. Describe how Rotter's principles of expectancy, reinforcement value, and locus of control can be used to change an undesirable behaviour that you have.

Internet Scavenger Hunt

1. There are several measures of personality available on the WWW. Evaluate the items with regard to the perspective you think they may be representing.

2. Conduct a search on some of the Key People (e.g., Sigmund Freud, Carl Jung, Carl Rogers) in the area of personality. Note the sites you find and their content.

Practice Test

Multiple Choice Items: *Please write the letter corresponding to your answer in the space to the left of each item.*

1. Trevor releases his anger and aggressive impulses by playing ice hockey. According to Freud, this would be an example of _____.

   a. projection
   b. displacement
   c. reaction formation
   d. sublimation

2. During a conversation with a friend, Al starts to get angry but this is an emotion that he considers inappropriate and childish. As a result, instead of noticing his own anger, he unknowingly starts to believe that his friend is becoming angry and excited, even though she is doing no such thing. This example **best demonstrates** the defence mechanism of

_____.

   a. reaction formation
   b. projection
   c. sublimation
   d. displacement

_____ 3. Freud speculated that someone who receives very lax toilet training during the anal stage of development will tend to be _____.

    a. a messy, negative, and dominant adult
    b. an obsessive and orderly adult
    c. a talkative, orally-focused adult
    d. a well-adjusted, healthy adult

_____ 4. Neoanalytic theorists such as Alfred Adler and Carl Jung departed from traditional psychoanalytic theory in that they _____.

    a. were less optimistic than Freud regarding human nature
    b. assumed that personality is almost entirely shaped during childhood
    c. believed childhood sexuality needed to emphasized even more
    d. believed that Freud did **not** place enough emphasis on social and cultural factors

_____ 5. Bob thinks that he is a good tennis player and his results support this belief. His is better than almost all of the people in his tennis club and he wins most of his tennis matches. This agreement between Bob's beliefs and his actual experience would **best be considered** as an example of Carl Roger's concept of _____.

    a. self-actualization
    b. congruence
    c. self-consistency
    d. a condition of worth

_____ 6. Sarah has the belief that she is good in math, but she has just received her first D grade in her freshman calculus class. This inconsistency between Sarah's self-belief and her actual experience will most likely generate what Carl Rogers termed _____.

    a. self-actualization
    b. a condition of worth
    c. threat
    d. a need for unconditional self-regard

_____ 7. A person who is intellectual, imaginative, and has a broad range of interests would **mostly likely** score highly on a measure of _____.

    a. Openness
    b. Agreeableness
    c. Extraversion
    d. Conscientiousness

_____ 8. Research conducted by Cloninger has linked the following 3 broad personality traits with the functioning of neurotransmitter systems:

    a. sensation-seeking, obstinacy, and optimism
    b. novelty-seeking, harm avoidance and reward dependence
    c. extraversion, openness, and optimism
    d. conscientiousness, novelty seeking, and optimism

_____ 9. Greg doesn't think he has much of a chance of getting into his top choice for medical school. However, he still very much likes this school and desires very much to go there. Based on Rotter's concept of _____, we would expect Greg **not** to apply to this school while Rotter's concept of _____ suggests that Greg would apply to this school.

a. internal locus of control; external locus of control
b. expectancy; reinforcement value
c. self-consistency; self-efficacy
d. reinforcement value; self-efficacy

_____ 10. Ralph tends to be a rather passive person. Though he is happy and content with himself, he doesn't really believe that his actions make much of a difference in the word. For instance, he doesn't vote because he assumes that most governments are run by a few powerful people and there is very little he can do to change things. Ralph would **most accurately** be classified as having _____.

a. low self-esteem
b. high self-monitoring skills
c. an external locus of control
d. an internal locus of control

_____ 11. Which trait shows the most stability over time:

a. introversion-extraversion
b. emotionality
c. activity level
d. all of the above are more stable than other traits

_____ 12. When using _____ to assess personality and/or behaviours, researchers will create explicit coding systems that contain the particular behavioural categories in which they are interested.

a. the interview method
b. psychological tests
c. the behavioural assessment method
d. projective tests

_____ 13. The basic assumption underlying projective tests is that if you present someone with a(n) _____ stimulus, the interpretation for this stimulus will come from within and thus presumably represent or reflect their inner needs and feelings.

a. sexual
b. ambiguous
c. psychodynamically meaningful
d. provocative

_d___ 14. According to Freud, the ego _____.

     a.   is responsible for creating instincts
     b.   operates according to the pleasure principle
     c.   is created after the resolution of the Oedipal or Electra complexes
     d.   operates according to the reality principle

_____ 15. The psychoanalytic term for unconscious methods by which the ego distorts reality, thereby protecting a person from anxiety is a(n) _____.

     a.   catharsis
     b.   defence mechanism
     c.   extrinsic motivation
     d.   competence motivation

_____ 16. Having had it drummed into her for years that sex is bad, bad, bad, Frig Id has a very uncomfortable and unhappy wedding night. Freud would probably suggest that the major reason for Frig's problems is that she has a _____.

     a.   very strong libido
     b.   very strong superego
     c.   lot of neurotic anxiety
     d.   strong defence mechanism

_b___ 17. Which approach are you using if you select items for a personality test based on your conception of the personality trait to be measured:

     a.   empirical
     b.   rational
     c.   factor analytic
     d.   psychometric

_____ 18. Eysenck's trait theory includes all of the following dimensions of personality except _____.

     a.   introversion
     b.   neuroticism
     c.   agreeableness
     d.   psychoticism

_____ 19. In their Big 5 theory, Costa and McCrae (1988) have argued that there are five major personality factors. Of the following, the one which is not one of the Big 5 factors is _____.

     a.   neuroticism
     b.   extraversion
     c.   openness
     d.   dominance

✓ 20. Of the following, the person who is probably most <u>fully functioning</u> is a person who _____.

    a. is worried about his performance
    b. feels that she is free to realize her potential
    c. dislikes trying new things
    d. hates everyone

✓ 21. Of the following, the one which is an example of <u>conditional</u> positive regard is _____.

    a. helping another person with a problem
    b. trying to understand another person
    c. a parent giving approval to a child only if the child brings home straight "A's"
    d. a parent giving approval to a child regardless of what the child does

22. The personality dimension shared by both Eysenck's theory and Big 5 theory is _____.

    a. introversion-extraversion
    b. openness
    c. dominance
    d. psychoticism

✓ 23. How positively or negatively we feel about ourselves is called _____.

    a. self-esteem
    b. self-verification
    c. self-enhancement
    d. self-actualization

24. Personality traits exist in human beings today because they have historically aided in both survival and reproduction, according to _____ theory.

    a. humanistic personality
    b. Big 5
    c. evolutionary personality
    d. Cattell's sixteen personality factor

25. The personality trait that affects whether or not people tailor their behaviour to what is called for by the situation is called _____.

    a. self-verification
    b. self-enhancement
    c. self-actualization
    d. self-monitoring

26. A personality type that may be related to the propensity to develop cancer is called _____.

    a. Type A
    b. Type B
    c. Type C
    d. Type D

_____ 27. According to Bandura's principle of reciprocal determinism, _____.

    a.   behaviour determines personality but not vice-versa
    b.   personality determines behaviour but not vice-versa
    c.   the environment does not affect behaviour
    d.   the environment, person factors, and behaviour all affect each other

_____ 28. Bandura has suggested that performance experiences, observational learning, emotional arousal, and verbal persuasion all affect _____.

    a.   locus of control
    b.   self-efficacy beliefs
    c.   the cognitive-affective personality system
    d.   self-actualization

_____ 29. Consistent ways of responding to particular classes of situations are called _____.

    a.   CAPS
    b.   loci of control
    c.   behavioural signatures
    d.   personalities

_____ 30. Kama, a very capable student, arrived late for her psychology class. She noticed a set of inkblots on the overhead and assumed her instructor must have been lecturing about _____ tests.

    a.   projective
    b.   locus of control
    c.   social cognitive
    d.   humanistic

True/False Items: *Write T or F in the space provided to the left of each item.*

_____ 1. Personality is defined as the relatively enduring ways of thinking, feeling, and acting that characterize a person's response to life situations.

_____ 2. Freud believed that instincts generate psychic energy.

_____ 3. Freud believed that children are sexual beings.

_____ 4. Rogers believed that people are motivated for self-consistency but not for congruence.

_____ 5. Conditional positive regard communicates that a person is inherently worthy of love regardless of what he or she does.

_____ 6. Biological factors do not affect the development of personality traits.

_____ 7. The degree of behavioural consistency across situations is affected by how important a given trait is to a person.

_____ 8. Coronary heart disease has been associated with Type A personality.

_____ 9. Rotter argued that both expectancy and reinforcement value affect the likelihood that we will engage in a behaviour.

_____ 10. Through remote behaviour sampling, researchers and clinicians can collect samples of behaviour from respondents as they live their daily lives.

Short Answer Questions

1. What were Freud's ideas about psychic energy and mental events?

2. What did Rogers argue about positive regard?

3. What are the Big Five factors in the five-factor model of personality?

4. What is locus of control?

5. What are projective tests used for?

Essay Questions

1. What were Freud's ideas on the structure of personality?

2. How do the neoanalytic and object relations theories differ from Freudian theory?

3. What are the biological foundations of personality traits?

4. How are personality scales constructed?

Study Sheet 12.1
Real and Ideal Selves

Please rate both your actual self (your perception of yourself right now) and your ideal self (how you would like to be) by using the following scale:

1	2	3	4	5	6	7
poor						excellent

	Actual	Ideal
_____ 1. Sensitivity	4	4
_____ 2. Body	3	7
_____ 3. Sense of humour	5	7
_____ 4. Weight	3	7
_____ 5. Friendliness	6	7
_____ 6. Face	6	7
_____ 7. Honesty	5	7
_____ 8. Smile	5	7
_____ 9. Being understanding	6	7
_____ 10. Chest	6	7
_____ 11. Patience	7	7
_____ 12. Legs	6	7
_____ 13. Being Outgoing	5	7
_____ 14. Eyes	7	7
_____ 15. Being caring	7	7

Answer Keys

Answer Key for Key Terms

What is Personality?
The Psychodynamic Perspective

1. n	9. a
2. o	10. d
3. h	11. b
4. e	12. k
5. m	13. f
6. c	14. i
7. p	15. j
8. l	16. g

The Humanistic Perspective

1. i	8. a
2. d	9. c
3. j	10. m
4. n	11. k
5. f	12. l
6. h	13. e
7. b	14. g

Trait and Biological Perspectives

1. j	10. h
2. m	11. b
3. a	12. e
4. g	13. c
5. n	14. d
6. i	
7. l	
8. f	
9. k	

Answer Key for Review at a Glance

1. psychic energy	22. fully-functioning
2. id	23. self-esteem
3. pleasure	24. self-verification
4. ego	25. self-enhancing
5. reality principle	26. factor analysis
6. superego	27. OCEAN
7. defence mechanisms	28. evolutionary personality
8. repression	29. reciprocal determinism
9. sublimation	30. internal
10. psychosexual	31. external
11. Oedipus complex	32. self-efficacy

12. Electra complex
13. analytic
14. archetypes
15. Object relations
16. self-actualization
17. self-consistency
18. congruence
19. positive regard
20. Unconditional positive regard
21. conditions of worth

33. Interviews
34. behavioural assessment
35. remote behaviour sampling
36. MMPI
37. rational
38. empirical
39. Projective

Answer Key for Practice Test Multiple Choice Questions

1. d
2. b
3. a
4. d
5. b
6. c
7. a
8. b
9. b
10. c
11. d
12. c
13. b
14. d
15. b

16. b
17. b
18. c
19. d
20. b
21. c
22. a
23. a
24. c
25. d
26. c
27. d
28. b
29. c
30. a

Answer Key for Practice Test True/False Questions

1. T
2. T
3. T
4. F
5. F

6. F
7. T
8. T
9. T
10. T

Answer Key for Practice Test Short Answer Questions

1. Freud believed that instincts created psychic energy, which powers the mind and presses for direct or indirect release.

2. Rogers believed that all of us are born with a need for positive regard, a need for acceptance, sympathy and love from others. A need for positive self-regard also develops, whereby we want to feel good about ourselves. Unconditional positive regard promotes our sense of well-being, while conditions of worth impede our development.

3. The five factors can be remembered through use of the acronym OCEAN: Openness, Conscientiousness, Extraversion, Agreeableness, and Neuroticism.

4. Locus of control refers to our expectancies of the degree of personal control we believe we believe we have over our behaviour. People with an external locus of control believe that environmental circumstances control their behaviour, while people with an internal locus of control believe that they have internal control over their own behaviour.

5. Projective tests use ambiguous stimuli to help therapists and clients uncover unconscious aspects of their personalities.

Answer Key for Practice Test Essay Questions

1. Freud divided the personality into three separate but interacting structures: the id, the ego, and the superego. The id operates according to the pleasure principle, seeking immediate gratification, and is the source of all psychic energy. The ego has both unconscious and conscious aspects and seeks to satisfy the id's desires while dealing with environmental realities. Thus, the ego operates according to the reality principle. The superego is the moral arm of the personality and consists of values and ideals of society.

2. The neoanalysts, including Jung, Adler, Horney, Erikson, and Jung argued that Freud did not give social and cultural factors enough emphasis in his theories and that he stressed infantile sexuality and the events of childhood too much as explanations of adult personality. Object relationships theorists, in particular, focus on the images or mental representations that people form of themselves through interactions with caregivers. These images form "mental models" that influence their behaviour.

3. Eysenck believed that differences in biological arousal within the brain underscores personality trait differences. Twin and adoption studies have conclusively shown that genetics play an important role in the development of traits. Evolutionary personality theory suggests that the traits we see in humans today exist because they have been historically useful in both survival and reproduction.

4. Personality scales are constructed through two main approaches. In the rational approach, items are chosen for the test because of the way the theorist conceptualizes the trait. In the empirical approach, the items are chosen because they have previously been determined to distinguish those who have the trait from those who do not.

Chapter 13. Psychological Disorders

Learning Objectives

13.1   Describe the demonological perspective on abnormal behaviour and its implications for dealing with deviant behaviour.

13.2   Describe the historical importance of the discovery of the cause of general paresis.

13.3   Describe the vulnerability-stress model of abnormal behaviour.

13.4   Cite and define the "Three Ds" that enter into diagnoses of abnormal behaviour.

13.5   Define reliability and validity as these terms apply to diagnostic classification systems.

13.6   Indicate how the five axes of DSM-IV are used to describe an individual's abnormal behaviour, and factors that may contribute to it, or predict its future course.

13.7   Describe the effects of psychiatric labeling on social and self-perceptions.

13.8   Differentiate between the legal concepts of competency and insanity and explain how they affected recent court cases.

13.9   Describe the three components of anxiety.

13.10   Describe characteristics of anxiety disorders, including phobic disorder, generalized anxiety disorder, panic disorder, obsessive-compulsive disorder, and post-traumatic stress disorder.

13.11   Describe the purpose, method, and results of the research study on recovery from trauma by Gilboa-Schectman and Foa (2001).

13.12   Describe the biological, psychodynamic, cognitive, behavioural, and sociocultural factors involved in causing anxiety disorders.

13.13   Describe three types of somatoform disorders and their causal factors.

13.14   Describe three types of dissociative disorders and their causal factors, including a discussion on the validity of the diagnosis.

13.15   Describe the four classes of symptoms that characterize depression.

13.16   Differentiate between major depressive disorder and bipolar disorder.

13.17   Describe the biological, psychodynamic, humanistic, cognitive, behavioural, and sociocultural factors involved in causing mood disorders.

13.18   Describe the motives for suicide, identify the warning signs of suicide, and state four guidelines for helping a suicidal person.

13.19 Describe the major cognitive, behavioural, emotional, and perceptual features of schizophrenia.

13.20 Describe the differences between the four major types of schizophrenic disorders.

13.21 Describe the biological, psychodynamic, cognitive, environmental, and sociocultural factors involved in causing schizophrenic disorders.

13.22 Differentiate the various personality disorders.

13.23 Describe the characteristics of antisocial personality disorder.

13.24 Describe the biological, psychodynamic, and behavioural factors involved in causing antisocial personality disorders.

13.25 Describe factors associated with dangerousness in people with psychological disorders.

13.26 Describe the various externalizing and internalizing disorders of childhood.

13.27 Describe characteristics and causes of dementia.

Chapter Overview

Historical Perspectives on Psychological Disorders

Ancient humans believed that abnormal behaviour was caused by supernatural forces. Up until fairly recent history, people with psychological disorders were branded as witches and hunted down and often killed. Early biological views, such as those of the Greek physician Hippocrates, suggested that psychological disorders are diseases just like physical disorders. Early psychological theories focused on the use of psychoanalytic, behavioural, cognitive, and humanistic theories to explain abnormality. Today most clinical psychologists and counsellors believe in the vulnerability/stress model, which suggests that biological, psychological, and environmental and sociocultural factors all play a role in the development of psychological disorders.

Defining and Classifying Psychological Disorders

Judgements about how to define an "abnormal" behaviour are often difficult to make and can vary from culture to culture, and can change as societies develop. A current working definition for abnormal behaviour is "behaviour that is personally distressful, personally dysfunctional, and/or so culturally deviant that other people judge it to be inappropriate or maladaptive." The most widely used diagnostic system for classifying mental disorders in the United States is called the Diagnostic and Statistical Manual of Mental Disorders (DSM-IV). DSM-IV uses five axes (primary diagnosis, personality/developmental disorders, relevant physical disorders, severity of psychosocial stressors, and global assessment of functioning) to help clinicians understand disorders.

Anxiety Disorders

In anxiety disorders, the frequency and intensity of anxiety responses are out of proportion to the situations that trigger them, and the anxiety interferes with daily life. Anxiety disorders have cognitive, physiological, and behavioural components. Phobias are strong and irrational fears of certain objects or situations. Generalized anxiety disorder is a chronic state of anxiety (called 'free-floating') that is not attached to specific situations or objects. Panic disorders involve sudden and unpredictable anxiety that is extremely intense. Obsessive-compulsive disorder involves repetitive and unwelcome thoughts, images, and impulses and repetitive behavioural responses. People who have been exposed to traumatic live events may develop posttraumatic stress disorder. Biological factors including genetics, neurotransmitters, and evolutionary factors have all been implicated in the development of anxiety disorders. Psychological factors such as cognitive processes and learning also play important roles in the development of anxiety disorders, while sociocultural factors can also play a role.

Mood (Affective Disorders)

Depression involves emotional, cognitive, motivational, and somatic (body) symptoms. Major depression may lead people to be unable to function, while a less intense form of depression called dysthymia has less dramatic effects on personal functioning. Bipolar disorder involves both depression and periods of mania, which is a state of excited mood and behaviour. Biological factors, including genetics and neurotransmitters play an important role in the development of mood disorders. Low levels of neurotransmitters such as serotonin, dopamine, and norepinephrine may be particularly likely to influence the development of mood disorders. Psychological factors including personality, cognitive processes, and learning also play roles. Sociocultural factors can affect the prevalence of depressive disorders and the ways in which depression is manifested.

Somatoform Disorders

Somatoform disorders involve physical complaints or disabilities that suggest a medical problem, but which have no known biological cause.

Dissociative Disorders

Dissociative disorders involve a breakdown of the normal integration of personality. These disorders include psychogenic amnesia, psychogenic fugue, and dissociative identity disorder, which used to be called multiple personality disorder. According to trauma-dissociation theory, dissociative disorders develop due to response to severe stress in a person's life.

Schizophrenia

Schizophrenia is a psychotic disorder that involves severe disturbances in thinking, speech, perception, emotion, and behaviour. DSM-IV differentiates between four major types of schizophrenia: paranoid type, disorganized type, catatonic type, and undifferentiated type. Strong evidence exists for the role of genetic factors in the development of schizophrenia. Studies of the brain have shown that brain atrophy (a loss of neurons in the cerebral cortex) and overactivity of the dopamine system may play roles in the development of schizophrenia. Psychological factors such as family dynamics and a high level of expressed emotion (high levels of criticism, hostility, and overinvolvement) may also play a role. Studies of sociocultural factors have indicated that the prevalence of schizophrenia is highest in lower socioeconomic populations.

Personality Disorders

People diagnosed with personality disorders exhibit stable, ingrained, inflexible, and maladaptive ways of thinking, feeling, and behaving. Studies of people with antisocial personality disorder have focused on the role of genetics and psychological factors such as classical conditioning and modelling to understand the development of that disorder.

Disorders of Childhood and Old Age

Children and the elderly are not exempt from the experience of psychological disorders. In fact, many adults suffering a mental disorder experienced mental problems during childhood. In childhood, two main categories of disorders are those that are directed outward toward the environment (externalizing) and those that are directed inward (internalizing). The most common childhood disorder is the externalizing disorder of ADHD. Anxiety and depression, two internalizing disorders, are also found in childhood. In the elderly, dementia is especially prevalent. There are many types and causes of dementia, but the leading cause is Alzheimer's disease, accounting for about 60% of dementia cases in those over 65.

Chapter Outline

Mood (Affective) Disorders
 Depression
 Bipolar Disorder
 Prevalence and Course of Mood Disorders
 Causal Factors in Mood Disorders
  Biological Factors
  Psychological Factors
   Psychological Applications: Understanding and Preventing Suicide

Somatoform Disorders

Dissociative Disorders
   Research Frontiers: Dissociative Identity Disorder: A Clinical and Scientific Puzzle

Schizophrenia
 Characteristics of Schizophrenia
 Subtypes of Schizophrenia
 Causal Factors in Schizophrenia
  Biological Factors
  Psychological Factors
  Environmental Factors
  Sociocultural Factors

Personality Disorders
 Antisocial Personality Disorder
 Causal Factors
  Biological Factors
  Psychological and Environmental Factors

Disorders of Childhood and Old Age
 Childhood Disorders
  Externalizing Disorders
  Internalizing Disorders
 Dementia in Old Age

Problem-Based Learning

Disorders

http://www.mentalhealth.com
Internet Mental Health-This website, created by Canadian psychiatrist Dr. Phillip Long, is an encyclopedia of mental health information. It contains information about disorders, diagnosis, medications, and research resources.

http://www.schizophrenia.com
Schizophrenia Home Page-This is a non-profit website that contains information, discussions, chats, and links to other resources.

Law and Psychology

http://www.sfu.ca/psyc/law/
This is a Simon Fraser University based website with information about law and psychology and links to related sites. It also contains information about the SFU program.

Regression

http://www.cyberpsych.org/apf/index.html
American Psychoanalytic Foundation-This site contains information about news and events, programs, links to other sites, and a bibliography of books and journal literature on psychoanalysis.

Psychology Associations

http://www.cpa.ca/contents.html
Canadian Psychological Association-This is the CPA's website and it contains information about careers, regulatory bodies, professional associations, clinical disorders, and issues that concern psychology in Canada. This site contains a Canadian report on the terrorist attacks in the United States.

http://www.apa.org
American Psychological Association-This is the APA's website and it contains information about careers, student concerns, some full text articles, news and events, and information about many areas such as clinical disorders, aids, violence and anger.

Key Terms: *Write the letter of the definition next to the term in the space provided.*

Historical Perspectives on Psychological Disorders
Defining and Classifying Psychological Disorders

1. ___ abnormal behaviour

2. ___ competency
3. ___ insanity
4. ___ reliability

5. ___ stressor
6. ___ validity

7. ___ vulnerability

8. ___ vulnerability-stress model

a. stresses that each of us have some degree of vulnerability to develop a psychological disorder, given sufficient stress
b. predisposition to a disorder
c. some recent or current event that requires a person to cope
d. behaviour that is personally distressful, personally dysfunctional, and/or so culturally deviant that other people judge it to be inappropriate or maladaptive
e. high levels of agreement in diagnostic decisions
f. when diagnostic categories accurately capture the essential features of the various disorders
g. refers to a defendant's state of mind at the time of a judicial hearing by which a person is judged as to his or her ability to understand the nature of the proceedings
h. a legal judgement that a person was so severely impaired during the commission of a crime that they lacked the capacity to appreciate the wrongfulness of their acts or to control their conduct

Anxiety Disorders
Mood (Affective) Disorders

1. ___ agoraphobia

2. ___ anxiety
3. ___ anxiety disorder
4. ___ biological preparedness
5. ___ bipolar disorder

6. ___ compulsions
7. ___ culture-bound disorder
8. ___ depressive triad
9. ___ dysthymia

10. ___ generalized anxiety disorder
11. ___ learned helplessness theory
12. ___ major depression

13. ___ mania

14. ___ mood disorder

15. ___ neurotic anxiety

a. disorder in which the frequency and intensity of anxiety responses are out of proportion to the situations that trigger them
b. state of tension and apprehension
c. strong and irrational fears of certain objects or situations
d. fear of public places and open areas
e. excessive fear of situations in which a person might be evaluated and embarrassed
f. fears of specific stimuli
g. a chronic state of "free-floating" anxiety
h. sudden, unpredictable, and intense anxiety
i. disorders consisting of repetitive uncontrollable thoughts and behaviours
j. repetitive and unwelcome thoughts, images, or impulses that invade consciousness
k. repetitive behavioural responses

l. a disorder in which a person experiences severe anxiety, flashbacks, numbness, and guilt
m. evolution makes it easier for us to learn to fear certain stimuli
n. occurs when unacceptable impulses threaten to overwhelm the ego's defences
o. disorder that only occurs in certain places

16. ___ obsessions
17. ___ obsessive-compulsive disorder
18. ___ panic disorder
19. ___ phobias
20. ___ posttraumatic stress disorder
21. ___ social phobia

22. ___ specific phobia
23. ___ suicide

p. emotion-based disorders involving depression or mania
q. a type of depression that leaves people unable to function effectively in their lives
r. a less intense form of depression that has less dramatic effects on personal and occupational functioning
s. a disorder in which depression alternates with periods of mania
t. a state of highly excited mood and behaviour

u. theory that holds that depression occurs when people expect that bad events will occur and that prevention and coping are impossible
v. the willful taking of one's own life
w. a cognitive triad of negative thoughts concerning the world, oneself, and the future

Somatoform Disorders
Dissociative Disorders
Schizophrenia
Personality Disorders

1. ___ catatonic type

2. ___ conversion disorder

3. ___ delusions

4. ___ disorganized type

5. ___ dissociative disorders

6. ___ dissociative identity disorder
7. ___ dopamine hypothesis

8. ___ expressed emotion

9. ___ hallucinations

10. ___ hypochondriasis

11. ___ negative symptoms
12. ___ pain disorder
13. ___ paranoid type

14. ___ personality disorder

a. disorder that suggests a medical problem but has no known biological cause
b. disorder in which people become unduly alarmed about symptoms and are concerned that they will have a serious illness
c. disorder in which people experience intense pain that is out of proportion to the medical condition they have or for which no physical basis can be found
d. a somatoform disorder in which serious neurological symptoms suddenly occur with no apparent physical cause
e. disorders that involve a breakdown of the normal integration of facets of the self
f. a person responds to a stressful event with extensive but selective memory loss
g. a dissociative disorder in which a person loses all sense of personal identity
h. a disorder in which two or more separate personalities coexist within the same person
i. theory that the development of new personalities occurs in response to severe stress
j. a psychotic disorder that involves severe disturbances in thinking, speech, perception, emotion, and behaviour
k. false beliefs
l. false perceptions
m. type of schizophrenia that prominently features delusions of persecution and grandeur
n. type of schizophrenia that features confusion, incoherence, and severe deterioration of adaptive behaviour

15. ___ positive symptoms

o. type of schizophrenia that features striking motor disturbances

16. ___ psychogenic amnesia

p. type of schizophrenia in which people exhibit some schizophrenic symptoms but not enough to be diagnosed into a particular category

17. ___ psychogenic fugue

q. type of schizophrenia that is characterized by positive symptoms

18. ___ regression

r. delusions, hallucinations, and disorganized speech and thinking

19. ___ schizophrenia

s. type of schizophrenia that features negative symptoms

20. ___ somatoform disorder

t. normal reactions that seem to be missing

21. ___ trauma-dissociation theory

u. hypothesis that the symptoms of schizophrenia are produced by overactivity of the dopamine system

22. ___ Type I schizophrenia

v. a retreat to an earlier stage of psychosocial development

23. ___ Type II schizophrenia

w. involves high levels of criticism, hostility, and overinvolvement

24. ___ undifferentiated type

x. disorders in which people exhibit stable, ingrained, inflexible, and maladaptive ways of thinking, feeling, and behaving

Disorders of Childhood and Old Age

1. ___ Alzheimer's disease

a. disorder in which problems may take the form of attention difficulties, hyperactivity-impulsivity, or a combination of the two that results in impaired functioning

2. ___ attention-deficit/hyperactivity disorder (ADHD)

b. disorder in which children consistently behave in a disobedient, defiant, and hostile manner that interferes with the child's functioning and interpersonal relationships

3. ___ conduct disorder

c. disorders directed toward the environment in the form of behaviours that are disruptive and often aggressive

4. ___ dementia

d. disorder in which children violate important social norms and show disregard for the rights of others

5. ___ externalizing disorders

e. the gradual loss of cognitive abilities that accompanies brain deterioration and interferes with normal functioning

6. ___ internalizing disorders

f. disorders, such as anxiety disorders and mood disorders, that involve maladaptive thoughts and emotions

7. ___ oppositional defiant disorder (ODD)

g. the leading cause of dementia in the elderly, accounting for about 60 percent of senile dementias

Review at a Glance: *Write the term that best fits the blank to review what you learned in this chapter.*

Historical Perspectives on Psychological Disorders

The belief that abnormal behaviour is caused by supernatural forces is called the (1) _____ view. Early biological views stressed that psychological disorders have the same causes as physical diseases. In today's (2) _____ - _____ model, each and every one of us has some degree of vulnerability for the development of a particular psychological disorder.

Defining and Classifying Psychological Disorders

When diagnosing psychological disorders, clinicians must use criteria that is both valid and reliable. (3) _____ means that clinicians using the system should show high levels of agreement in their diagnostic decisions, while (4) _____ means that the diagnostic categories should capture the essential features of the various disorders. The most widely used classification system in North America is called (5) _____. Psychiatric diagnoses can have important legal consequences. A defendant's state of mind at the time of a judicial hearing is called his or her (6) _____. The presumed state of mind of a defendant at the time the crime was committed is determined in the legal (not psychological) determination of (7) _____.

Anxiety Disorders

Strong and irrational fears of certain objects or situations are called (8) _____. Fear of public spaces is called (9) _____; excessive fear of situations in which the person might be evaluated and possibly embarrassed is called (10) _____ phobia. Fears of dogs, snakes, spiders, airplanes and other objects are called (11) _____ phobias. When a person experiences a chronic state of "free-floating" anxiety that is not tied to any specific thing, that person is diagnosed with (12) _____ _____ disorder. Sudden, unpredictable, and intense anxiety is a symptom of (13) _____ _____. Repetitive, unwelcome thoughts images, or impulses that invade consciousness are called (14) _____, while repetitive behavioural responses are called (15) _____. When a person suffers from both, he or she is diagnosed as having (16) _____ - _____ disorder. People who have been exposed to traumatic live events may experience (17) _____ - _____ _____ disorder. The search for biological processes associated with anxiety disorders have pointed to abnormally low levels of the neurotransmitter (18) _____. According to Freudian psychodynamic theory, (19) _____ anxiety occurs when unacceptable impulses threaten to overwhelm the ego's defences. Social and cultural factors likely also play a role in the development of anxiety. Certain disorders that only occur in certain places are called (20) _____ - _____ disorders.

Mood (Affective) Disorders

A type of depression that leaves people unable to function effectively in their lives is called (21) _____ depression. A less intense form of depression is called (22) _____. In (23) _____ _____, periods of depression alternate with periods of (24) _____, a state of highly excited mood and behaviour. A cognitive explanation of depression known as (25) _____ _____ theory suggests that depression occurs when people expect that bad events will occur and that there is nothing that they can do to prevent or cope with them.

Somatoform Disorders

In (26) _____, people notice and become unduly alarmed about any symptom they detect. People with (27) _____ disorder experience pain that is out of proportion to their medical condition or for which no physical problem can be found.
(28) _____ disorder is diagnosed for people in which serious neurological symptoms occur for no physical reason.

Dissociative Disorders

Dissociative disorders involve a breakdown of the normal integration of personality. In (29) _____ _____, a person responds to a stressful event with extensive but selective memory loss. (30) _____ _____ involves a loss of personal identity and the establishment of a new identity in a new location. A disorder formerly known as multiple personality disorder is known in DSM-IV as (31) _____ _____ disorder. An explanation of this disorder called (32) _____ - _____ theory suggests that the development of new personalities occurs in response to severe stress.

Schizophrenia

Schizophrenics sometimes have (33) _____, false beliefs that are sustained in the face of evidence to the contrary and (34) _____, false perceptions that have a compelling sense of reality. There are several types of schizophrenia. Delusions of persecution and grandeur are features of the (35) _____ type. Confusion, incoherence, and severe deterioration of adaptive behaviour are characteristic of the (36) _____ type. The (37) _____ type involves striking motor disturbances. A predominance of positive symptoms is present in (38) _____ schizophrenia, while a predominance of negative symptoms occurs in
(39) _____ schizophrenia. Schizophrenia is thought to have a biological basis, including the influence of genetic factors. Other researchers believe that an excess of the neurotransmitter (40) _____ is a cause of schizophrenia. Environmental factors may also play a role in the development of the disorder. Schizophrenics are more likely to relapse after treatment if they return to a home with a high degree of (41) _____ _____.

Personality Disorders

People with (42) _____ _____ disorder seem to lack a conscience.

Disorders of Childhood and Old Age

Two broad categories of psychological disorders in children are called (43) _____ and (44) _____. ADHD is the most common childhood disorder and falls under the broad category of (45) _____ disorders. Two internalizing disorders of childhood are (46) _____ and anxiety. Many of the childhood disorders are precursors of disorders experienced in (47) _____. Whereas, approximately 74% of children with a physical handicap receive professional treatment, only (48) _____ % of children with a psychological problem do. The elderly are susceptible to the disorders seen in adulthood, and are considered at risk for (49) _____. The leading cause of dementia is Alzheimer's disease, accounting for about (50) _____ % of dementia cases in those over 65.

Apply What You Know

1. Women are generally about twice as likely than men to suffer from both anxiety and mood disorders. Research the prevalence rates for both sets of disorders in Canada. Using what you have learned about biological, psychological, and environmental factors in the development of disorders, explain why you think this difference occurs.

Internet Scavenger Hunt

1. Go to the web site "News of the Weird" at http://www.newsoftheweird.com and find three cases of behaviours that you would consider to be abnormal. Using the criteria for what an abnormal behaviour is, explain why each behaviour is "abnormal."

2. "Abnormality" is a somewhat relative concept. Do some research to find five behaviours that are considered normal in Canadian culture, but are considered abnormal in other cultures.

Practice Test

Multiple Choice Items: *Please write the letter corresponding to your answer in the space to the left of each item.*

_____ 1. A recent immigrant to Canada has been having some problems in living and after some initial hesitation, decides to see a therapist for some assistance. After the interview, the therapist makes a particular diagnosis and is discussing the case with a colleague when the colleague raises some concerns. She points out that the therapist may need to reconsider his diagnosis because the behaviours involved are much more common and are even considered "normal" in the country from which the person came. The views of the colleague are **most consistent** with the _____ perspective on psychological disorders.

    a. sociocultural
    b. behavioural
    c. biological
    d. cognitive

_____ 2. Sara lost both of her parents when she was a young child. Primarily because of this historical factor, she develops an anxiety disorder when she learns that the life of her best friend is threatened by cancer. This example provides the **best illustration** of _____.

    a. learned helplessness
    b. the vulnerability-stress model
    c. the demonological perspective
    d. the trauma dissociation model

_____ 3. During a psychological assessment, a client shares that she just lost her job and recently ended a long-term romantic relationship. Such information would be recorded on Axis _____ by the psychologist using the DSM-IV.

    a. I
    b. II
    c. III
    d. IV

_____ 4. The serial murderer Paul Bernardo had a charismatic personality and felt no remorse or sympathy for his victims. These characteristics best typify which disorder?.

    a. schizophrenia
    b. bipolar disorder
    c. dissociative identity disorder
    d. anti-social personality disorder

_____ 5. Roger is tense and anxious almost everyday. Though he is frequently worried and often has the sense that something bad is about to happen, he can't relate his anxiety to any particular situation or setting. He has difficulty getting restful sleep at night and often takes antacids for his upset stomach. Roger would **most likely** be diagnosed as having _____.

a. social phobia
b. an environmental or situational phobia
c. generalized anxiety disorder
d. post traumatic stress disorder

_____ 6. Annette is very afraid of germs and disease, so much so that she washes her hands over 100 times a day to make sure that she can avoid infection. Usually she doesn't show much anxiety but if she is in a place where she is unable to clean her hands, such as the wilderness, she can become very distressed and upset. Annette would most likely be diagnosed as having _____.

a. obsessive-compulsive disorder
b. schizophrenia paranoid type
c. generalized anxiety
d. a health-related phobia

_____ 7. Research conducted with people suffering from panic disorder has revealed that these individuals may possess an abnormally low levels of _____ that can trigger increased brain activity in the _____ areas of the brain.

a. dopamine; right
b. GABA; arousal
c. lactic acid, left
d. epinephrine; temporal

_____ 8. Steve has a rather strong fear of social situations. He used to try to go to parties and other social events but his anxiety would usually overwhelm him. When experiencing these negative motions, he would often leave parties early, a behaviour that allowed him to reduce or eliminate his anxiety. According to the principles of operant conditioning, Steve's escape behaviour is being _____ and this means that it will be more likely to occur in the future.

a. positively reinforced
b. negatively reinforced
c. aversively punished
d. response-cost punished

_____ 9. A person with a euphoric mood, a decreased need for sleep, and grandiose or exaggerated cognitions would **most likely** be diagnosed as having _____.

a. psychogenic fugue
b. schizophrenia
c. major depression
d. mania

_____ 10. Twin studies suggest that approximately _____ of the variation in clinical depression can be accounted for by genetic factors.

    a. 10%
    b. 50%
    c. 67%
    d. 80%

_____ 11. Martin Seligman has theorized that an increased focus on individuality and personal control and a loss of interest in traditional family and religious values have combined to produce a dramatic increase in _____ since 1960.

    a. dissociative identity disorder
    b. schizophrenia
    c. anxiety disorders
    d. depression

_____ 12. Jane has recently managed to earn a spot on her highly competitive high school basketball team. Research on psychological disorders suggests that if Jane is depressed, she will attribute her success to _____ while if she is not depressed, she will most likely attribute her achievement to _____.

    a. external factors; external factors as well
    b. external factors; personal factors
    c. personal factors; external factors
    d. personal factors; personal factors as well

_____ 13. All of the following are different types of somatoform disorders except _____.

    a. conversion disorder
    b. psychogenic fugue
    c. hypochondriasis
    d. pain disorder

_____ 14. After surviving a particularly violent tornado, Dean experiences a selective memory loss for specific traumatic events that occurred just before and during the disaster. Other than these specific memory losses, Dean's personality and subjective sense of identity are essentially unchanged. Dean is **most likely** to be diagnosed with _____.

    a. psychogenic fugue
    b. dissociative identity disorder
    c. schizophrenia, disorganized type
    d. psychogenic amnesia

_____ 15. Aaron has been diagnosed with schizophrenia. He appears to be confused most of the time and it is very difficult to communicate with him because it is often hard to understand exactly what he means. He frequently acts childlike and also displays inappropriate affect, such as the time that he laughed throughout the funeral of his uncle. Aaron would **most likely** be diagnosed with the _____ type of schizophrenia.

a. paranoid
b. undifferentiated
c. disorganized
d. catatonic

_____ 16. Many Vietnam veterans came back from the war suffering from a great deal of stress and anxiety. Psychiatrists would likely note that the stressful episodes the soldiers encountered during the war contribute to their current concerns about anxiety. The disorder that most approximates the problems of these soldiers is known as _____.

a. posttraumatic stress disorder
b. borderline personality disorder
c. schizotypal personality disorder
d. panic disorder

_____ 17. A functional MRI study by Ross and co-workers at the University of British Columbia found that, compared to criminal non-psychopaths and non-criminal control subjects, criminal psychopaths

a. had greater left hemisphere activation.
b. were more physiologically aroused.
c. had less activity in the occipital region.
d. had weaker limbic input to the frontal cortex.

_____ 18. According to one survey, what percentage of Canadian students reported having had at least one panic attack in the previous year?

a. 2
b. 13
c. 34
d. 78

_____ 19. Symptoms of schizophrenia include all of the following <u>except</u> _____.

a. delusions of grandeur (false beliefs that a person is famous)
b. disturbances of affect
c. distortions of perception
d. multiple personalities

20. Santa, trying to hurry through his rounds this Christmas Eve so that he can hurry home and let some home-cooked lovin' from Mrs. Claus, worries about staying clean because of all of those leaps down people's dirty chimneys. He also worries about smelling bad for Mrs. Claus because of all of the time he's spending around those reindeer. Thus, in every house that Santa delivers presents he takes a shower and helps himself to some cologne. If this behaviour persists in Santa's daily life over the next year, Dr. Jack Frost is likely to diagnose Santa as having _____.

a. generalized anxiety disorder
b. obsessive-compulsive disorder
c. a panic disorder
d. bipolar depression

21. People with multiple personalities, such as Eve White (Eve Black, Jane), the subject of the movie "The Three Faces of Eve," are said to have _____.

a. dissociative amnesia
b. dissociative fugue
c. dissociative identity disorder
d. schizophrenia

22. The Grinch regularly steals everyone's Christmas presents, puts the stockings on his own feet, tells impressionable children that department store Santas aren't actually the real thing, rips decorations off of Christmas trees, and buys up all the local Christmas turkeys to use in place of bowling balls on his weekly bowling night. During all of these escapades, the Grinch feels no remorse whatsoever for his actions, despite the angry mobs that descend on his humble abode. We might most likely diagnose the Grinch as suffering from _____.

a. catatonic schizophrenia
b. residual schizophrenia
c. obsessive-compulsive disorder
d. antisocial personality disorder

23. When clinicians agree in their diagnostic decisions, _____ has been established.

a. validity
b. reliability
c. DSM-IV
d. Axis V of DSM-IV

24. Competency is _____.

a. a type of anxiety disorder
b. a term that refers to the defendant's state of mind at the time of a judicial hearing
c. the same thing as insanity
d. a type of dissociative disorder

25. A fear of public spaces is called _____.

a. social phobia
b. specific phobia
c. generalized anxiety disorder
d. agoraphobia

26. According to Freud, neurotic anxiety occurs when _____.

a. the ego uses defence mechanisms
b. unacceptable impulses threaten to overwhelm the ego's defences
c. a child reaches the oral stage of psychosexual development
d. a person experiences a panic attack

27. In Canada and the United States, the lifetime prevalence of obsessive-compulsive disorder is approximately _____ per 100 people.

a. 22
b. 31.5
c. 2.5
d. 18

28. Beck's depressive triad of negative thoughts concerns all of the following except _____.

a. the world
b. oneself
c. the future
d. perceptions of a strong self of self-efficacy

29. Rosita has been diagnosed with schizophrenia and shows almost no emotion compared to most people. She tends to speak in a monotonous voice and has an impassive face. Rosita could best be described as having _____ affect.

a. flat
b. blunt
c. inappropriate
d. repressive

30. Back in the 1970's, Texas Ranger pitcher Rogelio Moret suddenly became extremely rigid, not moving a muscle, one day in spring training. Moret was subsequently found to have schizophrenia and had to retire from baseball. Based on these symptoms, you would expect that Moret was diagnosed with _____ schizophrenia.

a. paranoid
b. disorganized
c. catatonic
d. undifferentiated

True/False Items: *Write T or F in the space provided to the left of each item.*

_____ 1. According to the demonological view, psychological disorders are diseases just like physical disorders.

_____ 2. Reliability means that the diagnostic categories accurately capture the essential features of the various disorders.

_____ 3. Competency refers to a defendant's state of mind at the time of a judicial hearing.

_____ 4. A fear of riding in airplanes would be a type of specific phobia.

_____ 5. The mood disorders involve depression and mania.

_____ 6. Conversion disorder is a type of dissociative disorder.

_____ 7. In psychogenic amnesia, a person develops multiple personalities.

_____ 8. Hallucinations are false perceptions.

_____ 9. Type I schizophrenia is characterized by negative symptoms.

_____ 10. There is no evidence for a biological basis for schizophrenia.

Short Answer Questions

1. What does the vulnerability-stress model argue?

2. What is "insanity?"

3. How is anxiety a learned response?

What are the differences between the three major types of mood disorders?

4.   What are the main characteristics of schizophrenia?

Essay Questions

1.   What is "abnormal?"

2.   What are the psychological factors involved in causing anxiety disorders?

3.   What biological factors cause mood disorders?

4.   Describe the subtypes of schizophrenia.

5.   What are the causal factors in schizophrenia?

Answer Keys

Answer Key for Key Terms

Historical Perspectives on Psychological Disorders
Defining and Classifying Psychological Disorders

1. d
2. g
3. h
4. e

5. c
6. f
7. b
8. a

Anxiety Disorders
Mood (Affective) Disorders

1. d
2. b
3. a
4. m
5. s
6. k
7. o
8. w
9. r
10. g
11. u
12. q

13. t
14. p
15. n
16. j
17. i
18. h
19. c
20. l
21. e
22. f
23. v

Somatoform Disorders
Dissociative Disorders
Schizophrenia
Personality Disorders

1. o
2. d
3. k
4. n
5. e
6. h
7. u
8. w
9. l
10. b
11. t
12. c

13. m
14. x
15. r
16. f
17. g
18. v
19. j
20. a
21. i
22. q
23. s
24. p

Disorders of Childhood and Old Age

1. g
2. a
3. d
4. e
5. c
6. f
7. b

Answer Key for Review at a Glance

1. demonological
2. vulnerability-stress
3. Reliability
4. validity
5. DSM-IV
6. competency
7. insanity
8. phobias
9. agoraphobia
10. social
11. specific
12. generalized anxiety
13. panic disorder
14. obsessions
15. compulsions
16. obsessive-compulsive
17. post-traumatic stress
18. GABA
19. neurotic
20. culture-bound
21. major

22. dysthymia
23. bipolar disorder
24. mania
25. learned helplessness
26. hypochondriasis
27. pain
28. conversion
29. psychogenic amnesia
30. Psychogenic fugue
31. dissociative identity
32. trauma-dissociation
33. delusions
34. hallucinations
35. paranoid
36. disorganized
37. catatonic
38. Type I
39. Type II
40. dopamine
41. expressed emotion
42. antisocial personality
43. externalizing
44. internalizing
45. externalizing
46. depression
47. adulthood
48. 40
49. dementia
50. 60

Answer Key for Practice Test Multiple Choice Questions

1. a
2. b
3. d
4. d

16. a
17. d
18. c
19. d

5. c	20. b
6. a	21. c
7. b	22. d
8. b	23. b
9. d	24. b
10. c	25. d
11. d	26. b
12. b	27. c
13. b	28. d
14. d	29. a
15. b	30. c

Answer Key for Practice Test True/False Questions

1. F	6. F
2. F	7. F
3. T	8. T
4. T	9. F
5. T	10. F

Answer Key for Practice Test Short Answer Questions

1. The vulnerability-stress model suggests that each of us has some degree of vulnerability for the development of a psychological disorder. The vulnerability may have a biological basis, such as genetics, a brain abnormality, or a hormonal factor. Personality factors, such as low self-esteem or pessimism, may also increase vulnerability. Finally, sociocultural factors can also increase vulnerability. Vulnerability combines with an experience with a stressor or stressors to trigger the appearance of a disorder.

2. "Insanity" is a legal rather than a psychological or psychiatric definition. It refers to the presumed state of mind of a defendant *at the time of a judicial hearing*.

3. From the behavioural perspective, anxiety disorders develop because of conditioning processes. For example, phobic reactions may occur because of associating a specific object or event (CS) with pain and trauma (UCS), producing a fear response. Phobias can also be acquired through observation (modelling). Finally, behaviours that produce anxiety reduction are negatively reinforced, which is an aspect of operant conditioning.

4. Major depression is a disorder that leaves people unable to function effectively in their lives. Dysthymia is a milder form of mood disorder which has less severe effects. Bipolar disorder is a disorder in which periods of depression alternate with periods of mania, a state of highly excited mood and behaviour.

5. Schizophrenia is a psychotic disorder that involves severe disturbances in thinking, speech, perception, emotion, and behaviour. It is characterized by delusions, hallucinations, disorganized speech and thought, and inappropriate, blunted, or flat affect.

Answer Key for Practice Test Essay Questions

1. Decisions about what behaviours are "abnormal" are surprisingly difficult to make. Most psychologists and psychiatrists would agree to examine the three "D's" in determining whether a behaviour should be considered abnormal. Behaviours that are distressing to self or others, deviant (i.e. violate social norms), and dysfunctional (for person and/or society) are considered to be abnormal. If only one or two of the "D's" are present, judgements of abnormality are less likely.

2. According to Freud, neurotic anxiety occurs when unacceptable impulses threaten to overwhelm the ego's defences. Cognitive theorists stress the role of maladaptive thought patterns in anxiety disorders. As mentioned in the answer to question #3 above, anxiety can be a learned response.

3. Both genetic and neurochemical factors have been linked to depression. Twin studies have shown that MZ twins have concordance rates of up to 67% for experiencing clinical (major) depression. Low levels of neurotransmitters such as serotonin, dopamine, and norepinephrine have also been found to be associated with mood disorders. One theory holds that when a person experiences low levels of these neurotransmitters, the brain regions responsible for reward and pleasure are not stimulated. Many drugs that treat mood disorders work by increasing neurotransmitter levels.

4. The paranoid type of schizophrenia is characterized by delusions of persecution and grandeur. Suspicions and anxiety often accompany the delusions, and hallucinations may occur. The disorganized type is characterized by confusion, incoherence, and severe deterioration of adaptive behaviour. The catatonic type is characterized by severe motor disturbances ranging from muscular rigidity to random or repetitive movements. The undifferentiated category is for people who exhibit symptoms of schizophrenia but do not neatly fall into any of the first three categories. Type I schizophrenia is characterized by the predominance of positive symptoms, such as delusions and hallucinations, while Type II schizophrenia is characterized by the absence of normal behaviours, which are known as negative symptoms.

5. Strong evidence exists for a biological basis for schizophrenia. The disorder tends to run in families, and twin studies show higher concordance rates between MZ twins than between DZ twins. Brain studies have indicated brain atrophy in the brains of schizophrenics. According to the dopamine hypothesis, excess levels of dopamine may cause schizophrenia. Freud believed that the disorder was caused by regression to early stages of psychosexual development because of life stress. Cognitive theorists believe that schizophrenics have a defect in attentional mechanisms. Stressful life events seem to precede much schizophrenic behaviour. Family dynamics, particularly the level of expressed emotion, may play a role. Finally, sociocultural factors may play a role. Schizophrenia tends to be found more among those in lower socioeconomic classes. It is not clear if being in that class causes or influences the development of schizophrenia or whether schizophrenics are just more likely to end up in lower socioeconomic classes.

Chapter 14. Treatment of Psychological Disorders

Learning Objectives

14.1   Describe the goals of therapy and the types of mental health professionals that conduct them.

14.2   Describe psychoanalysis and the associated techniques of free association and dream analysis.

14.3   Describe how psychoanalysts employ interpretation to overcome resistance and transference.

14.4   Describe how brief psychodynamic therapies differ from psychoanalysis.

14.5   Outline the goal of humanistic therapies, describing the client-centreed therapy of Rogers and Gestalt therapy.

14.6   Describe the four steps (ABCD) in rational-emotive behaviour therapy, and explain how the model is used in therapy.

14.7   Describe Beck's cognitive therapy and the focus of this therapeutic approach.

14.8   Outline the classical and operant conditioning procedures used in exposure therapy.

14.9   Describe the purpose, methods, and results of the study examining exposure treatment of fear of flying using virtual reality by Rothbaum and colleagues (2002).

14.10   Compare and contrast systematic desensitization and exposure in treating anxiety disorders.

14.11   Explain how classical conditioning underlies aversion therapy.

14.12   Describe how operant conditioning underlies token economies, punishment, and modeling therapies and outline the efficacy for these approaches.

14.13   Describe and give an example of eclecticism and the integration of therapeutic techniques.

14.14   Describe how therapy is conducted with families or couples.

14.15   Outline barriers to therapy for ethnic minorities and how they can be overcome with culturally-competent therapists.

14.16   Describe the importance of the "specificity question" in psychotherapy research.

14.17   Describe various methods for assessing treatment outcome, including randomized clinical trials, meta-analytic methods, and client evaluations of treatment.

14.18 List and describe the client variables, therapist factors, and technique variables that have been shown to be important to treatment outcome.

14.19 Define and give examples of common factors.

14.20 Describe drug therapies for treating psychological disorders and their side effects, including antianxiety drugs, antidepressant drugs, and antipsychotic drugs.

14.21 Describe electroconvulsive therapy and the disorder for which it is effective.

14.22 Describe the various types of psychosurgery and how and when they are used.

14.23 Outline research regarding the psychological and biological outcomes of drug treatments versus psychotherapy.

14.24 Describe the rationale for deinstitutionalization and explain why it has not been achieved.

14.25 Describe the positive and negative effects of managed care on mental health treatment.

14.26 Compare and contrast the two major approaches to prevention.

14.27 Describe the steps a person should take in seeking treatment for psychological disorders.

Chapter Overview

The Helping Relationship
> The goal of all therapy is to help people change maladaptive thinking, feeling, and behavioural patterns. Therapeutic techniques vary widely and depend on the theories that therapists use to understand psychological disorders.

Psychodynamic Therapies
> The goal of psychoanalysis is to help clients achieve insight, the conscious awareness of the psychodynamics that underlie problems. Freudian Psychoanalysts use free association techniques and dream interpretation in therapy. Clients may experience resistance to dealing with unconscious conflicts but eventually will transfer the conflicts associated in dealing with others to the therapist. Psychoanalytic therapists provide interpretation to the clients in an effort to help them achieve insight. Brief psychodynamic therapies utilize basic concepts from psychoanalysis, but conversation between therapist and client typically replace free association and therapy occurs more frequently than it does in traditional psychoanalysis.

Humanistic Psychotherapies
> Client-centred therapy, developed by Carl Rogers, focuses on unconditional positive regard, empathy, and genuineness (therapist consistency of feelings and behaviours). The characteristics of therapists have indeed been found to have important effects on therapeutic outcomes. Gestalt therapy is another approach to helping people get in touch with their selves.

Cognitive Therapies

Cognitive therapies focus on maladaptive ways of thinking about oneself and the world. Ellis' rational-emotive therapy stresses the roles of activating events, belief systems, emotional and behavioural consequences of appraisal in the development of psychological disorders and the importance of disputing, or challenging, erroneous beliefs in treatment. Similarly, Beck's cognitive therapy is designed to help clients point out logical errors in thinking that underlie disturbances such as mood disorders.

Behaviour Therapies

Behaviour therapies use basic principles of classical and operant conditioning in therapy. For example, anxiety responses can be eliminated through extinction procedures. Systematic desensitization is a technique used for treating anxiety disorders. Aversion therapy is used to reduce deviant behaviours. Behaviour modification techniques such as the use of positive reinforcement and punishment can also be used in therapy. The modelling of social skills can be used to help people to function effectively in society.

Integrating and Combining Therapies

To an increasing extent, therapists are becoming eclectic in their use of treatments and theoretical orientations to help people in therapy.

Cultural and Gender Issues in Psychotherapy

Cultural factors play a number of roles in the use of psychotherapy. Cultural norms can affect the likelihood of turning to professionals in time of need. A lack of access to services and a lack of skilled counsellors who can provide culturally responsive forms of treatment can hinder people in getting treatment. Therapists must understand the external barriers deeply embedded in the culture that may be involved in the development of psychological disorders in women.

Evaluating Psychotherapies

Today, researchers use the specificity question: "Which types of therapy, administered by which types of therapists to which types of clients having which kinds of problems, produce which kinds of effects. This question stresses the interactions between all variables in producing successful therapy. Randomized clinical trials and placebo control groups are considered critical for good research into the effectiveness of psychotherapy. Meta-analyses are used to combine the results of many studies.

Biological Approaches to Treatment

Antianxiety drugs such as Valium and Xanax are used to help people deal with anxiety. Antidepressant drugs fall into three major categories: tricyclics, MAO inhibitors, and SSRIs (selective serotonin reuptake inhibitors). Electroconvulsive therapy (ECT) is a technique used for treating major depression. Psychosurgery refers to surgical procedures that remove or destroy brain tissue.

Psychological Disorders and Society

A deinstitutionalization movement began in the 1960's to transfer the primary focus of treatment from the hospital to the community. Unfortunately, many patients have been released into communities that are unable to care for them, resulting in an increase in the homeless population and a revolving door phenomenon involving repeated hospitalizations and releases. Preventive mental health programs focus on both situation-focused prevention, which is directed at reducing or preventing environmental causes of disorders and competency-focused prevention, which is designed to increase personal resources and coping skills.

Chapter Outline

The Helping Relationship

Psychodynamic Therapies
        Psychoanalysis
                Free Association
                Dream Interpretation
                Resistance
                Transference
                Interpretation
        Brief Psychodynamic Therapies

Humanistic Psychotherapies
        Client-Centered Therapy
        Gestalt Therapy

Cognitive Therapies
        Ellis's Rational-Emotive Therapy
        Beck's Cognitive Therapy

Behaviour Therapies
        Classical Conditioning Procedures
                Exposure: An Extinction Approach
                Systematic Desensitization: A Counterconditioning Approach
                Aversion Therapy
        Operant Conditioning Treatments
                Positive Reinforcement
                Therapeutic Use of Punishment
        Modelling and Social Skills Training

Integrating and Combining Therapies
        Research Frontiers: Virtual Reality as a Therapeutic Technique

Cultural and Gender Issues in Psychotherapy
        Cultural Factors in Treatment Utilization
        Gender Issues in Therapy

Evaluating Psychotherapies
        Psychotherapy Research Methods
                What is a Good Psychotherapy Research Design?
                Meta-analysis: A Look at the Big Picture
        Factors Affecting the Outcome of Therapy
                Research Foundations: The Effectiveness of Psychotherapy: Feedback From the Consumer

Biological Approaches to Treatment
        Drug Therapies
                Antianxiety Drugs
                Antidepressant Drugs
                Antipsychotic Drugs

Electroconvulsive Therapy
Psychosurgery
Mind, Body, and Therapeutic Interventions

Psychological Disorders and Society
Deinstitutionalization
Preventive Mental Health
Psychological Applications: When and Where to Seek Therapy

Problem-Based Learning

Treatment
http://www.mentalhealth.com
Internet Mental Health-This website, created by Canadian psychiatrist Dr. Phillip Long, is an encyclopedia of mental health information. It contains information about disorders, diagnosis, medications, and research resources.

http://www.schizophrenia.com
Schizophrenia Home Page-This is a non-profit website that contains information, discussions, chats, and links to other resources.

http://www.cpa.ca/contents.html
Canadian Psychological Association-This is the CPA's website and it contains information about careers, regulatory bodies, professional associations, clinical disorders, and issues that concern psychology in Canada. This site contains a Canadian report on the terrorist attacks in the United States.

http://www.apa.org
American Psychological Association-This is the APA's website and it contains information about careers, student concerns, some full text articles, news and events, and information about many areas such as clinical disorders, aids, violence and anger.

http://www.cyberpsych.org/apf/index.html
American Psychoanalytic Foundation-This site contains information about news and events, programs, links to other sites, and a bibliography of books and journal literature on psychoanalysis.

Key Terms: *Write the letter of the definition next to the term in the space provided.*

The Helping Relationship   Psychodynamic Therapies
Humanistic Therapies   Cognitive Therapies   Behaviour Therapies

1. ___ aversion therapy

    a. conscious awareness of the psychodynamics that underlie problems

2. ___ behaviour modification

    b. Freud's technique asking clients to verbally report without censorship any thoughts, feelings, or images that entered awareness

3. ___ counterconditioning

    c. defensive maneuvers that hinder the process of therapy

4. ___ eclectic

    d. occurs when the client reacts to the therapist as if he or she were an important figure from the person's past

5. ___ empathy

    e. any statement by the therapist intended to provide the client with insight into behaviour or dynamics

6. ___ exposure

    f. a brief psychodynamic therapy that focuses on a client's interpersonal problems

7. ___ free association

    g. communicated when therapists show clients that they genuinely care about and accept them without judgement or evaluation

8. ___ genuineness

    h. willingness and ability to view the world through the client's eyes

9. ___ insight

    i. consistency between the way a therapist feels and the way he or she behaves

10. ___ interpersonal therapy

    j. presenting the feared CS in the absence of the UCS

11. ___ interpretation

    k. a technique to keep the avoidance response from occurring

12. ___ psychodynamic behaviour therapy

    l. a learning-based treatment for anxiety disorders

13. ___ resistance

    m. a procedure in which a new response that is incompatible with anxiety is conditioned to the anxiety-producing CS

14. ___ response prevention

    n. an ordering of anxiety-producing events

15. ___ social skills training

    o. therapy in which the therapist pairs an attractive stimulus with a noxious UCS in an attempt to condition an aversion to the CS

16. ___ stimulus hierarchy

    p. treatment techniques that involve the application of operant conditioning procedures

17. ___ systematic desensitization

    q. a system for strengthening desired behaviours through the application of positive reinforcement

18. ___ token economy

    r. learning new skills by observing and imitating a model who performs a socially skillful behaviour

19. ___ transference

    s. combining treatments and making use of various orientations and therapeutic techniques

20. ___ unconditional positive regard

    t. Wachtel's integration of psychodynamic and behaviour therapies

21. ___ virtual reality

    u. involves the use of computer technology to simulate real experiences

Integrating and Combining Therapies
Evaluating Psychotherapies
Psychological Disorders and Society

Cultural and Gender Issues in Psychotherapy
Biological Approaches to Treatment

1. ___ common factors

2. ___ competency-focused intervention

3. ___ cultural competence

4. ___ deinstitutionalization

5. ___ deterioration effect

6. ___ effect size statistic

7. ___ effectiveness

8. ___ efficacy

9. ___ electroconvulsive therapy

10. ___ meta-analysis

11. ___ openness

12. ___ placebo control group

13. ___ psychosurgery

14. ___ randomized clinical trial

15. ___ self-relatedness

16. ___ situation-focused intervention

17. ___ specificity question

18. ___ spontaneous remission

19. ___ tardive dyskinesia

a. ability to use knowledge about the client's culture to achieve a broad understanding of the client, at the same time understanding how the client may be different from the stereotype

b. "Which type of therapy, administered by which kinds of therapists to which kinds of clients, having which kinds of problems, produce which kinds of effects?"

c. symptom reduction in the absence of any treatment

d. studies in which individuals are randomly assigned to an experimental condition which receives the treatment or to a control condition

e. the group which gets a treatment they think will be effective but does not actually work

f. a statistical technique that allows researchers to combine the results of many studies to arrive at an overall conclusion

g. represents a common measure of treatment effectiveness in meta-analysis

h. clients' general willingness to invest themselves in therapy and take risks

i. refers to ability to experience and understand internal states, to be attuned to relational processes with therapists, and to apply what is learned in therapy to life

j. as a result of hostile interchanges between therapist and client, the client gets worse

k. shared by diverse forms of therapy that might contribute to therapeutic success, such as a caring therapist

l. refers to whether therapy can produce scientifically-demonstrated positive outcomes

m. outcomes that psychotherapy has in real-life settings of clinical practice

n. a severe movement disorder produced by antipsychotic drugs

o. seizure induction effective in treating major depression

p. procedures to remove or destroy brain tissue to change disordered behaviour

q. a movement to transfer the primary focus of treatment from the hospital to the community

r. directed at reducing or eliminating the environmental causes of behaviour disorders or enhancing situational factors that help prevent the development of disorders

s. designed to increase personal resources and coping skills

Review at a Glance: Write the term that best fits the blank to review what you learned in this chapter.

Psychodynamic Therapies

The goal of psychoanalysis is to help clients achieve (1) _____, the conscious awareness of the psychodynamics that underlie their problems. Freud asked his clients to recline on a couch and to verbally report their thoughts, a technique called (2) _____ _____. Through this technique, as well as (3) _____ _____, Freud believed that the therapist could help the client understand the unconscious motivations of their behaviour. Clients were expected to engage in defensive maneuvers called (4) _____ that hinder the process of therapy. If therapy is successful, (5) _____ should occur. In a brief psychodynamic therapy called (6) _____ therapy, the therapist focuses on the client's current interpersonal problems.

Humanistic Psychotherapies

In client-centered therapy, (7) _____ _____ _____ is communicated when therapists show clients that they genuinely care about and accept them. A second vital factor in therapy is called (8) _____, the willingness and ability of a therapist to see the world through the client's eyes. The third important therapist characteristic is (9) _____, which refers to consistency between a therapist's feelings and his or her behaviours.

Cognitive Therapies

Ellis' rational emotive therapy is embodied in his (10) _____ model. (11) _____ cognitive therapy revolves around pointing out logical errors in thinking that underlie emotional disturbance.

Behaviour Therapies

Classical conditioning approaches are often used in treatment of psychological disorders. In the extinction approach called (12) _____, the feared CS is presented without the UCS while using (13) _____ _____ to prevent the response from occurring. (14) _____ _____ is a technique developed by Joseph Wolpe to treat anxiety disorders, particularly phobias. In this procedure, the client is first trained in relaxation techniques and is then helped to construct a (15) _____ _____ of low-anxiety to high-anxiety scenes relating to the fear. The client then practices the relaxation techniques while progressing through the stimulus hierarchy. In (16) _____ therapy, the therapist pairs a stimulus that is attractive to a person with a noxious UCS in an attempt to condition an aversion to the CS. (17) _____ _____ techniques are operant conditioning treatments that involve trying to increase or decrease a specific behaviour. In (18) _____ _____ training, clients learn new skills by observing and then imitating a model who performs a behaviour.

Integrating and Combining Therapies

Today, therapists use a wide variety of techniques and approaches in treatment, which is called the (19) _____ approach. For example, (20) _____ _____ therapy involves an integration of psychoanalysis and behaviour therapy.

Cultural and Gender Issues in Psychotherapy

Stanley Sue (1998) suggests that (21) _____ _____ therapists are able to use their knowledge about the client's culture to achieve a broad understanding of the client while at the same time being attentive to how the client might be different from the cultural stereotype.

Evaluating Psychotherapies

Good research designs to evaluate the effectiveness of psychotherapy involve both (22) _____ _____ trials and (23) _____ _____ groups. The statistical technique of (24) _____ - _____ allows researchers to combine the results of many studies to arrive at an overall conclusion. Several factors have been found to affect the outcome of therapy. (25) _____ involves client's willingness to invest themselves in therapy, while (26) _____ - _____ refers to ability to experience and understand internal states, to be attuned to relational processes with therapists, and ability to apply what is learned in therapy to life outside treatment. Hostile interchanges between therapists and clients can lead to a (27) _____ effect in therapy. Various therapies tend to enjoy similar success rates, suggesting that there are (28) _____ _____ shared by these therapies.

Biological Approaches to Treatment

Valium, Xanax, and BuSpar are examples of (29) _____ drugs. Antidepressant drugs fall into three major categories: (30) _____, (31) _____, and (32) _____. (33) _____ drugs are used to treat schizophrenia. These drugs can produce a severe movement disorder called (34) _____ _____. (35) _____ therapy, or ECT, is used to treat severe major depression. (36) _____ refers to procedures to remove or destroy brain tissue in an attempt to change disordered behaviour.

Psychological Disorders and Society

Concerns about the inadequacies of mental hospitals and the ability of antipsychotic drugs to "normalize" patients' behaviour led to a (37) _____ movement to transfer the primary focus of treatment to the community from the hospital. Preventive mental health programs have become increasingly important. In (38) _____ - _____ prevention, the focus is on reducing or eliminating the environmental causes of behaviour disorders or on enhancing situational factors that help to prevent the development of disorders. (39) _____ - _____ prevention programs are designed to increase personal resources and coping skills.

Apply What You Know

1. Think of three behaviours that you would like to change. Describe each of them. Using what you have learned in this chapter, describe which forms of therapy would be most effective in helping you make the desired changes.

Internet Scavenger Hunt

1. Stanley Sue's and others' work have suggested that cultural factors can play a role in treatment utilization and therapeutic interventions. Enter the phrase 'culturally competent therapist' into Google and see which cultural factors are identified as playing a role in therapy. Are their other groups identified that would not normally be considered a 'culturally' distinct?.

2. Enter the phrase 'residential schools' in your search engine and view the history of residential schools
   in your province. You should be able to identify some of the psychological problems that arose within the Aboriginal people of Canada as a result of their treatment at residential schools, and the government's provisions for treatment.

Practice Test

<u>**Multiple Choice Items:**</u> *Please write the letter corresponding to your answer in the space to the left of each item.*

_____ 1. The primary therapeutic goal of _____ is to help a person achieve greater insight, which is the awareness of the underlying dynamics of their problems.

    a. humanistic therapy
    b. cognitive therapy
    c. behaviour modification
    d. psychoanalysis

_____ 2. Susan has an anxiety disorder and has sought help from a therapist, Dr. Jones. Dr. Jones believes that Susan's anxiety is related to her unconscious fear of her unmet sexual impulses and that in order for Susan to get over her anxiety problem, she needs to have greater awareness of this unconscious dynamic. Dr. Jones is most likely associated with the _____approach to therapy and appears to be trying to produce positive changes by fostering more _____.

    a. psychodynamic; transference
    b. interpersonal; empathy
    c. psychoanalytic; insight
    d. humanistic; unconditional positive regard

_____ 3. A therapist who takes to a humanistic approach to psychotherapy would **most likely** have the goal of creating a therapeutic environment that _____.

    a. encourages insight
    b. challenges irrational thoughts
    c. reinforces desired behaviours
    d. allows for self-exploration

_____ 4. Josh is visiting a friend when he accidentally breaks a valuable plate. He begins to berate himself for his clumsiness and stupidity and almost instantaneously he starts to feel embarrassed and upset. According to Ellis' ABCD model of emotion, the breaking of the plate would represent the _____.

    a. A
    b. B
    c. C
    d. D

_____ 5. Exposure therapies operate on the assumption that _____ is the most direct way to reduce or eliminate a learned anxiety response.

    a. classical extinction
    b. positive reinforcement
    c. operant extinction
    d. response cost punishment

_____ 6. Janice has a phobia of dogs and decides to consult with a behaviour therapist in order to get some help. The therapist first teaches her a muscle relaxation technique. After she has learned this, they create a list of increasingly fearful situations involving dogs. Starting with the least feared situation, the therapist has Janice imagine it and then use her relaxation training to eliminate any anxiety that arises. This therapist is using the general technique called _____ and the list that they have created is an example of _____.

    a. aversive conditioning; a punishment
    b. systematic desensitization; a stimulus hierarchy
    c. exposure therapy; flooding
    d. behaviour modification; positive reinforcer

_____ 7. Great flexibility and an increased sense of what is called presence are characteristics of _____, which has recently been used to treat a limited number of psychological disorders.

    a. systematic desensitization
    b. psychodyanamic behaviour therapy
    c. virtual reality
    d. aversion therapy

_____ 8. The process where some individuals experience complete symptom reduction in the absence of any treatment is known as _____.

    a. the placebo effect
    b. natural recovery
    c. spontaneous remission
    d. automatic adjustment

_____ 9. Dr. Stone designs a study to test the effectiveness of a new treatment for anxiety disorders. After making sure that her participants are roughly similar on important demographic variables, people are randomly assigned to receive her new therapy or another therapy technique that has already been proven to be effective. Of the following statements, the one which **best describes** Dr. Stone's study is that her study _____.

    a. uses randomized clinical trials and it has a placebo control group
    b. uses randomized clinical trials but does not have a placebo control group
    c. does not use randomized clinical trials but it does have a placebo control group
    d. does not use randomized clinical trials and it does not have a placebo control group

_____ 10. Modern meta-analyses comparing the effectiveness of various types of therapies have concluded that _____.

    a. behavioural and psychodynamic therapies are the most effective
    b. client-centered therapies are the most effective
    c. most therapies are no more effective than receiving no treatment at all
    d. with some exceptions, most different therapies are equally effective

_____ 11. The fact that vastly different types of therapies often produce similar outcomes has led some researchers to search for what are called _____, which are similar elements shared by each of the approaches that may account for their common successes.

a. meta-factors
b. joint components
c. common factors
d. shared components

_____ 12. Tricyclics, MAO inhibitors, and SSRIs were all mentioned as drug treatments for _____.

a. anxiety disorders
b. schizophrenia
c. depression
d. somatoform disorders

_____ 13. Harpreet has been seeing his analyst for about 6 months and he feels he is falling in love with her. A psychoanalyst would view Harpreet's behaviour as an example of

a. positive resistance.
b. positive transference.
c. negative resistance.
d. negative transference.

_____ 14. According to Health Canada about _____ percent of Canadians have taken tranquilizers.

a. 4
b. 18
c. 32
d. 57

_____ 15. When clients project their anxieties, fears, or other impulses onto the therapist during psychoanalytic therapy, _____ has occurred.

a. insight
b. free association
c. transference
d. resistance

_____ 16. Of the following, which is not part of humanistic psychotherapy.

a. unconditional positive regard
b. conditional positive worth
c. empathy
d. genuineness

_____ 17. In Ellis' rational-emotive therapy, the key to changing maladaptive emotions and behaviours is thought to be _____.

a. dream analysis
b. insight
c. disputing erroneous beliefs
d. somatic therapy

_____ 18. In extinction, the phobic object is _____.

a. the UCS
b. paired with a noxious UCS
c. presented in the absence of the UCS
d. the UCR

_____ 19. In aversion therapy, the behaviour to be changed is _____.

a. paired with a noxious UCS
b. considered to be a UCS
c. presented in the absence of the UCS
d. negatively reinforced

_____ 20. Dr. Wong asked Tamara to lie on a couch and report all images, thoughts and feelings that came to her and to avoid censoring them. This therapeutic technique is called

a. systematic desensitization
b. transference
c. resistance
d. free association.

_____ 21. Studies of punishment with severely disturbed autistic children have found that _____.

a. self-destructive behaviours can be controlled through punishment procedures
b. punishment makes autistic behaviour more likely to occur
c. punishment is ineffective in changing autistic behaviour
d. punishment doesn't work nearly as well with autistic children as it does with mentally retarded children

_____ 22. Eclectic therapists _____.

a. use psychodynamic behavioural therapy exclusively
b. believe strongly that therapists should use a single theoretical orientation in their therapy
c. believe strongly that therapists should use a single therapeutic technique in their therapy
d. use several different orientations and techniques in their therapy

_____ ✓ 23. It is estimated that approximately _____ percent of the homeless in Canada have been hospitalized in the past three years.

    a. 2 to 4
    b. 10 to 15
    c. 40 to 45
    d. 84 to 90

_____ ✓ 24. A _____ allows researchers to combine the results of many studies to arrive at an overall conclusion.

    a. placebo control group
    b. randomized clinical trial
    c. meta-analysis
    d. correlational study

_____ ✓ 25. Common factors in successful psychotherapy include _____.

    a. faith in the therapist
    b. a lack of self-efficacy
    c. a lack of self-relatedness
    d. a decreased optimistic outlook on life

_____ 26. _____ is a scientific term that refers to whether a therapy can produce positive outcomes exceeding those in appropriate control conditions.

    a. Meta-analysis
    b. Placebo
    c. Effectiveness
    d. Efficacy

_____ ✓ 27. The first provincial hospital in Nova Scotia for those with mental disorders was established in

    a. 1852
    b. 1901
    c. 1923
    d. 1947

_____ ✓ 28. SSRIs _____.

    a. increase MAO levels
    b. decrease MAO levels
    c. have more serious side effects than either tricyclics or MAO inhibitors
    d. increase levels of serotonin in the synapse

_____ 29. ECT is used to _____.

    a. increase MAO levels
    b. treat severely depressed people when other measures fail
    c. surgically remove parts of the brain
    d. place patients in a vegetative state

_____ 30. Procedures that are used to increase people's self-efficacy are part of _____.

    a. ECT
    b. competency-focused intervention
    c. situation-focused intervention
    d. deinstitutionalization

True/False Items: _Write T or F in the space provided to the left of each item._

_____ 1. Freud believed that dream interpretation was "the royal road to the unconscious."

_____ 2. Interpersonal therapy, a brief psychodynamic therapy, focuses on the client's current interpersonal problems.

_____ 3. Genuineness refers to a therapist's ability to view the world through a client's eyes.

_____ 4. In Ellis' ABCD model, the "C" stands for cognitions.

_____ 5. Systematic desensitization is a learning-based treatment for anxiety disorders.

_____ 6. Culturally sensitive therapy is therapy designed to make people sensitive to people from other cultures.

_____ 7. Clinicians who are eclectic stick to one tried-and-true technique in therapy.

_____ 8. A placebo control group is used to control for client expectations of improvement.

_____ 9. A meta-analysis allows researchers to combine the results of many studies to arrive at an overall conclusion.

_____ 10. Self-relatedness refers to a client's willingness to invest themselves in therapy and to take the risks required to change themselves.

Short Answer Questions

1. What is free association?

2. What are the processes of client-centered therapy?

3. How is social skills training accomplished?

4. How is virtual reality being used as a therapeutic technique?

5. What is electroconvulsive therapy?

Essay Questions

1. How do cognitive therapies work?

2. What is systematic desensitization?

3. What is a good psychotherapy research design?

4. Describe the factors affecting the outcomes of therapy.

5. Describe preventive mental health programs.

Answer Keys

Answer Key for Key Terms

The Helping Relationship
Psychodynamic Therapies
Humanistic Therapies
Cognitive Therapies
Behaviour Therapies
Group, Family, and Marital Therapies

1.	o	12.	t
2.	p	13.	c
3.	m	14.	k
4.	s	15.	r
5.	h	16.	n
6.	j	17.	l
7.	b	18.	q
8.	i	19.	d
9.	a	20.	g
10.	f	21.	u
11.	e		

Integrating and Combining Therapies
Cultural and Gender Issues in Psychotherapy
Evaluating Psychotherapies
Biological Approaches to Treatment
Psychological Disorders and Society

1.	k	11.	h
2.	s	12.	e
3.	a	13.	p
4.	q	14.	d
5.	j	15.	i
6.	g	16.	r
7.	m	17.	b
8.	l	18.	c
9.	o	19.	n
10.	f		

Answer Key for Review at a Glance

1.	insight	21.	culturally competent
2.	free association	22.	randomized clinical
3.	dream interpretation	23.	placebo control
4.	resistance	24.	meta-analysis
5.	transference	25.	Openness
6.	interpersonal	26.	self-relatedness
7.	unconditional positive regard	27.	deterioration
8.	empathy	28.	common factors

9. genuineness
10. ABCD
11. Beck's
12. exposure
13. response prevention
14. Systematic desensitization
15. stimulus hierarchy
16. aversion
17. Behaviour modification
18. social skills
19. eclectic
20. psychodynamic behaviour

29. antianxiety
30. tricyclics
31. MAO inhibitors
32. SSRIs
33. Antipsychotic
34. tardive dyskinesia
35. Electroconvulsive
36. Psychosurgery
37. deinstitutionalization
38. situation-focused
39. competency-focused

Answer Key for Practice Test Multiple Choice Questions

1.	d		16.	b
2.	c		17.	c
3.	d		18.	c
4.	a		19.	a
5.	a		20.	d
6.	b		21.	a
7.	c		22.	d
8.	c		23.	c
9.	b		24.	c
10.	d		25.	a
11.	c		26.	d
12.	c		27.	a
13.	b		28.	d
14.	a		29.	b
15.	c		30.	b

Answer Key for Practice Test True/False Questions

1.	T		6.	F
2.	T		7.	F
3.	F		8.	T
4.	F		9.	T
5.	T		10.	F

Answer Key for Practice Test Short Answer Questions

1. Free association refers to verbal reports without any censorship of thoughts, feelings, or images that enter awareness. It was a technique pioneered by Freud.

2. Three things are important in client-centered therapy. First, the therapist should communicate unconditional positive regard. Second, the therapist should express empathy for the client's point-of-view. Finally, the therapist, should be genuine and make sure that there is congruence between his or her feelings and his or her behaviours.

3. In social skills training, clients learn new skills by observing and then imitating a model who performs socially skillful behaviours.

4. Virtual reality involves the use of computer technology to create highly realistic environments in which behaviour and emotions can be studied. Virtual reality is highly flexible, meaning that it can be used to create a number of environments in which a therapist can study a client's reactions.

5. Electroconvulsive therapy (or ECT) is a technique in which a person receives electric shock to the brain. This shock, which lasts less than a second, causes a seizure of the central nervous system. Such treatments can help people with major depression but may cause permanent memory loss in some cases.

Answer Key for Practice Test Essay Questions

1. Cognitive therapies stress the importance of maladaptive thought processes in the development of psychological disorders. As such, the therapies attempt to change the thought processes. Clients are given help in identifying the maladaptive thoughts, are encouraged to challenge the thoughts, and change them. Both Ellis's rational-emotive therapy and Beck's cognitive therapy work this way.

2. Systematic desensitization is a counterconditioning technique that is most useful in treating anxiety disorders, particularly phobias. The first step in the technique is to train the client in the skill of muscle relaxation. The client then constructs a stimulus hierarchy of ten to fifteen scenes relating to the fear. Then, while practicing the relaxation techniques he or she has just learned, the client progresses through practicing behaviours in the stimulus hierarchy, starting with the least anxiety-provoking ones.

3. Sound psychotherapy research designs use both randomized clinical trials and placebo control groups. Randomized clinical trials involve making sure that both experimental and control group participants are similar on various variables that might affect the response to treatment. Placebo control group participants receive an intervention that is not expected to work but controls for client expectancies because the client <u>does</u> believe that the treatment will work. Treatment is standardized through manuals containing procedures that therapists involved in the study must follow exactly. Finally, sound designs include follow-ups to determine the long-term effects of the treatment.

4. Openness involves willingness to invest in therapy and take risks necessary for change. Self-relatedness refers to ability to experience and understand internal states. Common factors shared by successful therapies include faith in the therapist and treatment, receiving a plausible explanation for problems, alternative ways of looking at problems, a protective setting, an opportunity to practice new behaviours, and increased optimism and self-efficacy.

5. Preventive mental health programs are designed to prevent problems from occurring. Situation-focused prevention is directed at reducing or eliminating the environmental causes of behaviour disorders or enhancing situational factors important in the prevention of the development of disorders. Competency-focused prevention programs are designed to improve people's personal resources and coping skills.

Chapter 15. Stress, Coping, and Health

Learning Objectives

15.1   Describe the three ways that theorists have defined stress.

15.2   Describe the work of Holmes and Rahe (1967) and their Social Readjustment Rating Scale.

15.3   List and describe four types of appraisal that occur in response to a potential stressor, and explain how they correspond to primary and secondary appraisal.

15.4   Describe the three stages of Selye's General Adaptation Syndrome (GAS).

15.5   Describe three possible causal paths between self-reported stress and distress.

15.6   Describe the physiological and behavioural mechanisms that can allow stress to contribute to illness.

15.7   Discuss evidence regarding various vulnerability and protective factors, including social support, physiological reactivity, hardiness, coping self-efficacy, optimism, and religious beliefs.

15.8   Describe the physiological toughness endocrine pattern.

15.9   Define and give an example of the three major classes of coping strategies.

15.10   Discuss how controllability influences the effectiveness of various coping strategies.

15.11   Describe the relationship between emotional constraint and health.

15.12   Explain how gender and cultural factors affect the tendency to use particular coping strategies.

15.13   Describe cognitive coping skills and relaxation techniques that comprise effective stress management training programs.

15.14   Describe the biological mechanisms involved in the experience of pain, including gate control theory.

15.15   Describe the cultural and psychological influences in the experience of pain and how they help explain the placebo effect.

15.16   Describe research regarding the specific use of cognitive and behavioural strategies for controlling pain.

15.17 Outline how the leading causes of death have changed over the past century.

15.18 Describe the six stages of the Transtheoretical Model of behaviour change.

15.19 Describe research that has focused on increasing health-enhancing behaviours like exercise and weight control.

15.20 Describe research that has focused on decreasing health-impairing behaviours like unsafe sexual practices and substance abuse.

15.21 Describe effective treatments for substance abuse problems, including motivational interviewing and multimodal treatment approaches.

15.22 Describe methods for preventing health problems, including harm reduction strategies and relapse prevention.

Chapter Overview

This chapter examines the mind-body connection between psychological stress and physiological well-being, how we experience stress and how we can best cope with it. It also examines the experience of pain and pain management, and strategies to promote health and prevent illness.

Stressors are stimuli that place strong demands on us or threaten us. Stress involves a pattern of cognitive appraisals, physiological responses, and behavioral tendencies in response to a perceived imbalance between situational demands and the resources needed to cope with them. Stressors can be major or minor, catastrophic or ongoing. Four aspects of the appraisal process are: appraisal of demands of a situation (primary appraisal), appraisal of coping resources (secondary appraisal), judgment of the consequences of the situation, and appraisal of the personal meaning of the situation. Early stress researcher Hans Selye posited the general adaptation syndrome (GAS), which comprises alarm, resistance, and exhaustion.

Stress has important effects on health. For example, traumatic events correlate with long-term anxiety, depression, and unhappiness. Stress can combine with other factors to influence physical illnesses such as heart disease and cancer. Physiological studies suggest a connection between stress and lowered immune system activity. Psychologists look for vulnerability factors, which increase people's susceptibility to stressful events; and protective factors, which help people cope. Social support is a strong protective factor; the Type A behavior pattern, and particularly its hostility component, is a vulnerability factor. Beliefs such as hardiness, coping self-efficacy, optimism, and finding spiritual meaning in stressful life events can be protective factors.

Methods of coping with stress can be categorized as problem-focused (dealing with the stressor directly), emotion-focused (dealing with the emotions evoked by the stressor), and social support coping. A sense of controllability and coping efficacy seem to be particularly important, but if the stress is outside the individual's control then emotion-focused coping and social support are generally more helpful. Research suggests that physiological health is enhanced by recognizing and disclosing negative feelings about traumatic experiences and ongoing stress. Highly resilient children have been found to have good intellectual function, social skills, self-efficacy; and at least one caring adult in their lives who provided social support. There are gender differences in coping: Men are more likely to be problem-focused ("fight or flight"), while women are more likely to be emotion-focused and to seek social support ("tend and befriend"). Cultural differences in coping styles have also been observed, with Asians and Hispanics using more emotion-focused coping, and African-Americans seeking more social support, than White Americans. Stress management training methods include cognitive coping strategies such as cognitive restructuring and self-instructional training, and relaxation techniques such as somatic relaxation and meditation.

Pain is influenced by biological, psychological, and sociocultural factors. At the biological level, free nerve endings are pain receptors. Gate control theory attributes pain to the opening and closing of "gates" in the spinal cord. The nervous system contains endorphins, which play a major role in pain reduction. Placebos can produce expectations that reduce medical symptoms and pain. Cultural factors also influence the appraisal of painful stimuli. Negative emotional states decrease pain tolerance. Psychological techniques for pain control include (1) cognitive strategies, such as dissociative and associative techniques; (2) sensory and procedural information that increase cognitive control and support; and (3) increasing activity level to counter chronic pain.

Behavioral change is a key process in health promotion and illness prevention. The transtheoretical model identifies six stages of change: precontemplation, contemplation, preparation, action, maintenance, and termination. Exercise enhances both physical and psychological well-being. People who adhere to an exercise program for 3-6 months have a better chance of continuing thereafter. About a third of the American population is obese, as are one in 6 children and adolescents. Behavioral weight control programs feature self-monitoring, stimulus control procedures, and strategies that encourage people to eat less but enjoy it more. Exercise also enhances weight control.

HIV infection is spread by high-risk sexual and drug abuse behaviors. Behavioral changes have been accomplished in some, but not all, high-risk populations. Cultural factors may conflict with safer-sex practices, increasing the difficulty of reducing STD-linked behaviors. Substance abuse is often part of a larger pattern of maladjustment. Multimodal substance abuse treatments combine techniques such as aversion training, stress management and coping skills training, and positive reinforcement. Motivational interviewing uses the person's own motivation to change self-defeating behaviors. Harm reduction approaches focus on reducing the negative consequences that a behavior produces, rather than stopping the behavior itself. Relapse prevention is designed to keep occasional lapses from becoming full-blown relapses. Health psychologists have made important contributions to helping people reduce health-impairing behaviors and acquire healthier life styles, but many challenges remain.

Chapter Outline

THE NATURE OF STRESS
    Stressors
        Measuring Stressful Life Events
    The Stress Response
    Chronic Stress and the GAS

STRESS AND HEALTH
    Stress and Psychological Well-Being
    Stress and Illness

VULNERABILITY AND PROTECTIVE FACTORS
    Social Support
    Cognitive Protective Factors: The Importance of Beliefs
        Hardiness
        Coping Self-efficacy
        Optimism
        Finding Meaning in Stressful Life Events
    Physiological Reactivity
        Research Frontiers: Stress and Working Memory

COPING WITH STRESS
    Effectiveness of Coping Strategies
    Controllability and Coping Efficacy
    Bottling up Feelings: The Cost of Constraint
    Gender, Culture, and Coping
        Psychological Applications: Stress Management

PAIN AND PAIN MANAGEMENT
    Biological Mechanism of Pain
        Gate Control Theory
        The Endorphins
    Cultural and Psychological Influences on Pain
        Cultural Factors
        Meanings and Beliefs
        Personality Factors and Social Support
    Psychological Techniques for Controlling Pain and Suffering
        Cognitive Strategies
        Hospital Interventions: Giving Patients Informational Control
        A Key Behavioural Strategy: Becoming Active Again

HEALTH PROMOTION AND ILLNESS PREVENTION
    How People Change: The Transtheoretical Model
    Increasing Behaviours That Enhance Health
        Exercise
        Weight Control
    Reducing Behaviours That Impair Health
        Prevention Programs

COMBATTING SUBSTANCE ABUSE
    Psychological Approaches to Treatment and Prevention
        Relapse Prevention
        Motivational Interviewing
        Multimodal Treatment Approaches
        Harm Reduction Approaches to Prevention

Problem-Based Learning

Health

www.healthpsych.com
Health Psychology and Rehabilitation-This site contains research, viewpoints and links to other
sites on health psychology.

http://www.hc-sc.gc.ca
Health Canada-This excellent site contains a vast amount of information on Canadian health
issues.

Professional Associations
http://www.cpa.ca/contents.html
Canadian Psychological Association-This is the CPA's website and it contains information about
careers, regulatory bodies, professional associations, clinical disorders, and issues that concern
psychology in Canada. This site contains a Canadian report on the terrorist attacks in the United
States.

www.psychologicalscience.org
American Psychological Society-This site is the home page for the American Psychological
Society and it contains a wealth of information including student tips, teaching resources, journal
articles, news and events and links to many areas of psychology.

http://www.apa.org
American Psychological Association-This is the APA's website and it contains information about
careers, student concerns, some full text articles, news and events, and information about many
areas such as clinical disorders, aids, and anger.

Key Terms: *Write the letter of the definition next to the term in the space provided.*

Stress and well-being

1. ___ coping self-efficacy

2. ___ general adaptation syndrome (GAS)

3. ___ hardiness

4. ___ life event scales

5. ___ neuroticism

6. ___ physiological toughness

7. ___ primary appraisal

8. ___ protective factor

9. ___ rape trauma syndrome

10. ___ secondary appraisal

11. ___ stress

12. ___ stressors

13. ___ vulnerability factors

a. a pattern of cognitive appraisals, physiological responses, and behavioral tendencies that occurs in response to a perceived imbalance between situational demands and the resources available to cope with them

b. a protective stress hormone pattern involving (a) a low resting level of cortisol and low levels of cortisol secretion in response to stressors, and (b) a low resting level of catecholamines, but a quick and strong catecholamine response when the stressor occurs, followed by a quick decline in catrecholamine secretion and arousal when the stressor is over

c. situations that places demands on organisms that tax or exceed their resources

d. a stress-resistant personality pattern that involves the factors of commitment, control, and challenge

e. beliefs relating to our ability to deal effectively with a stressful stimulus or situation, including pain

f. environmental or personal resources that help people fare better in the face of stress

g. one's judgment of the adequacy of personal resources needed to cope with a stressor; occurs after primary appraisal

h. Selye's description of the body's responses to a stressor, which includes successive phases of alarm, resistance, and exhaustion

i. situational or physical factors that increase susceptibility to the negative impact of stressful events

j. the initial appraisal of a situation as benign, irrelevant, or threatening; a perception of the severity of demands

k. questionnaires that measure the number (and, sometimes, the intensity) of positive and negative life events that have occurred over a specific period of time

l. a pattern of cognitive, emotional, and behavioural responses that occurs in response to the trauma of being raped

m. a personality trait that involves the tendency to experience high levels of negative affect and to behave in self-defeating ways

COPING WITH STRESS
PAIN AND PAIN MANAGEMENT

1. ___ emotion-focused coping
2. ___ endorphins

3. ___ gate control theory
4. ___ placebos

5. ___ problem-focused coping
6. ___ seeking social support
7. ___ stress-induced analgesia

a. a reduction in sensitivity that occurs when endorphins are released under stressful conditions
b. a theory of pain that postulates the existence of gating mechanisms in the spinal cord and brain that can increase or decrease the experience of pain by regulating the flow of pain impulses to the brain
c. inactive or inert substances
d. attempts to turn to others for assistance or emotional support in times of stress
e. coping strategies directed at minimizing or reducing emotional responses to a stressor
f. coping strategies that involve direct attempts to confront and master a stressful situation
g. natural opiate-like substances that are involved in pain reduction

HEALTH PROMOTION AND ILLNESS PREVENTION

1. ___ abstinence violation effect

2. ___ aerobic exercise

3. ___ harm reduction

4. ___ health-compromising behaviours
5. ___ health-enhancing behaviours

6. ___ health psychology

7. ___ lapse

8. ___ motivational interviewing

9. ___ multimodal treatment approaches
10. ___ relapse

11. ___ transtheoretical model
12. ___ yoyo dieting

a. a model of behavior change that includes the phases of precontemplation, contemplation, preparation, action, maintenance, and termination
b. a prevention strategy that is designed not to eliminate a problem behavior, but to reduce its harmful consequences
c. a response to a lapse in which a person blames him/herself and concludes that he or she is incapable of resisting high-risk situations
d. behaviours, such as exercise and good dietary habits, that support and increase health and longevity
e. a treatment approach that avoids confrontation and leads the clients to their own realization of a problem and increased motivation to change
f. substance abuse interventions that combine a number of treatments, such as aversion therapy and coping skills training
g. sustained activity that elevates the heart rate and body's need for oxygen
h. the study of psychological and behavioral factors in the prevention and treatment of illness and in the maintenance of health
i. a complete return to a previous undesirable behaviour and an abandonment of attempts to change
j. a one-time return to an undesirable behaviour pattern, usually in a high-risk situation
k. behaviours, such as poor dietary habits and unprotected sexual activity, that impair health and reduce longevity
l. severe intermittent dieting that results in large weight fluctuations

Key People: *Write the letter of the ideas associated with the person in the space provided.*

1. ___ Hans Selye
2. ___ Thomas Holmes and Richard Rahe
3. ___ Suzanne Kobasa
4. ___ Richard Lazarus
5. ___ Ronald Melzack & Patrick Wall
6. ___ James Prochaska & Carlo DiClemente

a. "3 Cs" of hardiness: commitment, control, & challenge
b. Canadian who discovered the General Adaptation Syndrome
c. gate control theory of pain
d. Social Readjustment Rating Scale (SRRS)
e. primary, secondary appraisals of stress
f. transtheoretical model identifies 6 stages of behavior change

Review at a Glance: *Write the term that best fits the blank to review what you learned in this chapter.*

Stress and Well-Being

Stimuli that place strong demands on us are called (1) _____. (2) _____ is a pattern of cognitive appraisals, physiological responses, and behavioral tendencies that occurs in response to a perceived imbalance between situational demands and the resources needed to cope with them. Lazarus suggests that when we first encounter a situation, we engage in (3) _____ appraisal, by which we perceive the situation as either benign, neutral, or threatening. Our perception of our ability to cope with a situation is called (4) _____ appraisal. Hans Selye, a pioneer in examining the body's response to stress, found three phases: alarm, resistance, and exhaustion in a system he called the (5) _____ _____ syndrome. Long-term difficulties such as (6) _____, anxiety, and unhappiness are common in people who have experienced catastrophic events. Physiological studies have found a correlation between stress and lowered (7) _____ _____ function. Factors that increase susceptibility to stress, such as Type A behavior pattern, are called (8) _____ factors, while those that decrease susceptibility, such as social support, are (9) _____ factors.

Coping with Stress

Some individuals cope better with stress than do others. A stress-protective factor identified by Kobasa and termed (10) _____ consists of commitment, control, and challenge. The belief that we have the ability to do what is necessary to cope is called coping (11) _____ - _____. (12) _____ - _____ coping strategies attempt to directly deal with the problem, while (13) _____ - _____ strategies attempt to manage the emotional aspects of the problem. A third class of coping strategies involves (14) _____ _____ _____, turning to others for assistance and emotional support in times of stress. In examining what makes children highly resilient to stress, Masten identified the presence of a caring adult who provided (15) _____ _____, among other factors, as key. Coping behaviors may vary according to (16) _____ and culture. Stress management training includes (17) _____ coping strategies, which deal with thoughts and beliefs; and relaxation techniques such as somatic relaxation and (18) _____.

Pain: A Major Health Issue

Pain involves a complex set of sensations and perceptions. (19) _____ _____ theory describes how the nervous system transmits pain impulses. To help us deal with pain, the brain has its own built-in analgesics called (20) _____. A phenomenon attributed to endorphins is (21) _____ - _____ _____, a dramatic lack of perception of pain under extreme circumstances. Psychological pain control strategies include dissociative and (22) _____ techniques, increasing cognitive control and support, and increasing one's activity level.

Health Promotion and Illness Prevention

A key process in health promotion and illness prevention is (23) _____ change. The (24) _____ model identifies six stages of change: precontemplation, contemplation, preparation, action, maintenance, and (25) _____. People often quit exercise programs, but those who keep exercising for (26) _____ _____ _____ months are more likely to continue over the long term. About (27) _____ _____ of the U.S. population is obese; another third is overweight. (28) _____ weight control programs feature self-monitoring, stimulus control procedures, and strategies that encourage people to eat less but enjoy it more. Apart from improved eating habits, another contributor to weight control is (29) _____.

HIV infection is spread by high-risk (30) _____ and drug abuse behaviors. According to the United Nations in 2002, (31) _____ made up one half of all AIDS cases. Behavioral changes have effectively increased condom use among (32) _____ _____, but other high-risk populations continue to challenge health advocates. Particularly among adolescents and young adults, many individuals continue to have an irrational sense of (33) _____ _____ _____, and this belief contributes to a failure to (34) _____ from sex or to engage in protected sexual practices. Substance abuse is often part of a larger pattern of (35) _____. Multimodal substance abuse treatments combine techniques such as aversion training, stress management and coping skills training, and positive (36) _____. Motivational interviewing uses the person's own (37) _____ to change self-defeating behaviors. (38) _____ _____ approaches focus on reducing the negative consequences a behavior produces, not stopping the behavior itself. Relapse prevention is designed to keep occasional (39) _____ from becoming full-blown relapses. (40) _____ _____ have made important contributions to helping people reduce health-impairing behaviors and acquire healthier life styles, but many challenges remain.

Apply What You Know

1.   Using the general adaptation syndrome (GAS) model, classify some typical responses that people are likely to have to the following stressors. Notice which kinds of stressors lend themselves better to this model than others.

Stressor	Alarm	Resistance	Exhaustion
Being attacked by a stranger who tries to rob and sexually assault you			
Being involved in a bus accident in which others are seriously injured but you are not			
Living for several years in extreme poverty			
Being the bride or groom in a large traditional wedding			
Going to an important job interview and not being offered the job			
Preparing for and getting through a week of final exams			

2. The next time you experience pain (such as a headache, heartburn, sore muscles from exercising, menstrual cramps, etc.), try implementing one or more of the psychological pain management strategies outlined in this chapter. Make notes below of the nature of the pain, the intervention(s) you tried, and how well you were able to manage the pain.

	Source of Pain	How Well Managed
Dissociative technique:		
Associative technique:		
Cognitive control procedure:		
Social support procedure:		
Increasing activity:		

3. How regularly do you exercise? Record your exercise for a week on the following chart. Note your reasons for exercising, any obstacles you overcame to stick with your exercise program, and any supportive factors that helped you adhere to it.

	Type and Duration of Exercise	Obstacles; How I Overcame Them	Supportive Motivators
Sunday			
Monday			
Tuesday			
Wednesday			
Thursday			
Friday			
Saturday			

Internet Scavenger Hunt: *Here's a chance to explore the multi-faceted field of psychology in the context of the World Wide Web. As with any Internet research, it is important to consider how legitimate a given source is before you rely on the information it presents. Your instructor or librarian may give you some specific guidelines for distinguishing which kinds of websites tend to be reputable.*

A. Take another look at the Key Terms and Key People for this chapter. In the space below, make a list of any whose definitions or associations you are not yet confident of, and any you'd like to learn more about. Try entering the terms on your list into your search engine. Make notes of any helpful information you find.

Key Term or Key Person / Information Found

B. Explore the websites of several professional organizations related to the study of stress and health, including the following. In the space provided, make note of the resources offered by each of these organizations to professionals, students, and the general public.

- American Psychological Association Division 38 (Health Psychology) its journal, *Health Psychology*, and its newsletter, *The Health Psychologist*

- STAR (Stress and Anxiety Research) Society

- International Stress Management Association (U.K.)

- American Institute of Stress

- Association for Applied and Therapeutic Humor

Practice Test

Multiple Choice Items: *Write the letter corresponding to your answer in the space to the left of each item.*

_____ 1. According to research by Janet Kielcot-Glaser and co-workers, stressful experiences, such as final exams, _____.

    a.   correlated with depression and anxiety for years afterward
    b.   increased self-efficacy beliefs
    c.   led to primary but not secondary appraisal
    d.   lowered immune system function

_____ 2. According to Statistics Canada (2000) _____ percent of Canadians between 20 and 64 years of age are overweight.

    a.   8
    b.   48
    c.   74
    d.   23

_____ 3. Roberta is undergoing cancer treatment. When she tells her oncologist she feels depressed, he brushes aside the comment and talks about her latest MRI. When she tells her husband she feels depressed, he says, "Look, I've got enough on my mind without having to listen to your complaining." When she tells her mother she feels depressed, her mother says, "You need to get right with God, then God will stop punishing you." Roberta is a strong candidate for _____.

    a.   high resilience
    b.   increased activity for pain reduction
    c.   problem-focused coping strategies
    d.   seeking social support through a cancer patients' support group

_____ 4. According to Statistics Canada childhood obesity has increased _____ % between 1980 and 2004.

    a.   10
    b.   50
    c.   100
    d.   500

_____ 5. Aware that the other castaways on Gilligan's island look to him as a leader in their stressful predicament, the skipper is highly committed to doing the best possible job, has a sense of control, and views difficulties that arise as challenges. A health psychologist would most likely classify the skipper as a(n) ____ individual.

a. Type A
b. optimistic
c. vulnerable
d. hardy

_____ 6. The well-known "serenity prayer" ("God grant me the serenity to accept the things I cannot change, the courage to change the things I can, and the wisdom to know the difference") may help to reduce stress by ____.

a. increasing emotion-focused coping behavior
b. increasing social support
c. increasing wisdom
d. differentiating between stressors that are, and are not, amenable to problem-focused coping

_____ 7. According to Statistics Canada (2000), nearly ___ percent of Canadians aged 20 to 64 are obese:

a. 30%
b. 50%
c. 15%
d. 40%

_____ 8. Ralph grew up with a verbally abusive mother and neglectful father. When he was 16, he was robbed and brutally beaten by an assailant who was never caught. He is working his way through community college with a sales job that pays him commissions but no salary. His older brother, with whom he has always had a positive relationship, recently got married and moved away. Ralph maintains, however, that he does not feel any negative emotions from these stressful experiences. According to research, Ralph is likely to be _____.

a. a Type A person
b. in need of training to express his negative emotions
c. a highly resilient child
d. in need of problem-focused coping strategies

_____ 9. The pain-free state, sometimes called "runner's high," that many people experience during sustained exercise is due to ____.

a. naloxone
b. stress-induced analgesia
c. gate control theory
d. endorphins

_____ ✓ 10. Research has shown that excessive levels of stress can have detrimental effects on both psychological and physical health. Evolutionary theorists speculate that this may be because the physical mobilization system that was shaped by evolution to help people cope with life-threatening _____ stressors may not be adaptive for coping with the _____ stressors that characterize the modern world.

    a. emotional; physical
    b. physical; psychological
    c. psychological; emotional
    d. emotional; physical

_____ 11. People who are high in the personality trait of _____ have a heightened tendency to experience negative emotions and to get themselves into stressful situations. This variable may explain in part why there is a positive correlation between negative life events and distress.

    a. depression
    b. neuroticism
    c. anxiety
    d. pessimism

_____ 12. A return to the undesirable behaviour pattern is called _____.

    a. a lapse
    b. a relapse
    c. the abstinence violation effect
    d. harm reduction

_____ ✓ 13. Jan is about to compete in a triathlon. Though such a competition would likely inspire fear and nervousness in most people, Jan is feeling good about the race because she believes she has the skills to complete it successfully. Psychologist Albert Bandura would most likely say that Jan has high _____.

    a. self-efficacy
    b. self-esteem
    c. self-confidence
    d. self-control

_____ 14. Research on the influence of religious beliefs has suggested that they have the most positive effects in helping people to deal with _____, but can increase the stress of people dealing with _____.

    a. illnesses; losses
    b. losses; marital problems and abuse
    c. marital problems and abuse; personal setbacks
    d. marital problems and abuse; illnesses

_____ 15. Norm and Cliff have both recently been through relationship breakups. Norm decides to go to his favorite bar and talk with his friends about what's been happening. Cliff on the other hand, decides to deal with his negative feelings through meditation. Based on the information provided, we would say that the coping strategy Norm uses is ___ while Cliff's strategy is ___.

    a. seeking social support; emotion-focused coping
    b. seeking social support; problem-focused coping
    c. emotion-focused coping; seeking social support
    d. emotion-focused coping; problem-focused coping

_____ 16. In experiments with pain control, patients sometimes report pain relief after being given a(n) _____ that is equal to the relief they report after being given an actual pain-killing drug.

    a. naloxone
    b. placebo
    c. endorphin
    d. emotion-focused coping strategy

_____ 17. Selye, in his general adaptation syndrome theory, argued that animals will go through all of the following stages except _____ in dealing with an environmental stressor.

    a. empathy
    b. resistance
    c. exhaustion
    d. alarm

_____ 18. The first three of the six stages in the transtheoretical model of behavior change are _____.

    a. primary appraisal, secondary appraisal, and action
    b. contemplation, preparation, and action
    c. precontemplation, contemplation, and preparation
    d. precontemplation, preparation, and change

_____ 19. The last three of the six stages in the transtheoretical model of behavior change are _____.

    a. action, maintenance, and termination
    b. change, maintenance, and review
    c. action, maintenance, and relapse
    d. action, sustenance, and disengagement

_____ 20. A health-enhancing behavior that affects both psychological and physical well-being is _____.

    a. cognitive restructuring
    b. portion control
    c. exercise
    d. harm reduction

_____ 21. Women who are _____ percent overweight are more than _____ as likely to develop heart disease than are normal-weight women.

a. 30; twice
b. 20; twice
c. 10; four times
d. 30; three times

_____ 22. Charlie is overweight and has started a behavioral weight control program. He is recording what he eats, how much, and under what circumstances. This phase of the program is called _____.

a. feedback
b. portion control
c. stimulus control
d. self-monitoring

_____ 23. A substance abuse treatment program that combines aversion training, stress management and coping skills, and positive reinforcement would be called a(n) _____.

a. success
b. multimodal program
c. culturally based program
d. harm reduction program

_____ 24. Loni is seeing a counselor about her habit of using amphetamines to stay awake and study. The counselor avoids confrontation but encourages Loni herself to describe how often she uses the drug, how it affects her life, and how she might want to change her behavior to rely less on the drug. The counselor is most likely using a _____ approach.

a. harm reduction
b. multimodal
c. motivational interviewing
d. culture-fair

_____ 25. Factors that increase people's susceptibility to stressful events are known as _____ factors.

a. protective
b. stress
c. vulnerability
d. stressor

_____ 26. The conviction that we can perform the behaviors necessary to cope with a stressor successfully is known as _____.

a. hardiness
b. optimism
c. coping self-efficacy
d. primary appraisal

_____ 27. All of the following except _____ seem to be involved in a person's hardiness.

    a. commitment
    b. primary appraisal
    c. control
    d. challenge

_____ 28. Studies of stressors suggest that _____.

    a. everyone experiences stress in the same way
    b. there is little evidence that stressors have long-term effects
    c. stressors can have long-term and strong psychological impact
    d. there is little evidence that environmental factors produce stress

_____ 29. According to United Nations 2002 data, half of all HIV cases are found in _____.

    a. men who have sex with men, including those who do not consider themselves homosexual
    b. intravenous drug users
    c. women
    d. children

_____ 30. Self-blaming failure to prevent an undesirable behaviour and believing that the failure indicates an inability to resist temptation is called _____.

    a. a lapse
    b. a relapse
    c. increased self-efficacy
    d. the abstinence violation effect

True/False Items: _Write T or F in the space provided to the left of each item._

_____ 1. Alarm, resistance, and exhaustion are the phases of the GAS.
_____ 2. Gate control theory is a model for analyzing stress control strategies.
_____ 3. Decreased pain tolerance is correlated with a negative emotional state.
_____ 4. The transtheoretical model uses non-judgmental interviewing to change a self-defeating behaviour through the client's own motivation.
_____ 5. Harm reduction approaches include needle-exchange programs for intravenous drug users and condom distribution programs for teenagers.
_____ 6. Stressors are specific kinds of eliciting stimuli that place demands on us and endanger our well-being.
_____ 7. Appraising our ability to cope with the demands of a situation is called primary appraisal.
_____ 8. Social support is an example of a vulnerability factor.
_____ 9. The factor called hardiness comprises three factors: commitment, control, and challenge.
_____ 10. Studies of coping suggest that both emotion-focused coping and seeking social support are used by women more frequently than by men.

Short Answer Questions

1. How do psychologists define (a) a stressor and (b) stress?

2. Distinguish between primary and secondary appraisal.

3. What protective factors help people cope with stress?

4. Describe the transtheoretical model of behavior change and how it works.

5. Describe some of the strategies that health psychologists use in prevention of HIV and substance abuse.

Essay Questions

1. Describe a stressful situation that you recently encountered. Using Lazarus's model, describe how the processes of primary appraisal and secondary appraisal were involved in your experience. Were the third and fourth processes of appraisal involved as well? Which of the coping strategies outlined in this chapter did you use?

2. What do you think about the findings of research on highly resilient children that are described in Chapter 15 of your textbook? What can teachers, clergy, and other concerned adults do to increase the likelihood that a challenged child will be highly resilient?

3. Why do you think HIV/AIDS continues to be a major public health problem even though most people are well aware of the behaviors that spread the infection? Of the illness prevention strategies outlined in this chapter, which ones do you think are most likely to be effective in reducing the spread of HIV/AIDS, and why?

Answer Keys

Answer Key for Key Terms

STRESS AND WELL-BEING

1.	e	5.	m	9.	l	13.	i
2.	h	6.	b	10.	g		
3.	d	7.	j	11.	a		
4.	k	8.	f	12.	c		

COPING WITH STRESS / PAIN AND PAIN MANAGEMENT

1.	e	4.	c	7.	a
2.	g	5.	f		
3.	b	6.	d		

HEALTH PROMOTION AND ILLNESS PREVENTION

1. c	2. g	3. b	4. k
5. h	6. j	7. e	8. f
9. l	10. a	11. l	

Answer Key for Key People

1. b
2. d
3. a
4. e
5. c
6. f

Answer Key for Review at a Glance

1. stressors
2. Stress
3. primary
4. secondary
5. general adaptation
6. depression
7. immune system
8. vulnerability
9. protective
10. hardiness
11. coping self-efficacy
12. Problem-focused
13. emotion-focused
14. seeking social support
15. social support
16. gender
17. cognitive
18. meditation
19. Gate control
20. endorphins
21. stress-induced analgesia
22. associative
23. behavior
24. transtheoretical
25. termination
26. three to six
27. one third
28. Behavioral
29. exercise
30. sexual
31. women
32. homosexual men
33. invulnerability to infection
34. abstain
35. maladjustment
36. reinforcement
37. motivation
38. Harm reduction
39. lapses
40. Health psychologists

Answer Key for Practice Test Multiple Choice Items

1. d	7. c	13. a	19. a	25. c
2. b	8. b	14. b	20. c	26. c
3. d	9. d	15. a	21. d	27. b
4. d	10. b	16. b	22. d	28. c
5. d	11. b	17. a	23. b	29. c
6. d	12. b	18. c	24. c	30. d

Answer Key for Practice Test True/False Items

1. T	3. T	5. T	7. F	9. T
2. F	4. F	6. T	8. F	10. T

Answer Key for Practice Test Short Answer Questions

1. A stressor is a stimulus that places strong demands on us or threatens us. Stress is defined as a pattern of cognitive appraisals, physiological responses, and behavioral tendencies that occur in response to a perceived imbalance between situational demands and the resources needed to cope with them. Stress may be major or minor, event-focused or ongoing. The effects of ongoing stress are often cumulative.

2. Primary appraisal involves determining the extent to which a situation is benign, neutral, irrelevant, or threatening. Secondary appraisal involves determining one's ability to cope with the situation by examining one's coping resources. Additional appraisal steps are judging the consequences of the situation, and determining the personal meaning of the situation.

3. Protective factors are environmental or personal resources that help people to cope more effectively with stressful events. These include social support, coping skills, and optimism. Coping skills such as hardiness and coping self-efficacy are important resources. Having a sense of control, part of hardiness, seems to be particularly important in helping us to cope with stressful circumstances.

4. The transtheoretical model outlines six stages of behavior change: precontemplation, contemplation, preparation, action, maintenance, and termination (which means success – not quitting, as one might think). Notice that half the model goes by before we reach "action." However, the stages do not necessarily occur in order. Many people move forward and backward through the stages as they try to change their behavior, and try repeatedly to change before they finally succeed. Still, failure at a given stage is likely if the person has not mastered previous stages.

5. Strategies for reducing high-risk sexual behavior and substance abuse include multimodal programs, which combine several techniques such as aversion, stress management, and positive reinforcement; motivational interviewing, which elicits the person's own motivation to change self-defeating behaviors; harm reduction, which focuses on reducing the ill effects of a behavior rather than stopping the behavior; and relapse prevention, which encourages the person to stick with the changed behavior even when an occasional lapse occurs.

Answer Key for Practice Test Essay Questions

As you may have guessed, there are no right or wrong answers to the essay questions in this practice test. That does not mean, however, that all essays are equally good. To get maximum learning benefit from the essay questions, do the following:

- Review each essay a day or two after you wrote it, noting any necessary corrections and any additional support for your points that you can think of.
- Review the section in your textbook that pertains to the topic of each essay. Annotate your essay with any corrections or additional support for your points that you find in the text.
- Spend a few minutes researching the topic of each essay on the Internet. Annotate your essay further with any additional (reliable) information you find.

Finally, reread each essay with the annotations you have added

Chapter 16. Behaviour in a Social Context

Learning Objectives

These questions, with a few additions (indicated with an asterisk), are taken from the directed questions found in the margins of the chapter. After reading the chapter, you should be able to answer these questions.

16.1 When does the mere presence of others people enhance or impair performance? Why?

16.2 How do norms and roles guide our behaviour?

16.3 Explain the difference between informational and normative social influence.

16.4 Identify some situational factors that influence people's degree of conformity.

16.5 When is the minority most likely to influence the majority?

16.6 Describe Milgram's obedience experiment. Do you believe the results would be similar today? Why or why not?

16.7 What situational factors increase obedience?

16.8 Describe deindividuation and how conditions in the Stanford Prison Study may have fostered it.

16.9 What is social loafing and when is it most likely to occur?

16.10 Identify two causes of group polarization.

16.11 What are some causes, symptoms, and consequences of groupthink?

16.12 Why did LePiere's study raise doubts about attitude-behaviour consistency?

16.13 Discuss the three broad conditions under which attitudes best predict behaviour.

16.14 What causes cognitive dissonance, and how can it produce attitude change?

16.15 According to self-perception theory, why does counterattitudinal behaviour produce attitude change?

16.16 What evidence supports dissonance theory? What evidence favours self-perception theory?

16.17 Identify communicator and message characteristics that increase persuasiveness.

16.18 Describe the central and peripheral routes to persuasion. For whom is the central route most likely to be effective?

16.19 How are the norm of reciprocity, door-in-the-face, and foot-in-the-door techniques, and lowballing used to manipulate behaviour?

16.20 What types of information lead us to form a situational, rather than personal attribution?

16.21 Describe the fundamental attribution error and the self-serving bias. How do cultural norms affect these attributional tendencies?

16.22   Why do primacy effects occur in impression formation? How can they be reduced?

16.23   How do mental sets shape the way we perceive people? How do stereotypes create mental sets?

16.24   Explain how our incorrect expectations can become self-fulfilling.

16.25   From evolutionary and social comparison viewpoints, why are humans such social creatures?

16.26   How does fear influence affiliation?

16.27   How and why does proximity influence affiliation and attraction?

16.28   Do birds of a feather flock together or do opposites attract? Describe the evidence.

16.29   Identify two factors that may underlie the desire to affiliate more with attractive people.

16.29.1* What is the matching effect and what predictions does it make regarding dating preferences?

16.30   Describe some gender differences in mate preferences.

16.31   How do evolutionary and social structure models explain gender differences in mate preferences?

16.32   How consistent are gender differences in mate preferences across cultures? How might this support both evolutionary and social structure views?

16.33   According to social penetration and social exchange theories, what factors influence whether a relationship will deepen, be satisfying, and continue?

16.34   How does Sternberg's model expand upon the passionate-companionate love distinction?

16.35   Explain how transfer of excitation can influence our feelings of love.

16.35.1* What percentage of marriages end in divorce? How well can marital researchers predict marriage outcomes?

16.36   Based on marital research, give some advice to a newlywed couple about behaviours that will help keep their relationship strong.

16.37   How do psychologists use reaction time tasks to detect people's covert prejudices?

16.38   Identify cognitive processes that foster prejudice.

16.39   How can people maintain their stereotypes in the face of contradictory information?

16.40   According to realistic conflict theory and social identity theory, what are the motivational roots of prejudice?

16.41   Discuss how self-fulfilling prophecies and stereotypes threaten to perpetuate prejudice.

16.42   According to sociobiologists, what is the evolutionary basis for helping behaviour?

16.43   How do social norms, self-reinforcers, and empathy influence helping behaviour?

16.44   Identify two key ways (2 stages of intervention) in which the "bystander effect" often inhibits people from responding to emergency.

16.44.1* What additional factors help to explain why bystanders may be helpful?

16.45   Who are we most likely to help? How might the belief in a just world inhibit us from helping?

16.45.1* What factors serve to increase prosocial behaviour?

16.46   What evidence supports a genetic role in aggression?

16.47   Discuss some brain regions and body chemicals that play a role in aggression.

16.48   Identify some major types of environmental stimuli that increase the risk of aggression.

16.49   Discuss how reinforcement and modelling contribute to aggression.

16.50   How do cognitive factors determine whether we respond to a stimulus aggressively?

16.50.1* Define the term catharsis and how it is related to Megargee's concept of overcontrolled hostility?

16.51   According to the catharsis and social learning viewpoints, what role does media violence play in regulating human aggression?

16.52   Based on research, how does media violence affect people's behaviour and attitudes?

16.53   According to learning principles, how might violent video games teach people to behave aggressively? Does evidence support this view?

Chapter Overview

Attributions are judgments about the causes of behavior. One distinction we make is between personal and situational attributions. When we make a personal attribution, we believe the cause of someone's behavior is a personal characteristic of theirs. Situational attributions are made to environmental causes. A number of biases, including the fundamental attribution error (the tendency to overestimate personal causes of behavior), affect our judgments. Forming and maintaining impressions is another aspect of social thinking and perception. The initial information we learn about a person greatly influences our perceptions of them (primacy effect). Stereotypes and self-fulfilling prophecies can bias the way that we perceive individuals.

Attitudes are positive or negative evaluative reactions toward stimuli. Attitudes are most predictive of behavior when situational factors are weak, when subjective norms support our attitudes, and when we believe behaviors are under our control, according to the theory of planned behavior. Additionally, attitudes best predict behavior when we are aware of them, and general attitudes best predict general classes of behavior, while specific attitudes best predict specific behaviors. Other theories such as cognitive dissonance theory and self-perception theory focus on how our behavior influences our attitudes. Specifically, they predict that we mold our attitudes to be consistent with how we have already behaved.

Studies of persuasion suggest three major components in the persuasive process: the communicator, the message, and the audience. Communicator credibility, largely determined by perceived expertise and trustworthiness, is a key to persuasion. Two-sided communications, which present both sides of an issue, have been found to be more persuasive than one-sided messages in many situations. Audience factors play a role in whether the central or the peripheral route to persuasion is a better technique for persuasion. When people are motivated to examine arguments critically, the central route is the better technique.

A major topic of social psychology is the study of how other people influence our behavior, which is called social influence. Studies of social facilitation suggest that both animals and humans have an increased tendency to perform their dominant response in the presence of others. When performing easy tasks or complex tasks that we have mastered, our dominant response usually is correct, so the presence of others enhances performance. At unlearned complex tasks, our dominant response usually is to make errors, so the presence of others impairs performance. We are also affected by both social norms and social roles, both of which prescribe how we *should* behave.

Conformity and obedience are two major topics in the area of social influence. We conform because of both informational social influence (i.e., conforming because we believe others are right) and because of normative social influence (i.e., conforming because we want others to accept us). Group size affects conformity to a certain point, and the presence of a dissenter can reduce conformity. Milgram's classic studies on obedience point to a number of situational factors that influence obedience, including remoteness of victims, closeness and legitimacy of an authority figure, and being a "cog in a wheel." Personal characteristics do not seem to explain obedience as well as such situational factors. Marketers use several compliance techniques to induce people to say yes when their inclination is to say no, including the norm of reciprocity, the door-in-the-face technique, the foot-in-the-door technique, and lowballing.

In groups, people may engage in social loafing, which is the tendency to expend less effort when working in a group than when working alone; or groupthink, which is the tendency for group members to suspend critical thinking to create a sense of group unanimity. Deindividuation, resulting from the increased anonymity that sometimes accompanies being in a crowd, can fuel destructive behavior.

Attraction, liking, and loving are an important part of our social interactions. Proximity, mere exposure, similarity of attitudes, and physical attractiveness typically enhance our attraction toward someone. Relationships deepen as partners self-disclose and exchanges between them become more intimate and broader. Social exchange theory analyzes relationships in terms of the rewards and costs experienced by each partner. The qualities that people find most attractive in a mate vary somewhat across cultures. Evolutionary theorists propose that gender difference in mate preferences reflect inherited biological tendencies, whereas sociocultural theorists believe that these differences result from socialization and gender inequities in economic opportunities. The triangular theory of love identifies passion, intimacy, and commitment as the components of various kinds of love. Partners are more likely to remain happily married when they understand each other and deal with conflicts by de-escalating their emotions and providing mutual support.

Prejudice, which is defined attitudinally; and discrimination, which is defined behaviorally; remain major problems in American society. Categorization into ingroups and outgroups and the use of the outgroup homogeneity bias (the belief that the members of our outgroups are all very similar to one another) are major cognitive sources of prejudice and discrimination. Realistic conflict theory explains the motivational source of prejudice and discrimination as due to competition between groups for limited resources, while social identity theory explains prejudice and discrimination as due to a need to enhance our self-esteem (by making sure that our ingroup does well and that our outgroup does poorly). Stereotype threat is the fear of being seen by others as "living up" to the stereotype they hold about one's group. An effective strategy for reducing prejudice is equal status contact.

Prosocial behavior is affected by biological predispositions, learning, and by personality characteristics such as empathy. According to the empathy-altruism hypothesis, empathy produces altruism. Other factors that influence helping include simply noticing a problem, social comparison, feeling a sense of responsibility to help, and a sense of self-efficacy in dealing with the situation. The bystander effect tends to reduce prosocial behavior by diffusing responsibility.

Aggressive behavior is influenced by biological, environmental, and psychological factors. The hypothalamus, amygdala, and other subcortical structures seem to affect the likelihood of engaging in aggression. Recent studies have also implicated the role of the frontal lobes (site of reasoning, forethought, and impulse control) in aggressive behavior. Low levels of serotonin and high levels of testosterone have also been found to correlated with aggression. Environmental stimuli that cause frustration or pain can increase aggression, as can other environmental factors such as provocation and exposure to aggressive models. Attributions of intentionality for someone's negative behavior toward us, a lack of empathy, and the inability to regulate emotions are important psychological factors in affecting aggressive behavior. Studies of media violence point to a link between media and violent behavior in children, adolescents, and adults. Several avenues of influence have been identified, including these: Viewers learn new aggressive behaviors through modeling, viewers believe that aggression is rewarded, and viewers become desensitized to violence and suffering.

Chapter Outline

SOCIAL THINKING
>   Attribution: Perceiving the Causes of Behavior
>>   Personal Versus Situational Attributions
>>   Attributional Biases
>>   Culture and Attribution
>   Forming and Maintaining Impressions
>>   Primacy versus Recency: Are First Impressions More Important?
>>   Mental Sets and Schemas: Seeing What We Expect to See
>>   Self-Fulfilling Prophecies: Creating What We Expect to See
>   Attitudes and Attitude Change
>>   Do Our Attitudes Influence Our Behavior?
>>   Does Our Behavior Influence Our Attitudes?
>>   Persuasion

SOCIAL INFLUENCE
>   The Mere Presence of Others
>   Social Norms: The Rules of the Game
>>   Culture and Norm Formation
>>   Why Do People Conform?
>>   Factors That Affect Conformity
>>   Minority Influence
>>   Obedience to Authority

Problem-Based Learning

General

www.socialpsychology.org
Social Psychology Network-This site which is maintained by Scott Plous of Wesleyan University is a very large database that covers all areas of social psychology. It offers links to professional organizations, graduate programs, online studies, journals and other resources.

Racial Conflict and Intergroup Hostility

http://www.jigsaw.org
Official website for the Jigsaw Classroom-Offers information and links related to Elliot Aronson's cooperative learning technique that was designed to reduce intergroup hostility and racial conflict.

Obedience and Persuasion

http://www.csj.org
AFF website (a secular, non-profit organization)-This site contains publications, workshops, and other resources about cults and psychological manipulation.

Media and Violence

http://www.cln.org/themes/media_violence.html
Part of the Open Learning Agency website-This site contains information on media and violence and is largely Canadian material.

http://www.crtc.gc.ca/eng/social/tv.htm
CRTC website-This site offers news releases, background on the issue of television violence in Canada, resources for parents and a bibliography of some of the available literature.

http://www.media-awareness.ca/
Media Awareness Network-This site offers information about media and violence from a Canadian perspective.

Key Terms: *Write the letter of the definition next to the term in the space provided.*

SOCIAL THINKING

1. ___ attitude
2. ___ attribution
3. ___ central route to persuasion
4. ___ communicator credibility
5. ___ fundamental attribution error
6. ___ peripheral route to persuasion
7. ___ primacy effect
8. ___ self-fulfilling prophecy
9. ___ self-perception theory
10. ___ self-serving bias
11. ___ stereotype
12. ___ theory of cognitive dissonance
13. ___ theory of planned behavior

a. (impression formation) our tendency to attach more importance to the initial information that we learn about a person

b. a generalized belief about a group or category of people

c. a judgment

d. a positive or negative evaluative reaction toward a stimulus (e.g., toward a person, action, object, or concept)

e. a tendency to underestimate the impact of the situation and overestimate the role of personal factors when explaining other people's behavior

f. occurs when people do not scrutinize a message, but are influenced mostly by other factors such as a speaker's attractiveness or a message's emotional appeal

g. occurs when people think carefully about a message and are influenced because they find the arguments compelling

h. occurs when people's erroneous expectations lead them to act toward others in a way that brings about the expected behaviors, thereby confirming the original impression

i. the degree to which an audience views a communicator as believable, largely based on the communicator's expertise and trustworthiness

j. the tendency to make relatively more personal attributions for success and situational attributions for failures

k. the theory that people strive to maintain consistency in their beliefs and actions, and that inconsistency creates dissonance—unpleasant arousal that motivates people to restore balance by changing their cognitions

l. the theory that we make inferences about our own attitudes by observing how we behave

m. the view that our intention to engage in a behavior is strongest when we have a positive attitude toward that behavior, when subjective norms (our perceptions of what other people think we should do) support our attitudes, and when we believe that the behavior is under our control

SOCIAL INFLUENCE

1. ___ deindividuation
2. ___ door-in-the-face technique
3. ___ foot-in-the-door technique

a. a manipulation technique in which a persuader gets you to commit to some action and then—before you actually perform the behavior—he or she increases the "cost" of that same behavior

b. a manipulation technique in which a persuader makes a large request, expecting you to reject it, and then presents a smaller request

c. a manipulation technique in which the persuader gets you to comply with a small request first, and later presents a larger request

4. ___ group polarization

d. a set of norms that characterizes how people in a given social position ought to behave

5. ___ groupthink

e. a state of increased anonymity in which a person, often as part of a group or crowd, engages in disinhibited behavior

6. ___ informational social influence

f. an increased tendency to perform one's dominant response in the mere presence of others

7. ___ lowballing

g. conformity motivated by gaining social acceptance and avoiding social rejection

8. ___ norm of reciprocity

h. following the opinions or behavior of other people because we believe they have accurate knowledge and what they are doing is "right"

9. ___ normative social influence

i. shared expectations about how people should think, feel, and behave

10. ___ social comparison

j. the norm that when other people treat us well, we should respond in kind

11. ___ social facilitation

k. the tendency for people to expend less individual effort when working collectively in a group than when working alone

12. ___ social loafing

l. the tendency of group members to suspend critical thinking because they are motivated to seek agreement

13. ___ social norm

m. when a group of like-minded people discusses an issue, the "average" opinion of group members tends to become more extreme

14. ___ social role

n. the act of comparing one's personal attributes, abilities, and opinions to those of other people

SOCIAL RELATIONS

1. ___ bystander effect

a. a form of love that involves intense emotional arousal and yearning for one's partner

2. ___ catharsis

b. a negative attitude toward people based on their membership in a group

3. ___ companionate love

c. a theory proposing that a social relationship can best be described in terms of exchanges of rewards and costs between the two partners

4. ___ cognitive arousal model of love

d. a theory proposing that as a relationship deepens, exchanges (including self-disclosure) become broader and more intimate

5. ___ discrimination

e. an affectionate relationship characterized by commitment and caring about the partner's well-being; sometimes contrasted with passionate love, which is more intensely emotional

6. ___ empathy-altruism hypothesis

f. behavior that involves treating people unfairly based on the group to which they belong

7. ___ frustration-aggression hypothesis

g. in romantic relationships, the tendency for partners to have a similar level of physical attractiveness

8. ___ equal status contact

h. the anxiety created by the perceived possibility that one's behavior or performance will confirm a negative stereotype about one's group

9. ___ just world hypothesis

i. the idea that performing an act of aggression discharges aggressive energy and temporarily reduces our impulse to aggress

10. ___ matching effect

    j.   the principle that prejudice between people is likely to be reduced when they engage in sustained close contact, have equal status within the context of their interaction, work to achieve a common goal that requires cooperation, and are supported by broader social norms that encourage prejudice reduction

11. ___ mere exposure effect

    k.   the principle that the presence of multiple bystanders inhibits each person's tendency to help, largely due to social comparison or diffusion of responsibility

12. ___ negative state relief model

    l.   the tendency to evaluate a stimulus more favorably after repeated exposure to it

13. ___ passionate love

    m.   the theory that competition for limited resources fosters prejudice

14. ___ prejudice

    n.   the theory that prejudice stems from a need to enhance our self-esteem

15. ___ realistic conflict theory

    o.   the theory that pure altruism does exist, and that it is produced by the capacity to empathize with the person in need of aid

16. ___ social exchange theory

    p.   the view that (1) frustration inevitably leads to aggression, and (2) all aggression is the result of frustration

17. ___ social identity theory

    q.   the view that various types of love result from different combinations of three core factors: intimacy, commitment, and passion

18. ___ social penetration theory

    r.   the theory that men and women behave differently, such as expressing different mate preferences, because society directs them into different social and economic roles

19. ___ stereotype threat

    s.   the view that passionate love has interacting cognitive and physiological components

20. ___ social structure theory

    t.   a misinterpretation of one's state of arousal that occurs when arousal actually is caused by one source, but the person attributes her or his arousal to another source

21. ___ transfer of excitation

    u.   the view that empathy does not lead to pure altruism, but instead, that high empathy causes us to feel distress when we learn of others' suffering, so that by helping them we reduce our own personal distress

22. ___ triangular theory of love

    v.   holds that because people want to view the world as fair, they perceive that people get what they deserve and deserve what they get

Key People: *Write the letter of the ideas associated with the person in the space provided.*

1. ___ Albert Bandura   a.   aggression can be learned by observing others
2. ___ C. Daniel Batson   b.   attributions comprise consistency, distinctiveness, and consensus
3. ___ Leon Festinger   c.   bystander intervention is a 5-step process
4. ___ Sigmund Freud   d.   catharsis discharges aggressive energy, temporarily reducing aggressive impulse
5. ___ Anthony Greenwald   e.   Chinese couple was refused service only once on 1930s cross-country trip
6. ___ David Grossman   f.   cognitive dissonance theory
7. ___ Harold Kelley   g.   empathy-altruism hypothesis
8. ___ Richard LaPiere   h.   Implicit Association Test reveals unconscious prejudice

9. ___ Bibb Latané & John Darley
10. ___ Stanley Milgram
11. ___ Max Ringelmann
12. ___ Muzafer Sherif
13. ___ Robert Sternberg
14. ___ Claude Steele
15. ___ Elaine Walster
16. ___ Robert Zajonc
17. ___ Philip Zimbardo

i. killing requires overcoming natural inhibition against killing members of our own species
j. participants exposed to the autokinetic effect developed group norms for distance they thought the light moved
k. participants obeyed in giving electric shocks to "learner"
l. physical attractiveness was the only predictor of being liked
m. social facilitation is the tendency to perform the dominant response in the presence of others
n. social loafing: 8 men pulled a rope with 51% less force than expected
o. Stanford Prison Study had to be stopped after 6 days
p. stereotype threat: fear of "living up" to others' stereotype about us
q. triangular theory of love: passion, intimacy, commitment

Review at a Glance: *Write the term that best fits the blank to review what you learned in this chapter.*

Social Thinking

Social psychologists study the process of (1) _____, by which we make judgments about the causes of our own and other's behaviors. One major distinction made by social psychologist Fritz Heider was between attributions to personal characteristics, called (2) _____ attributions, and attributions to environmental causes of behavior, called (3) _____ attributions. We can be quite biased in the way that we explain behavior. A bias by which we tend to underestimate situational factors of behavior when judging the causes of other people's behavior is called the (4) _____ _____ _____. When it comes to explaining our own behavior, we tend to protect our self-esteem by using the (5) _____ - _____ _____, making more personal attributions for success and more situational ones for failure. As social beings, we constantly form impressions of others. The tendency to attach more importance to the initial information we learn about a person is called the (6) _____ effect. Generalized beliefs about a group or category of people are called
(7) _____. When people's erroneous expectations about a person or group of people leads them to act toward others in a way that brings about the expected behavior, a
(8) _____ - _____ _____ has occurred.

Another major topic of social psychology is how people come to perceive their world. A(n)
(9) _____ is a positive or negative evaluative reaction toward a stimulus. Much research has been done to examine the relationship between attitudes and behaviors. According to the theory of (10) _____ _____, our intentions to engage in a behavior are strongest when subjective norms support our attitudes, when we have a positive attitude toward the behavior, and when we believe the behavior is under our control. We tend to believe that our attitudes cause our behaviors, but there is some evidence that behavior influences what we believe our attitudes to be. According to the theory of (11) _____ _____, people strive for consistency in their cognitions, such that, for example, when people's cognitions about their attitudes and behaviors are not consistent with one another, people are motivated to change either

attitudes or behaviors to bring them into line with one another. Similarly, Daryl Bem argued in his (12) _____ - _____ theory that we make inferences about our own attitudes by examining our own behavior.

Much research in social psychology has examined the process of persuasion. The three components that have been studied the most are the communicator, the message, and the audience. Studies of communicator credibility have indicated that communicators are most credible if we believe that they are (13) _____ and (14) _____. In general, studies of messages indicate that (15) _____ - _____ messages are the most effective kinds. Petty and Cacioppo have argued that there are two routes that audiences use when examining messages. The (16) _____ route occurs when people think carefully about the message, whereas the (17) _____ route occurs when people do not scrutinize the message but are persuaded by other factors, such as the speaker's attractiveness or the emotional content of the message.

Social Influence

Another major aspect of social psychology is the exploration of how other people influence our behavior, a phenomenon called (18) _____ _____.
Researchers such as Zajonc have found that the mere presence of others can affect the behavior of both animals and humans. When humans and animals perform simple tasks or complex learned tasks better in the presence of others but difficult or unlearned tasks worse in the presence of others, the phenomenon called (19) _____ _____ has occurred. All societies have rules for proper behavior.
(20) _____ _____ are shared expectations about how people should think, feel, and behave. (21) _____ _____ are sets of norms that characterize how people in a given social position "ought" to behave. People will generally conform to social norms and expectations because of both (22) _____ _____ _____, by which people conform because they think others are right; and (23) _____ _____ _____, by which people conform because they want to be accepted by others. Milgram's studies of (24) _____ point to situational factors including remoteness of victim, closeness of authority figure, and being a (25) "_____ in a wheel."

Social psychologists have also studied tactics used by salespersons to get compliance. People often feel that if someone has done something nice for them, they should do the same for that person, a phenomenon known as the (26) _____ _____ _____. When someone firsts asks you for a large request, which you typically refuse, and then asks you to comply with a smaller request (the real target behavior), that individual is using the
(27) _____ - _____ - _____ - _____ technique. The opposite technique, which requires compliance first with a small request before a larger request is made, is called the (28) _____ - _____ - _____ - _____ technique. When a persuader gets us to commit to an action and then increases the cost of the behavior before we actually have performed the behavior, (29) _____ has occurred.

People's behavior can also be affected by the greater sense of anonymity they feel in crowds, leading to disinhibition. This phenomenon is called (30) _____. Yet another phenomenon of social influence by which people work less hard in groups than they do when working alone is called (31) _____ _____. Good decision-making is sometimes impaired by group dynamics. When a group of like-minded people discusses an issue, the initial tendency of the group tends to become more extreme, a process called (32) _____ _____. Social psychologist Irving Janis described a process by which groups suspend good critical thinking in the name of group unanimity, a process he calls (33) _____.

Social Relations

We tend to be (34) _____ to people when we are exposed to their presence, have similar attitudes, and consider them physically attractive. Sternberg's triangular theory of love identifies (35) _____, intimacy, and (36) _____ as key ingredients that combine to produce various kinds of love. According to (37) _____ _____ theory, we evaluate relationships in terms of their rewards and costs to us. Evolutionary theorists propose that gender differences in mate selection reflect (38) _____ _____ tendencies, whereas (39) _____ theorists attribute these differences to socialization. A key to a satisfactory marriage seems to be the ability to deal with conflicts by (40) _____ - _____ emotions and providing mutual support.

(41) _____ refers to a negative attitude toward people based on their membership in a certain group. Social categorization of individuals leads to a differentiation between groups to which we believe we belong, or (42) _____ - _____, and groups to which we believe we do not belong, or (43) _____ - _____. A tendency to view the members of groups to which we believe we do not belong as being more similar to one another than members of groups to which we believe we do belong is called the (44) _____ _____ bias. Two major theories of why prejudice occurs have been identified. According to (45) _____ _____ theory, competition for limited resources fosters prejudice. According to (46) _____ _____ theory, prejudice occurs because of our basic need to maintain and enhance our self-esteem, which is done by making sure our in-group succeeds (often at the expense of our out-group).

Social psychologists have also studied why and when people help each other. According to (47) _____ _____, people (and animals) are most likely to help others with whom they share the most genes. According to the (48) _____ - _____ hypothesis, helping is influenced by our ability to understand things from another's perspective. Studies of helping in crowds suggest a (49) _____ _____, by which the presence of many people decreases the likelihood of any individual helping, largely because of a lack of individual felt responsibility to help.

Studies of aggression have suggested both biological and psychological causes. Psychological factors in aggression include (50) _____ - _____, by which aggressors blame the victim for some problem, thus convincing themselves that the victims deserved the aggression; and (51) _____ _____ _____, by which aggressors believe that they have been deliberately provoked by others. Research supports a link between media (52) _____ and aggressive behavior in children, adolescents, and adults.

Apply What You Know

1. Choose three television commercials. Describe each commercial and how communicator, message, and audience factors play roles in the persuasive process of the ad. Record your findings on the chart below.

Commercial	Communicator	Message	Audience

2. Describe how you would design a study to examine whether the primacy or recency effect was more important in the forming of impressions.

3. Watch three children's cartoons and record the number of aggressive acts that you see in each program. Make sure that you operationally define each category. What aggressive acts occur most often? Did the results surprise you? Why or why not?

Cartoon	Physical Aggression (Definition:)	Verbal Aggression (Definition:)

Internet Scavenger Hunt

1. Take another look at the Key Terms and Key People for this chapter. In the space below, make a list of any whose definitions or associations you are not yet confident of, and any you'd like to learn more about. Try entering the terms on your list into your search engine. Make notes of any helpful information you find.

Key Term or Key Person / Information Found

2. Conflicts between ethnic groups in various parts of the world (e.g., the Balkans, Israel, or Northern Ireland) have been sources of international concern for many years. Choose a long-standing ethnic conflict and use the Internet to gather information about its causes and effects, focusing on the prejudices and discrimination that occur on both sides. Summarize your findings in the space below, citing your sources.

3. Using the American Psychological Association website as your starting point, examine the table of contents of a recent issue in the <u>Journal of Personality and Social Psychology</u> and make note of the proportion of social psychology-related articles versus those on personality topics. Next, navigate to the APA homepage for Divisions. You will see that the APA does not have a social psychology division, but instead links social psychology issues to a variety of different APA divisions. Make note of these various divisions and their importance to the study of social psychology.

Practice Test

Multiple Choice Items: *Write the letter corresponding to your answer in the space to the left of each item.*

1. The fact that Japanese individuals typically sit farther apart when conversing than Americans do, and that Greeks are more likely than Britons to touch during a social interaction, are **best considered** as examples of _____.

   a. groupthink
   b. stereotype threat
   c. social norms
   d. informational social influence

2. Suppose you were designing an obedience study and wanted to reduce or lower the obedience rates found by Milgram. Of the following, the one which would **most likely** decrease participants' obedience would be to _____.

   a. have an authority figure that is perceived to be legitimate
   b. have the participants feel fully responsible for the victim's welfare
   c. place the victims in a separate room where the participant can't see them
   d. have your participants all be women

3. The fact that guards in the Stanford Prison study did not use their actual names, did not know that they were being observed, and wore reflective sunglasses that prevented direct eye contact all suggest that _____ may have played a key role in producing the results obtained in this experiment.

   a. the self-fulfilling prophecy
   b. social facilitation
   c. perceived legitimacy of the authority figures
   d. deindividuation

4. The belief that one's individual performance within a group is **not** being monitored, and having a task goal that is not very meaningful or valuable to a person, are two factors that are **most likely** to increase the chance of _____.

   a. groupthink
   b. social loafing
   c. minority influence
   d. group polarization

5. A group of public officials is meeting to decide what to do about a budget shortage. The principle of group polarization would predict that this group of people would be **most likely** to reach a highly conservative decision if _____.

   a. the group has a relatively small number of people in it (4-5)
   b. the group members believe that their individual performance with in the group is being monitored
   c. the group members are generally conservative to begin with
   d. the group has an authority figure who is perceived to be legitimate

_d_ 6. In the case of the Space Shuttle Challenger disaster, the NASA official who gave the final go-ahead for the mission was never informed about the many engineers who initially opposed the launch. The fact that this information never reached the official **best illustrates** the groupthink process of _____.

a. direct pressure
b. the illusion of unanimity
c. self-censorship
d. mind guarding

_d_ 7. Don went to three different dances this past week. Prior to this, he had a slightly negative attitude towards dancing, but after observing his behavior he starts to conclude that he must in fact enjoy it otherwise he wouldn't have attended so many. This change in Don's attitude is **most consistent** with the predictions of _____.

a. social identity theory
b. cognitive dissonance theory
c. the theory of planned behavior
d. self-perception theory

_c_ 8. Alison is at a workshop where a presenter is attempting to persuade people to make a rather risky but potentially profitable financial investment. After carefully considering the presenter's arguments, Alison finds this person's idea sound and compelling and decides to invest. This example **best demonstrates** the _____.

a. peripheral route to persuasion
b. norm of reciprocity
c. central route to persuasion
d. door-in-the-face technique

_a_ 9. A phone solicitor calls and asks if you would be interested in volunteering to work on a local political campaign. The job involves working 20 hours per week, you must work on the both Saturday and Sunday for the next 6 months, and you receive no financial compensation. After you politely refuse this request, the solicitor asks if you would be willing to work one evening a month on the campaign. This example **best demonstrates** the persuasion strategy known as _____.

a. the foot-in-the-door technique
b. the door-in-the-face technique
c. the norm of reciprocity
d. lowballing

_b_ 10. A person on campus walks up to you and asks if you would be willing to wear a ribbon to show support for her cause. Though the ribbon is a bit unattractive, it is small so you agree to wear it. After you agree to this request, the solicitor then asks you if you would be willing to make a donation of $15. This example best demonstrates the persuasion technique called _____.

    a.   the foot-in-the-door
    b.   the door-in-the-face
    c.   the norm of reciprocity
    d.   lowballing

_c_ 11. Juan is in the process of forming an opinion about someone he has just met when a friend who is taking a psychology class tells him to avoid making snap judgments and to consider the evidence carefully. The net result of this advice is that Juan feels more accountable for his opinions. The advice of Juan's friend should **most likely** decrease the _____.

    a.   recency effect
    b.   primacy effect
    c.   fundamental attribution error
    d.   self-serving bias

_d_ 12. A person with covert prejudicial feelings against gays and lesbians would most likely have the **slowest** reaction times to which of the following word pairs presented using the implicit association test? _____.

    a.   gay-wrong
    b.   straight-right
    c.   lesbian-bad
    d.   gay-good

_a_ 13. Dustin found himself particularly attracted to a woman he met just after crossing Vancouver's Capilano Suspension Bridge, a narrow bridge that sways on cables high above a ravine. Which model of love does Dustin's behaviour best support?

    a.   cognitive-arousal
    b.   triangular
    c.   social exchange
    d.   social penetration

_a_ 14. In his study of murderers, Adrian Raine (1998) found that impulsive murderers had _____ than murders who had committed their crimes as a planned predatory act.

    a.   lower frontal lobe activity
    b.   greater frontal lobe activity
    c.   less subcortical activity
    d.   more subcortical activity

_C_ 15. Realistic conflict theory argues that _____.

    a. we use the outgroup homogeneity bias to classify outgroups
    b. prejudice is due to illusory correlations
    c. prejudice and discrimination exist because groups of people are competing for the same things
    d. prejudice and discrimination are due to repressed frustrations that people have

_C_ 16. The likelihood that Person A will be attracted to Person B is enhanced by all of the following except _____.

    a. similarity of attitudes between Persons A and B
    b. physical attractiveness of Person B
    c. absence of Person B, which makes the heart grow fonder
    d. mere exposure to each other

_c_ 17. Sternberg's triangular theory of love proposes _____.

    a. that love progresses through separate, consecutive phases of passion, intimacy, and commitment
    b. that love will become more passionate if a third party gets involved, forming a love triangle
    c. passion, intimacy, and commitment as ingredients of love
    d. that love requires equal amounts of passion, intimacy, and commitment to exist

_C_ 18. Bored with life on Gilligan's island, the Professor decides to do a case study of mate selection using the only married couple available, Mr. and Mrs. Howell, as his data source. His hypothesis is that they chose each other based on gender inequities in economic opportunity and socialization that promotes mating with a member of one's own social class. The Professor is most likely taking the _____ view of mate selection.

    a. cognitive
    b. evolutionary
    c. sociocultural
    d. situational attribution

_a_ 19. Shared expectations about how people should think, feel, and behave are called _____.

    a. social norms
    b. informational social influences
    c. normative social influences
    d. self-perceptions

_c_ 20. Going along with a group's opinion because we believe the group is "right" is called _____.

    a. social norming
    b. informational social influence
    c. normative social influence
    d. a self-perception

____ 21. Studies of the effect of group size on conformity suggest that _____.

   a. group size has no effect on conformity
   b. a group of twenty produces more conformity that a group of five
   c. the larger the group, the more likely there is to be just one dissenter
   d. increasing group size up to about five people increases conformity

____ 22. Studies of personal characteristics in obedience have found that _____.

   a. more intelligent people are less likely to be obedient
   b. more religious people are more likely to be obedient
   c. women are less likely than men to be obedient
   d. gender is not related to obedience rates

____ 23. A generalized belief about a group of category of people is called a(n) _____.

   a. stereotype
   b. self-perception
   c. self-schema
   d. self-fulfilling prophecy

____ 24. Research by Esses and Zanna (1995) found that English Canadians rated other ethnic groups more negatively when the English Canadians

   a. were wealthy.
   b. had very high self-esteem.
   c. were in a bad mood.
   d. were more educated.

____ 25. Research on violence on Canadian television found that

   a. Canadian television had far less violence than U.S. television.
   b. children's programming had more violence than programming overall.
   c. only 15 percent of the overall programming contained some type of violence.
   d. cartoons contained the least amount of violence.

____ 26. According to _____ theory, prejudice stems from a need to enhance our self-esteem.

   a. social facilitation
   b. social identity
   c. norm of reciprocity
   d. attribution

27. Ramanjeet is very physically attracted to Jason. Although she is committed to keeping her relationship with Jason she often complains that she does not feel close to him or share with him. Which type of love best describes Ramanjeet's feelings toward Jason?

   a. companionate
   b. fatuous
   c. infatuation
   d. empty

28. The idea that we help others because it helps us to reduce our own personal distress is called _____.

   a. the norm of reciprocity effect
   b. kin selection
   c. the negative state relief model
   d. the empathy-altruism hypothesis

29. Jack had just bought a new car and parked it outside his apartment. An hour later he happened to look out the window and see his neighbor, Mickey, walking past the car carrying a folded-up umbrella. Jack thought he saw Mickey's umbrella put a scratch on the car. He went outside and, sure enough, there was a faint, barely visible scratch in the area where he had seen the umbrella. Jack became furious and banged on Mickey's door, cursing and yelling, promising to repay Mickey for being jealous of his new car and wanting to ruin it. Jack's aggressive behavior is most likely due to _____.

   a. a lack of empathy
   b. an attribution of intentionality for Mickey's behavior
   c. an inability to regulate his emotions
   d. the negative-state relief model

30. Studies of the effects of media violence on viewers' behavior have found that _____.

   a. viewers learn new aggressive behaviors through modeling
   b. the fear of becoming a target of violent crime decreases with more TV watching
   c. viewers learn that aggression is rarely rewarded
   d. fears that viewers will become desensitized to violence are unfounded

True/False Items: *Write T or F in the space provided to the left of each item.*

_____ 1. The mere presence of others does not affect human behavior.

_____ 2. Normative social influence occurs when people conform because they want to be accepted by others.

_____ 3. The presence of a dissenter tends to increase conformity.

_____ 4. Personal characteristics have been found to be more important than situational characteristics in obedient behavior.

_____ 5. Social loafing is more likely to occur when people believe that individual performance is not being monitored.

_____ 6. A relationship that lacks passion, intimacy, and commitment is not a love relationship by Sternberg's definition.

_____ 7. According to social exchange theory, we evaluate personal relationships by the benefits and costs that they entail.

_____ 8. The peripheral route to persuasion occurs when people carefully scrutinize the content of a message.

_____ 9. Stereotypes are not types of schemas.

_____ 10. We are more likely to help people who are similar to us than those we perceive as different.

Short Answer Questions

1. What are the differences among social facilitation, social loafing, and social compensation?

2. Why do influence processes produce conformity?

3. What does cognitive dissonance theory argue?

4. What are the cognitive roots of prejudice?

5. How do people progress from initial attraction to relationships at deeper levels of liking and loving?

Essay Questions

1. What group dynamics affect group decision-making?

2. How do our attitudes influence our behaviour?

3. What processes are involved in forming and maintaining impressions?

4. Describe the triangular theory of love.

5. What psychological factors are involved in aggression?

Answer Keys

Answer Key for Key Terms

SOCIAL THINKING

1. d	5. e	9. l	13. m
2. c	6. f	10. j	
3. g	7. a	11. b	
4. i	8. h	12. k	

SOCIAL INFLUENCE

1. e	5. l	9. g	13. i
2. b	6. h	10. n	14. d
3. c	7. a	11. f	
4. m	8. j	12. k	

SOCIAL RELATIONS

1. k	6. o	11. l	16. c
2. i	7. p	12. u	17. d
3. e	8. j	13. a	18. h
4. s	9. v	14. b	19. r
5. f	10. g	15. m	20. t
			21. q

Answer Key for Key People

1. a	6. i	11. n	16. m
2. g	7. b	12. j	17. o
3. f	8. e	13. q	
4. d	9. c	14. p	
5. h	10. k	15. l	

Answer Key for Review at a Glance

1. attribution
2. personal
3. situational
4. fundamental attribution error
5. self-serving bias
6. primacy
7. stereotypes
8. self-fulfilling prophecy
9. attitude
10. planned behavior
11. cognitive dissonance
12. self-perception
13. trustworthy
14. expert
15. two-sided
16. central
17. peripheral
18. social influence
19. social facilitation
20. Social norms
21. Social roles
22. informational social influence
23. normative social influence
24. obedience
25. cog
26. norm of reciprocity
27. door-in-the-face
28. foot-in-the-door
29. lowballing
30. deindividuation
31. social loafing
32. group polarization
33. groupthink
34. attracted
35. passion
36. commitment
37. social exchange
38. inherited biological
39. sociocultural
40. de-escalating
41. Prejudice
42. in-groups
43. out-groups
44. outgroup homogeneity
45. realistic conflict
46. social identity
47. evolutionary theory
48. empathy-altruism
49. bystander effect
50. self-justification
51. attribution of intentionality
52. violence

Answer Key for Practice Test Multiple Choice Items

1. c
2. b
3. d
4. b
5. c
6. d
7. d
8. c
9. b
10. a
11. b
12. d
13. a
14. a
15. c
16. c
17. c
18. c
19. a
20. b
21. d
22. d
23. a
24. c
25. b
26. b
27. b
28. c
29. b
30. a

Answer Key for Practice Test True/False Questions

1.	F	6.	T
2.	T	7.	T
3.	F	8.	F
4.	F	9.	F
5.	T	10.	T

Answer Key for Practice Test Short Answer Questions

1. Social facilitation is an increased tendency to perform one's dominant response in the mere presence of others. Social loafing is the tendency for people to expend less effort when working in groups than when working alone. Social compensation, in contrast, is the tendency for people to expend <u>more</u> effort in groups than when working alone.

2. People conform because of both informational and normative social influence. When people conform because they believe others are right, informational social influence has occurred. When people conform because they want to be accepted by others, normative social influence has occurred.

3. Cognitive dissonance theory argues that people strive for consistency in their cognitions. When two or more cognitions contradict one another, people are motivated to change them so that they are consistent. Thus, cognitive dissonance motivates attitude and behavior change.

4. People tend to categorize the world into "in-groups," groups to which we feel we belong, and "out-groups," groups to which we don't feel that we belong. We tend to believe that the members of a given outgroup are quite similar to one another, which is called the outgroup homogeneity bias. Stereotypes are formed through this process. We tend to place exceptions to the stereotype in a special subcategory so that we may maintain the stereotype.

5. According to social penetration theory, relationships progress as interactions between people become broader (involving more areas of their lives) and deeper (involving more intimate and personally meaningful areas). Social exchange theory proposes that the course of a relationship is governed by rewards and costs that the partners experience. If they find that the rewards outweigh the costs, the relationship will continue. When liking progresses to love, passionate love involves intense emotion, arousal, and yearning for the partner; whereas companionate love involves affection and deep caring about the partner's well-being.

Answer Key for Practice Test Essay Questions

1. Group polarization effects occur when the group's initial position becomes more extreme with discussion. Both normative and informational social influence play a role in the process. Groupthink occurs when groups suspend critical thinking when they are striving to seek agreement. Janis has proposed that groupthink occurs when a group is under high stress to make a decision, is insulated from outside input, has a directive leader who promotes his or her personal agenda, and has high cohesion.

2. Attitudes have been found to influence behaviours more strongly when counteracting situational factors are weak, when we are aware of them and when they are strongly held, and when general attitudes are used to predict general classes of behaviour and specific attitudes are used to predict specific behaviours. According to the theory of planned behaviour,

behavioural intentions are predicted by subjective norms, attitudes toward the behaviour, and perceptions of personal control.

3. The primacy effect refers to our tendency to attach more importance to the initial information that we learn about a person. Mental sets and schemas can bias what we perceive about another person. Self-fulfilling prophecies occur when our expectations about others lead us to act toward others in such a way that brings about the expected behaviours, thus confirming the original impression.

4. Robert Sternberg's triangular theory of love suggests that three components: intimacy, passion and commitment are the most important aspects of love relationships. If we just have intimacy, we like a person. If we just have passion, we experience infatuation. If we just have commitment, we have an empty love. Other types of love are combinations of these components. Romantic love springs from a combination of intimacy and passion. Companionate love springs from intimacy and commitment. Fatuous love is a combination of passion and commitment. Finally, consummate love occurs if all three components are present in a relationship. Sternberg argues that consummate love is the ultimate form of love.

5. People often use self-justification in their aggressive behaviour by blaming victims for imagined wrongs. If we perceive that others have intentionally wronged us, we are more likely to aggress against them, as will a lack of empathy toward them. Finally, our ability to regulate our emotions influences our aggressive tendencies.